THE
SPRINGFIELD
READER

THE SPRINGFIELD READER

Edited by

David Cavitch

Tufts University

BEDFORD BOOKS ❧ BOSTON

For Bedford Books

President and Publisher: Charles H. Christensen
General Manager and Associate Publisher: Joan E. Feinberg
Managing Editor: Elizabeth M. Schaaf
Developmental Editor: Alanya Harter
Editorial Assistant: Aron Keesbury
Production Editor: Karen S. Baart
Production Assistant: Deborah Baker
Copyeditor: Jane Zanichkowsky
Text Design: George H. McLean
Cover Design: Richard Emery Design, Inc.
Cover Art: Hans Hofmann, *Burning Bush*, 1959. Oil on canvas, 60″ × 48″. Private Collection, Massachusetts.

Library of Congress Catalog Card Number: 96–86770

1   0   9   8   7   6
f   e   d   c   b   a

For information, write: Bedford Books, 75 Arlington Street, Boston, MA 02116 (617–426–7440)

ISBN: 0–312–14912–3

Acknowledgments

Diane Ackerman, "The Chemistry of Love." From *A Natural History of the Senses* by Diane Ackerman. Copyright © 1990 by Diane Ackerman. Reprinted by permission of Random House, Inc.
Maya Angelou, "Graduation." From *I Know Why the Caged Bird Sings* by Maya Angelou. Copyright © 1969 by Maya Angelou. Reprinted by permission of Random House, Inc.
Toni Cade Bambara, "The Lesson." From *Gorilla, My Love* by Toni Cade Bambara. Reprinted by permission of Random House, Inc.
Stephen L. Carter, "Schools of Disbelief." Excerpt from *The Culture of Disbelief* by Stephen L. Carter. Copyright © 1993 by Stephen L. Carter. Reprinted by permission of BasicBooks, a division of HarperCollins Publishers, Inc.

PREFACE
FOR INSTRUCTORS

Like many composition anthologies, *The Springfield Reader* assembles essays and stories that are meant to generate good class discussion and galvanize student writing. Its brevity and low cost are what make this reader unique. An education has become an expensive commodity, and this reader was assembled with the assumption that good things can come in a compact, affordable package. With many of the features offered by more expensive anthologies, *The Springfield Reader* contains essays and stories that provide strong examples of the power of good writing — more than enough material for a semester.

The twenty-nine selections are grouped into five thematic chapters, themes that strongly matter to students. Starting with issues of self-awareness, the chapters move from dealing with the sense of home in family and groups, to our relationships of love and friendship, the many languages we have for acquiring knowledge, and the moral issues we face when thinking about current social problems. Each chapter includes diverse perspectives on culture, race, and gender, and ends with a story addressing the theme imaginatively. While many selections are familiar favorites, six of the essays have never before appeared in a composition reader.

The editorial apparatus guides students into intelligent awareness, and it promotes their articulate responses. A biographical headnote introduces each selection. To help improve critical reading, every selection is followed by "Considerations" about meaning and methods. Each of these questions can stimulate extended dicussion in class. One or two challenging writing topics lead students into developing their ideas in thoughtful essays.

A succinct and encouraging Introduction for Students stresses the importance of critical reading to improve writing. It makes allowance for but does not spell out detailed instructions that teachers may prefer to originate in class. An Instructor's Manual coauthored by Debra Spark offers suggestions for dealing with each selection in class. A rhetorical index to the selections appears in the back of the book.

Acknowledgments

The idea for this reader originated with Chuck Christensen and Joan Feinberg. I am grateful for the opportunity to give it concrete form, and for their wise counsel as the work proceeded. It was also a pleasure to work with others at Bedford Books. The editor, Alanya Harter, demonstrated great skill and tact editing my drafts. Aron Keesbury assisted both of us speedily and flawlessly. For adroitly steering the manuscript through production, I owe thanks to managing editor Elizabeth Schaaf, production editor Karen Baart and her assistant Deborah Baker, and to Ellen Thibault for her work on the Instructor's Manual. Outside of Bedford, Karen Rose cleared permissions with efficient good humor and Jane Zanichkowsky copyedited with a light hand.

INTRODUCTION
FOR STUDENTS

This collection of essays and stories can help you write better. Each selection offers a good read, and better writing comes from better reading. Works that stimulate ideas and feelings rouse our desire to respond articulately about important matters. A good writer is probably someone who has found reasons to answer — and perhaps surpass — some good reading.

We acquire the skill to write well by practice, of course. Revising and polishing and correcting our writing are the fundamental processes of composition. But practice is more successful if we also read with close attention and active responses. Reading increases our awareness of the variety of styles and methods that serve different purposes in writing. We learn new patterns of expression and new models for organizing our thoughts. By analyzing examples, we learn how to develop ideas and how to present complicated thoughts clearly.

To help raise your level of critical awareness, each selection in this book is followed by "Considerations" about meaning and methods. Strategies for critical reading include underlining and commenting on the page of the text, or keeping a journal to note down your responses.

Whatever your techniques, the key is to concentrate all your attention. Take in the essay or story with all its details, the entire work and not just part of it. Don't skim or skip a thing. Remember that you are reading not merely to grasp a general point but to absorb the full range and variety of writing effects. The more you take in, the more tools you will possess for writing of your own.

Following each selection a writing topic suggests how you can further develop your responses to the reading. The topic might introduce a different approach or related matters to consider. The best way to think fruitfully about an idea is to write about it. Through all the phases of composition, such as pre-writing, drafting, revising, and proofreading, a writer discovers additional meanings. Each improvement adds substance, emphasis, and clarity. By becoming a critical reader of your own work you see that better writing comes from better readers.

CONTENTS

1

IDENTITY

Self-Image and Reflections   1

$$\boxed{2}$$

HOME

Family and Groups   29

"The motorcycle was a compendium of gears and springs and sprockets and cylinder heads and piston rings, which between my father and me acquired the force of more affectionate words that we could never seem to use in each other's presence."

"Without marriage, men also lose access to the social and emotional intelligence of women in building relationships. . . . In general, men need marriage in order to be good fathers."

"I can't remember ever hearing my grandfather say to my mother, 'Well done, Jane.' I can't remember my mother ever saying to my sister, 'Well done, Susie.' And I never gave my mother the chance to say it to me."

"Being both black and middle class becomes a double bind when class and race are defined in sharply antagonistic terms, so that one must be repressed to appease the other."

"'Maggie can't appreciate these quilts!' she said. 'She'd probably be backward enough to put them to everyday use.'"

$$\boxed{3}$$

RELATIONSHIPS

Friends and Lovers   58

"The beauty of best friendship, as opposed to, say, marriage, is that it's a totally grass-roots, creative effort that requires no help at all from the powers-that-be."

4

LESSONS

Language and Learning   97

$$\boxed{5}$$

DILEMMAS

IDENTITY

Self-Image and Reflections

JOHN UPDIKE

The Disposable Rocket

JOHN UPDIKE (b. 1932), one of America's most recognized and prolific writers, started his career on the staff of *The New Yorker* after graduating from Harvard in 1954. His contribution to this and other major magazines — of stories, poems, essays, and reviews — continues to this day. His major novels include four about Harry "Rabbit" Angstrom: *Rabbit, Run* (1960), *Rabbit Redux* (1971), *Rabbit Is Rich* (1981), and *Rabbit at Rest* (1990). His best-known novel may well be *The Witches of Eastwick* (1984), also adapted into a successful movie. As an essayist Updike often writes about painting and other visual art, his secondary interest. The following essay first appeared in a special issue of *The Michigan Quarterly Review* devoted to the topic of the male body.

Inhabiting a male body is like having a bank account; as long as it's healthy, you don't think much about it. Compared to the female body, it is a low-maintenance proposition: a shower now and then, trim the fingernails every ten days, a haircut once a month. Oh yes, shaving — scraping or buzzing away at your face every morning. Byron, in *Don Juan*, thought the repeated nuisance of shaving balanced out the periodic agony, for females, of childbirth. Women are, his lines tell us,

> Condemn'd to child-bed, as men for their sins
> Have shaving too entail'd upon their chins, —
>
> A daily plague, which in the aggregate
>   May average on the whole with parturition.

From the standpoint of reproduction, the male body is a delivery system, as the female is a mazy device for retention. Once the delivery is made, men feel a faint but distinct falling-off of interest. Yet against the enduring female heroics of birth and nurture should be set the male's superhuman frenzy to deliver his goods: He vaults walls, skips sleep, risks wallet, health, and his political future all to ram home his seed into the gut of the chosen woman. The sense of the chase lives in him as the key to life. His body is, like a delivery rocket that falls away in space, a disposable means. Men put their bodies at risk to experience the release from gravity.

When my tenancy of a male body was fairly new — of six or so years' duration — I used to jump and fall just for the joy of it. Falling — backwards, or down stairs — became a specialty of mine, an attention-getting stunt I was still practicing into my thirties, at suburban parties. Falling is, after all, a kind of flying, though of briefer duration than would be ideal. My impulse to hurl myself from high windows and the edges of cliffs belongs to my body, not my mind, which resists the siren call of the chasm with all its might; the interior struggle knocks the wind from my lungs and tightens my scrotum and gives any trip to Europe, with its Alps, castle parapets, and gargoyled cathedral lookouts, a flavor of nightmare. Falling, strangely, no longer figures in my dreams, as it often did when I was a boy and my subconscious was more honest with me. An airplane, that necessary evil, turns the earth into a map so quickly the brain turns aloof and calm; still, I marvel that there is no end of young men willing to become jet pilots.

Any accounting of male-female differences must include the male's superior recklessness, a drive not, I think, toward death, as the darker feminist cosmogonies would have it, but to test the limits, to see what the traffic will bear — a kind of mechanic's curiosity. The number of men who do lasting damage to their young bodies is striking; war and car accidents aside, secondary-school sports, with the approval of parents and the encouragement of brutish coaches, take a fearful toll of skulls and knees. We were made for combat, back in the postsimian, East-African days, and the bumping, the whacking, the breathlessness, the pain-smothering adrenaline rush form a cumbersome and unfashionable bliss, but bliss nevertheless. Take your body to the edge, and see if it flies.

The male sense of space must differ from that of the female, who has such interesting, active, and significant inner space. The space that interests men is outer. The fly ball high against the sky, the long pass spiraling overhead, the jet fighter like a scarcely visible pinpoint nozzle laying down its vapor trail at forty thousand feet, the gazelle haunch flickering just beyond arrow-reach, the uncountable stars sprinkled on their great black wheel, the horizon, the mountaintop, the quasar — these bring portents with them and awaken a sense of relation with the invisible, with the empty. The ideal male body is taut with lines of potential force, a diagram extending outward; the ideal female body curves around centers of repose. Of course, no one is ideal, and the sexes are somewhat androgynous subdivisions of a species: Diana the huntress is a more trendy body type nowadays than languid, overweight Venus, and polymorphous Dionysus poses for more underwear ads than Mars. Relatively, though, men's bodies, however elegant, are designed for covering territory, for moving on.

An erection, too, defies gravity, flirts with it precariously. It extends   5 the diagram of outward direction into downright detachability — objective in the case of the sperm, subjective in the case of the testicles and penis. Men's bodies, at this juncture, feel only partly theirs; a demon of sorts has been attached to their lower torsos, whose performance is erratic and whose errands seem, at times, ridiculous. It is like having a (much) smaller brother toward whom you feel both fond and impatient; if he is you, it is you in curiously simplified and ignoble form. This sense, of the male body being two of them, is acknowledged in verbal love play and erotic writing, where the penis is playfully given a pet name, an individuation not even the rarest rapture grants a vagina. Here, where maleness gathers to a quintessence of itself, there can be no insincerity, there can be no hiding; for sheer nakedness, there is nothing like a hopeful phallus; its aggressive shape is indivisible from its tender-skinned vulnerability. The act of intercourse, from the point of view of a consenting female, has an element of mothering, of enwrapment, of merciful concealment, even. The male body, for this interval, is tucked out of harm's way.

To inhabit a male body, then, is to feel somewhat detached from it. It is not an enemy, but not entirely a friend. Our being seems to lie not in cells and muscles but in the traces that our thoughts and actions inscribe on the air. The male body skims the surface of nature's deeps wherein the blood and pain and mysterious cravings of women perpetuate the species. Participating less in nature's processes than the female body, the male body gives the impression — false — of being exempt from time. Its powers of strength and reach descend in early adolescence, along with acne and sweaty feet, and depart, in imperceptible increments, after thirty or so. It surprises me to discover, when I remove my shoes and socks, the same paper-white, hairless ankles that struck me as pathetic when I observed them on my father. I felt betrayed when, in some tumble of touch football twenty years ago, I heard my tibia snap; and when, between two reading engagements in Cleveland, my appendix tried to burst; and when, the other day, not for the first time, there arose to my nostrils out of my own body the musty attic smell my grandfather's body had.

A man's body does not betray its tenant as rapidly as a woman's. Never as fine and lovely, it has less distance to fall; what rugged beauty it has is wrinkleproof. It keeps its capability of procreation indecently long. Unless intense athletic demands are made upon it, the thing serves well enough to sixty, which is my age now. From here on, it's chancy. There are no breasts or ovaries to admit cancer to the male body, but the prostate, that awkwardly located little source of seminal fluid, shows the strain of sexual function with fits of hysterical cell replication, and all that male-bonding beer and potato chips add up in the coronary arteries. A

writer, whose physical equipment can be minimal as long as it gets him to
the desk, the lectern, and New York City once in a while, cannot but be
grateful to his body, especially to his eyes, those tender and intricate sites
where the brain extrudes from the skull, and to his hands, which hold the
pen or tap the keyboard. His body has been, not himself exactly, but a
close pal, potbellied and balding like most of his other pals now. A man
and his body are like a boy and the buddy who has a driver's license and
the use of his father's car for the evening; one only goes along, gratefully,
for the ride.

CONSIDERATIONS

1. Does Updike oversimplify male and female self-images? Or does he accu-
   rately present basic facts? In your answer, consider the implications of the
   essay's emphasis on male and female biology.
2. How would the connotations of Updike's metaphor change if he referred
   to the male body as *the reusable rocket?* How would that metaphor change
   the central idea of the essay?
3. In the final two paragraphs, what is the author's attitude toward his aging
   body? How does it differ from his youthful attitude?

WRITING SUGGESTIONS

4. Updike refers to "ideal" forms of men and women, but he notes that
   "trendy" norms may differ (paragraph 4). What is currently considered attractive in women and men? Do popular images glamorize health and
   sportiness, delicateness and fragility, subtlety and mystery, or something
   else? What are the possibly negative effects of these images?
5. Choose a particular object, plant, or animal as a suitable metaphor for your
   sense of self. In explaining your choice of metaphor, include precise details
   that exemplify some of your complexities.

NORA EPHRON

Shaping Up Absurd

NORA EPHRON (b. 1941) grew up in the adult world of Hollywood screenwriters, entertainers, and celebrities. After graduating
from Wellesley College she began a career as a journalist in New
York by writing for *Newsweek* and contributing articles to enter-
tainment magazines, eventually joining the staff of magazines
such as *New York* and *Esquire*. Her essays have been collected in
Wallflower at the Orgy (1970), *Crazy Salad* (1975), and *Nora
Ephron Collected* (1991). She has also written a comic novel, *Heart-
burn* (1983), and several screenplays. Recently Ephron co-wrote
and directed the film *Sleepless in Seattle* (1992). "Shaping Up Absurd"[1] considers a troubling self-image in her early life.

I have to begin with a few words about androgyny. In grammar
school, in the fifth and sixth grades, we were all tyrannized by a rigid set
of rules that supposedly determined whether we were boys or girls. The
episode in *Huckleberry Finn* where Huck is disguised as a girl and gives
himself away by the way he threads a needle and catches a ball — that
kind of thing. We learned that the way you sat, crossed your legs, held a
cigarette, and looked at your nails — the way you did these things instinctively was absolute proof of your sex. Now obviously most children
did not take this literally, but I did. I thought that just one slip, just one
incorrect cross of my legs or flick of an imaginary cigarette ash would
turn me from whatever I was into the other thing; that would be all it
took, really. Even though I was outwardly a girl and had many of the
trappings generally associated with the field of girldom — a girl's name,
for example, and dresses, my own telephone, an autograph book — I
spent the early years of my adolescence absolutely certain that I might at
any point gum it up. I did not feel at all like a girl. I was boyish. I was
athletic, ambitious, outspoken, competitive, noisy, rambunctious. I had
scabs on my knees and my socks slid into my loafers and I could throw a
football. I wanted desperately not to be that way, not to be a mixture of
both things but instead just one, a girl, a definite indisputable girl. As
soft and as pink as a nursery. And nothing would do that for me, I felt,
but breasts.

I was about six months younger than everyone else in my class, and
so for about six months after it began, for six months after my friends had

---

[1]Editor's title. [All notes are the editor's unless identified otherwise.]

begun to develop — that was the word we used, develop — I was not particularly worried. I would sit in the bathtub and look down at my breasts and know that any day now, any second now, they would start growing like everyone else's. They didn't. "I want to buy a bra," I said to my mother one night. "What for?" she said. My mother was really hateful about bras, and by the time my third sister had gotten to the point where she was ready to want one, my mother had worked the whole business into a comedy routine. "Why not use a Band-Aid instead?" she would say. It was a source of great pride to my mother that she had never even had to wear a brassiere until she had her fourth child, and then only because her gynecologist made her. It was incomprehensible to me that anyone could ever be proud of something like that. It was the 1950s, for God's sake. Jane Russell. Cashmere sweaters. Couldn't my mother see that? *"I am too old to wear an undershirt."* Screaming. Weeping. Shouting. "Then don't wear an undershirt," said my mother. "But I want to buy a bra." "What for?"

I suppose that for most girls, breasts, brassieres, that entire thing, has more trauma, more to do with the coming of adolescence, of becoming a woman, than anything else. Certainly more than getting your period, although that too was traumatic, symbolic. But you could *see* breasts; they were there; they were visible. Whereas a girl could claim to have her period for months before she actually got it and nobody would ever know the difference. Which is exactly what I did. All you had to do was make a great fuss over having enough nickels for the Kotex machine and walk around clutching your stomach and moaning for three to five days a month about The Curse and you could convince anybody. There is a school of thought somewhere in the women's lib/women's mag/gynecology establishment that claims that menstrual cramps are purely psychological, and I lean toward it. Not that I didn't have them finally. Agonizing cramps, heating-pad cramps, go-down-to-the-school-nurse-and-lie-on-the-cot cramps. But unlike any pain I had ever suffered, I adored the pain of cramps, welcomed it, wallowed in it, bragged about it. "I can't go. I have cramps." "I can't do that. I have cramps." And most of all, gigglingly, blushingly: "I can't swim. I have cramps." Nobody ever used the hard-core word. Menstruation. God, what an awful word. Never that. "I have cramps."

The morning I first got my period, I went into my mother's bedroom to tell her. And my mother, my utterly-hateful-about-bras mother, burst into tears. It was really a lovely moment, and I remember it so clearly not just because it was one of the two times I ever saw my mother cry on my account (the other was when I was caught being a six-year-old kleptomaniac), but also because the incident did not mean to me what it meant to her. Her little girl, her firstborn, had finally become a woman. That was what she was crying about. My reaction to the event, however, was that I might well be a woman in some scientific, textbook sense (and could at least stop faking every month and stop wasting all those nickels). But in another sense — in a visible sense — I was as androgynous and as liable to tip over into boyhood as ever.

I started with a 28 AA bra. I don't think they made them any smaller   5
in those days, although I gather that now you can buy bras for five-year-olds that don't have any cups whatsoever in them; trainer bras they are called. My first brassiere came from Robinson's Department Store in Beverly Hills. I went there alone, shaking, positive they would look me over and smile and tell me to come back next year. An actual fitter took me into the dressing room and stood over me while I took off my blouse and tried the first one on. The little puffs stood out on my chest. "Lean over," said the fitter (to this day, I am not sure what fitters in bra departments do except to tell you to lean over). I leaned over, with the fleeting hope that my breasts would miraculously fall out of my body and into the puffs. Nothing.

"Don't worry about it," said my friend Libby some months later, when things had not improved. "You'll get them after you're married."

"What are you talking about?" I said.

"When you get married," Libby explained, "your husband will touch your breasts and rub them and kiss them and they'll grow."

That was the killer. Necking I could deal with. Intercourse I could deal with. But it had never crossed my mind that a man was going to touch my breasts, that breasts had something to do with all that, petting, my God, they never mentioned petting in my little sex manual about the fertilization of the ovum. I became dizzy. For I knew instantly — as naive as I had been only a moment before — that only part of what she was saying was true: the touching, rubbing, kissing part, not the growing part. And I knew that no one would ever want to marry me. I had no breasts. I would never have breasts.

My best friend in school was Diana Raskob. She lived a block from   10
me in a house full of wonders. English muffins, for instance. The Raskobs were the first people in Beverly Hills to have English muffins for breakfast. They also had an apricot tree in the back, and a badminton court, and a subscription to *Seventeen* magazine, and hundreds of games like Sorry and Parcheesi and Treasure Hunt and Anagrams. Diana and I spent three or four afternoons a week in their den reading and playing and eating. Diana's mother's kitchen was full of the most colossal assortment of junk food I have ever been exposed to. My house was full of apples and peaches and milk and homemade chocolate-chip cookies — which were nice, and good for you, but-not-right-before-dinner-or-you'll-spoil-your-appetite. Diana's house had nothing in it that was good for you, and what's more, you could stuff it in right up until dinner and nobody cared. Bar-B-Q potato chips (they were the first in them, too),

giant bottles of ginger ale, fresh popcorn with melted butter, hot fudge sauce on Baskin-Robbins jamoca ice cream, powdered-sugar doughnuts from Van de Kamp's. Diana and I had been best friends since we were seven; we were about equally popular in school (which is to say, not particularly), we had about the same success with boys (extremely intermittent), and we looked much the same. Dark. Tall. Gangly.

It is September, just before school begins. I am eleven years old, about to enter the seventh grade, and Diana and I have not seen each other all summer. I have been to camp and she has been somewhere like Banff with her parents. We are meeting, as we often do, on the street midway between our two houses and we will walk back to Diana's and eat junk and talk about what has happened to each of us that summer. I am walking down Walden Drive in my jeans and my father's shirt hanging out and my old red loafers with the socks falling into them and coming toward me is . . . I take a deep breath . . . a young woman. Diana. Her hair is curled and she has a waist and hips and a bust and she is wearing a straight skirt, an article of clothing I have been repeatedly told I will be unable to wear until I have the hips to hold it up. My jaw drops, and suddenly I am crying, crying hysterically, can't catch my breath sobbing. My best friend has betrayed me. She has gone ahead without me and done it. She has shaped up.

Here are some things I did to help:
Bought a Mark Eden Bust Developer.
Slept on my back for four years.
Splashed cold water on them every night because some French actress said in *Life* magazine that that was what *she* did for her perfect bustline.   15

Ultimately, I resigned myself to a bad toss and began to wear padded bras. I think about them now, think about all those years in high school I went around in them, my three padded bras, every single one of them with different sized breasts. Each time I changed bras I changed sizes: one week nice perky but not too obtrusive breasts, the next medium-sized slightly pointy ones, the next week knockers, true knockers; all the time, whatever size I was, carrying around this rubberized appendage on my chest that occasionally crashed into a wall and was poked inward and had to be poked outward — I think about all that and wonder how anyone kept a straight face through it. My parents, who normally had no restraints about needling me — why did they say nothing as they watched my chest go up and down? My friends, who would periodically inspect my breasts for signs of growth and reassure me — why didn't they at least counsel consistency?

And the bathing suits. I die when I think about the bathing suits. That was the era when you could lay an uninhabited bathing suit on the beach and someone would make a pass at it. I would put one on, an absurd swimsuit with its enormous bust built into it, the bones from the suit stabbing me in the rib cage and leaving little red welts on my body, and there I would be, my chest plunging straight downward absolutely vertically from my collarbone to the top of my suit and then suddenly, wham, out came all that padding and material and wiring absolutely horizontally.

Buster Klepper was the first boy who ever touched them. He was my boyfriend my senior year of high school. There is a picture of him in my high-school yearbook that makes him look quite attractive in a Jewish, horn-rimmed glasses sort of way, but the picture does not show the pimples, which were air-brushed out, or the dumbness. Well, that isn't really fair. He wasn't dumb. He just wasn't terribly bright. His mother refused to accept it, refused to accept the relentlessly average report cards, refused to deal with her son's inevitable destiny in some junior college or other. "He was tested," she would say to me, apropos of nothing, "and it came out 145. That's near-genius." Had the word "underachiever" been coined, she probably would have lobbed that one at me, too. Anyway, Buster was really very sweet — which is, I know, damning with faint praise, but there it is. I was the editor of the front page of the high-school newspaper and he was editor of the back page; we had to work together, side by side, in the print shop, and that was how it started. On our first date, we went to see *April Love* starring Pat Boone. Then we started going together. Buster had a green coupe, a 1950 Ford with an engine he had handchromed until it shone, dazzled, reflected the image of anyone who looked into it, anyone usually being Buster polishing it or the gas-station attendants he constantly asked to check the oil in order for them to be overwhelmed by the sparkle on the valves. The car also had a boot stretched over the back seat for reasons I never understood; hanging from the rearview mirror, as was the custom, was a pair of angora dice. A previous girlfriend named Solange who was famous throughout Beverly Hills High School for having no pigment in her right eyebrow had knitted them for him. Buster and I would ride around town, the two of us seated to the left of the steering wheel. I would shift gears. It was nice.

There was necking. Terrific necking. First in the car, overlooking Los Angeles from what is now the Trousdale Estates. Then on the bed of his parents' cabana at Ocean House. Incredibly wonderful, frustrating necking, I loved it, really, but no further than necking, please don't, please, because there I was absolutely terrified of the general implications of going-a-step-further with a near-dummy and also terrified of his finding out there was next to nothing there (which he knew, of course; he wasn't that dumb).

I broke up with him at one point. I think we were apart for about two weeks. At the end of that time I drove down to see a friend at a boarding school in Palos Verdes Estates and a disc jockey played "April Love" on the radio four times during the trip. I took it as a sign. I drove straight back to Griffith Park to a golf tournament Buster was playing in (he was the sixth-seeded teenage golf player in southern California) and presented myself back to him on the green of the eighteenth hole. It was all very dramatic. That night we went to a drive-in and I let him get his hand under my protuberances and onto my breasts. He really didn't seem to mind at all.

> *"Do you want to marry my son?" the woman asked me.*
> *"Yes," I said.*
> *I was nineteen years old, a virgin, going with this woman's son, this big strange woman who was married to a Lutheran minister in New Hampshire and pretended she was Gentile and had this son, by her first husband, this total fool of a son who ran the hero-sandwich concession at Harvard Business School and whom for one moment one December in New Hampshire I said — as much out of politeness as anything else — that I wanted to marry.*
> *"Fine," she said. "Now, here's what you do. Always make sure you're on top of him so you won't seem so small. My bust is very large, you see, so I always lie on my back to make it look smaller, but you'll have to be on top most of the time."*
> *I nodded. "Thank you," I said.*
> *"I have a book for you to read," she went on. "Take it with you when you leave. Keep it." She went to the bookshelf, found it, and gave it to me. It was a book on frigidity.*
> *"Thank you," I said.*

That is a true story. Everything in this article is a true story, but I feel I have to point out that that story in particular is true. It happened on December 30, 1960. I think about it often. When it first happened, I naturally assumed that the woman's son, my boyfriend, was responsible. I invented a scenario where he had had a little heart-to-heart with his mother and confessed that his only objection to me was that my breasts were small; his mother then took it upon herself to help out. Now I think I was wrong about the incident. The mother was acting on her own, I think: That was her way of being cruel and competitive under the guise of being helpful and maternal. You have small breasts, she was saying; therefore you will never make him as happy as I have. Or you have small breasts; therefore you will doubtless have sexual problems. Or you have small breasts; therefore you are less woman than I am. She was, as it happens, only the first of what seems to me to be a never-ending string of women who have made competitive remarks to me about breast size. "I would love to wear a dress like that," my friend Emily says to me, "but my bust is too big." Like that. Why do women say these things to me? Do I attract these remarks the way other women attract married men or alcoholics or homosexuals? This summer, for example. I am at a party in East Hampton and I am introduced to a woman from Washington. She is a minor celebrity, very pretty and Southern and blonde and outspoken and I am flattered because she has read something I have written. We are talking animatedly, we have been talking no more than five minutes, when a man comes up to join us. "Look at the two of us," the woman says to the man,

25

indicating me and her. "The two of us together couldn't fill an A cup." Why does she say that? It isn't even true, dammit, so why? Is she even more addled than I am on this subject? Does she honestly believe there is something wrong with her size breasts, which, it seems to me, now that I look hard at them, are just right? Do I unconsciously bring out competitiveness in women? In that form? What did I do to deserve it?

As for men.

There were men who minded and let me know that they minded.   30
There were men who did not mind. In any case, I always minded.

And even now, now that I have been countlessly reassured that my figure is a good one, now that I am grown up enough to understand that most of my feelings have very little to do with the reality of my shape, I am nonetheless obsessed by breasts. I cannot help it. I grew up in the terrible Fifties — with rigid stereotypical sex roles, the insistence that men be men and dress like men and women be women and dress like women, the intolerance of androgyny — and I cannot shake it, cannot shake my feelings of inadequacy. Well, that time is gone, right? All those exaggerated examples of breast worship are gone, right? Those women were freaks, right? I know all that. And yet here I am, stuck with the psychological remains of it all, stuck with my own peculiar version of breast worship. You probably think I am crazy to go on like this: Here I have set out to write a confession that is meant to hit you with the shock of recognition, and instead you are sitting there thinking I am thoroughly warped. Well, what can I tell you? If I had had them, I would have been a completely different person. I honestly believe that.

After I went into therapy, a process that made it possible for me to tell total strangers at cocktail parties that breasts were the hang-up of my life, I was often told that I was insane to have been bothered by my condition. I was also frequently told, by close friends, that I was extremely boring on the subject. And my girlfriends, the ones with nice big breasts, would go on endlessly about how their lives had been far more miserable than mine. Their bra straps were snapped in class. They couldn't sleep on their stomachs. They were stared at whenever the word "mountain" cropped up in geography. And *Evangeline,* good God what they went through every time someone had to stand up and recite the Prologue to Longfellow's *Evangeline:* "*. . . stand like druids of eld . . . /With beards that rest on their bosoms."* It was much worse for them, they tell me. They had a terrible time of it, they assure me. I don't know how lucky I was, they say.

I have thought about their remarks, tried to put myself in their place, considered their point of view. I think they are full of shit.

CONSIDERATIONS

1. Ephron establishes a very informal, chatty tone right from the start. Underline the key words and phrases in the opening paragraph that help set

this tone. What is the correlation between this tone and the subject of her essay?

2. As a child, Ephron felt sure that fateful disaster lurked around every corner. In addition to her breast size, what does she worry about? How does she express these worries?

3. What is the point of the section about her friend Diana? Does her name fit the effect that she has on Ephron? Similarly, what is the point of the section about Buster Klepper? And what are the connotations of his name? Do they fit his effect on her?

WRITING SUGGESTION

4. Being unusually tall or short, thin or fat, red-haired, freckled, pretty, or thoroughly average can seem to be the most important fact about you. Write an essay explaining how one trait came to have exaggerated importance for some period of your life. Be sure to examine the reasons for its importance at that time.

BRENT STAPLES

Black Men and Public Space

BRENT STAPLES (b. 1951) was born in Chester, Pennsylvania. He earned his undergraduate degree at Widener University and a Ph.D. in psychology from the University of Chicago. After working at the *Chicago Sun-Times* and several Chicago periodicals, he became an assistant metropolitan editor at the *New York Times* in 1985. He is now on the editorial board of that newspaper. Staples has published a memoir, *Parallel Time: Growing Up in Black and White* (1994). The following essay, which appeared first in *Ms.* magazine, describes his experience of "being forever the suspect" in urban America.

My first victim was a woman — white, well dressed, probably in her early twenties. I came upon her late one evening on a deserted street in Hyde Park, a relatively affluent neighborhood in an otherwise mean, impoverished section of Chicago. As I swung onto the avenue behind her, there seemed to be a discreet, uninflammatory distance between us. Not so. She cast back a worried glance. To her, the youngish black man — a broad six feet two inches with a beard and billowing hair, both hands shoved into the pockets of a bulky military jacket — seemed menacingly close. After a few more quick glimpses, she picked up her pace and was soon running in earnest. Within seconds she disappeared into a cross street.

That was more than a decade ago. I was twenty-two years old, a graduate student newly arrived at the University of Chicago. It was in the echo of that terrified woman's footfalls that I first began to know the unwieldy inheritance I'd come into — the ability to alter public space in ugly ways. It was clear that she thought herself the quarry of a mugger, a rapist, or worse. Suffering a bout of insomnia, however, I was stalking sleep, not defenseless wayfarers. As a softy who is scarcely able to take a knife to a raw chicken — let alone hold one to a person's throat — I was surprised, embarrassed, and dismayed all at once. Her flight made me feel like an accomplice in tyranny. It also made it clear that I was indistinguishable from the muggers who occasionally seeped into the area from the surrounding ghetto. That first encounter, and those that followed, signified that a vast, unnerving gulf lay between nighttime pedestrians — particularly women — and me. And I soon gathered that being perceived as dangerous is a hazard in itself. I only needed to turn a corner into a dicey situation, or crowd some frightened, armed person in a foyer somewhere, or make an errant move after being pulled over by a policeman. Where fear and weapons meet — and they often do in urban America — there is always the possibility of death.

In that first year, my first away from my hometown, I was to become thoroughly familiar with the language of fear. At dark, shadowy intersections in Chicago, I could cross in front of a car stopped at a traffic light and elicit the *thunk, thunk, thunk, thunk* of the driver — black, white, male, or female — hammering down the door locks. On less traveled streets after dark, I grew accustomed to but never comfortable with people crossing to the other side of the street rather than pass me. Then there were the standard unpleasantries with police, doormen, bouncers, cabdrivers, and others whose business it is to screen out troublesome individuals *before* there is any nastiness.

I moved to New York nearly two years ago and I have remained an avid night walker. In central Manhattan, the near-constant crowd cover minimizes tense one-on-one street encounters. Elsewhere — in SoHo, for example, where sidewalks are narrow and tightly spaced buildings shut out the sky — things can get very taut indeed.

After dark, on the warrenlike streets of Brooklyn where I live, I   5
often see women who fear the worst from me. They seem to have set their faces on neutral, and with their purse straps strung across their chests bandolier-style, they forge ahead as though bracing themselves against being tackled. I understand, of course, that the danger they perceive is not a hallucination. Women are particularly vulnerable to street violence, and young black males are drastically overrepresented among the perpetrators

of that violence. Yet these truths are no solace against the kind of alienation that comes of being ever the suspect, a fearsome entity with whom pedestrians avoid making eye contact.

It is not altogether clear to me how I reached the ripe old age of twenty-two without being conscious of the lethality nighttime pedestrians attributed to me. Perhaps it was because in Chester, Pennsylvania, the small, angry industrial town where I came of age in the 1960s, I was scarcely noticeable against a backdrop of gang warfare, street knifings, and murders. I grew up one of the good boys, had perhaps a half-dozen fistfights. In retrospect, my shyness of combat has clear sources.

As a boy, I saw countless tough guys locked away; I have since buried several, too. They were babies, really — a teenage cousin, a brother of twenty-two, a childhood friend in his mid-twenties — all gone down in episodes of bravado played out in the streets. I came to doubt the virtues of intimidation early on. I chose, perhaps unconsciously, to remain a shadow — timid, but a survivor.

The fearsomeness mistakenly attributed to me in public places often has a perilous flavor. The most frightening of these confusions occurred in the late 1970s and early 1980s when I worked as a journalist in Chicago. One day, rushing into the office of a magazine I was writing for with a deadline story in hand, I was mistaken for a burglar. The office manager called security and, with an ad hoc posse, pursued me through the labyrinthine halls, nearly to my editor's door. I had no way of proving who I was. I could only move briskly toward the company of someone who knew me.

Another time I was on assignment for a local paper and killing time before an interview. I entered a jewelry store on the city's affluent Near North Side. The proprietor excused herself and returned with an enormous red Doberman pinscher straining at the end of a leash. She stood, the dog extended toward me, silent to my questions, her eyes bulging nearly out of her head. I took a cursory look around, nodded, and bade her good night.

Relatively speaking, however, I never fared as badly as another black male journalist. He went to nearby Waukegan, Illinois, a couple of summers ago to work on a story about a murderer who was born there. Mistaking the reporter for the killer, police officers hauled him from his car at gunpoint and but for his press credentials would probably have tried to book him. Such episodes are not uncommon. Black men trade tales like this all the time. 10

Over the years, I learned to smother the rage I felt at so often being taken for a criminal. Not to do so would surely have led to madness. I now take precautions to make myself less threatening. I move about with care, particularly late in the evening. I give a wide berth to nervous people on subway platforms during the wee hours, particularly when I have exchanged business clothes for jeans. If I happen to be entering a building behind some people who appear skittish, I may walk by, letting them clear the lobby before I return, so as not to seem to be following them. I have been calm and extremely congenial on those rare occasions when I've been pulled over by the police.

And on late-evening constitutionals I employ what has proved to be an excellent tension-reducing measure: I whistle melodies from Beethoven and Vivaldi and the more popular classical composers. Even steely New Yorkers hunching toward nighttime destinations seem to relax, and occasionally they even join in the tune. Virtually everybody seems to sense that a mugger wouldn't be warbling bright, sunny selections from Vivaldi's *Four Seasons*. It is my equivalent of the cowbell that hikers wear when they know they are in bear country.

CONSIDERATIONS

1. What is the effect of the opening paragraph?
2. How does the author's presence "alter public space in ugly ways"? Describe the difference between Staples's image of himself and how he is perceived by others.
3. Why doesn't Staples assume that the suspicion he elicits as a young black man on the street is solely the result of racial prejudice?
4. How does the author defuse the explosive tensions his presence produces in other people? Do his methods compromise his own self-image and integrity?
5. What is the essay's overall purpose? Does Staples propose any remedies for the unjust assumptions he describes?

WRITING SUGGESTION

6. In what way have you been stereotyped? Perhaps as "a brain" or "a jock"; or as a black, a Jew, an Italian; or as someone who is always "good-natured" or always "responsible." In an essay, examine the stereotype that falsifies and denigrates something that is true in your nature.

E. B. WHITE

Once More to the Lake

ELWYN BROOKS WHITE (1899–1985) was one of America's leading essayists and the author of classic books for children. He
joined the staff of *The New Yorker* soon after graduating from
Cornell University, and in later years he wrote also for *Harper's*,
where the following essay first appeared. His essays are collected
in *Essays of E. B. White* (1977). His children's books include *Stuart
Little* (1945), *Charlotte's Web* (1952), and *The Trumpet of the Swan*
(1970).

One summer, along about 1904, my father rented a camp on a lake
in Maine and took us all there for the month of August. We all got ring-
worm from some kittens and had to rub Pond's Extract on our arms and
legs night and morning, and my father rolled over in a canoe with all his
clothes on; but outside of that the vacation was a success and from then on
none of us ever thought there was any place in the world like that lake in
Maine. We returned summer after summer — always on August 1 for one
month. I have since become a salt-water man, but sometimes in summer
there are days when the restlessness of the tides and the fearful cold of the
sea water and the incessant wind that blows across the afternoon and into
the evening make me wish for the placidity of a lake in the woods. A few
weeks ago this feeling got so strong I bought myself a couple of bass
hooks and a spinner and returned to the lake where we used to go, for a
week's fishing and to revisit old haunts.

I took along my son, who had never had any fresh water up his nose
and who had seen lily pads only from train windows. On the journey over
to the lake I began to wonder what it would be like. I wondered how time
would have marred this unique, this holy spot — the coves and streams,
the hills that the sun set behind, the camps and the paths behind the
camps. I was sure that the tarred road would have found it out, and I wondered in what other ways it would be desolated. It is strange how much
you can remember about places like that once you allow your mind to return into the grooves that lead back. You remember one thing, and that
suddenly reminds you of another thing. I guess I remembered clearest of
all the early mornings, when the lake was cool and motionless, remembered how the bedroom smelled of the lumber it was made of and of the
wet woods whose scent entered through the screen. The partitions in the
camp were thin and did not extend clear to the top of the rooms, and as I

was always the first up I would dress softly so as not to wake the others, and sneak out into the sweet outdoors and start out in the canoe, keeping close along the shore in the long shadows of the pines. I remembered being very careful never to rub my paddle against the gunwale for fear of disturbing the stillness of the cathedral.

The lake had never been what you would call a wild lake. There were cottages sprinkled about the shores, and it was in farming country although the shores of the lake were quite heavily wooded. Some of the cottages were owned by nearby farmers, and you would live at the shore and eat your meals at the farmhouse. That's what our family did. But although it wasn't wild, it was a fairly large and undisturbed lake and there were places in it which, to a child at least, seemed infinitely remote and primeval.

I was right about the tar: It led to within half a mile of the shore. But when I got back there, with my boy, and we settled into a camp near a farmhouse and into the kind of summertime I had known, I could tell that it was going to be pretty much the same as it had been before — I knew it, lying in bed the first morning, smelling the bedroom and hearing the boy sneak quietly out and go off along the shore in a boat. I began to sustain the illusion that he was I, and therefore, by simple transposition, that I was my father. This sensation persisted, kept cropping up all the time we were there. It was not an entirely new feeling, but in this setting it grew much stronger. I seemed to be living a dual existence. I would be in the middle of some simple act, I would be picking up a bait box or laying down a table fork, or I would be saying something, and suddenly it would be not I but my father who was saying the words or making the gesture. It gave me a creepy sensation.

We went fishing the first morning. I felt the same damp moss cov- 5 ering the worms in the bait can, and saw the dragonfly alight on the tip of my rod as it hovered a few inches from the surface of the water. It was the arrival of this fly that convinced me beyond any doubt that every-thing was as it always had been, that the years were a mirage and there had been no years. The small waves were the same, chucking the row-boat under the chine as we fished at anchor, and the boat was the same boat, the same color green and the ribs broken in the same places, and under the floorboards the same fresh-water leavings and debris — the dead helgramite, the wisps of moss, the rusty discarded fishhook, the dried blood from yesterday's catch. We stared silently at the tips of our rods, at the dragonflies that came and went. I lowered the tip of mine into the water, tentatively, pensively dislodging the fly, which darted two feet away, poised, darted two feet back, and came to rest again a little far-ther up the rod. There had been no years between the ducking of this dragonfly and the other one — the one that was part of memory. I looked at the boy, who was silently watching his fly, and it was my hands that held his rod, my eyes watching. I felt dizzy and didn't know which rod I was at the end of.

We caught two bass, hauling them in briskly as though they were mackerel, pulling them over the side of the boat in a businesslike manner without any landing net, and stunning them with a blow on the back of the head. When we got back for a swim before lunch, the lake was exactly where we had left it, the same number of inches from the dock, and there was only the merest suggestion of a breeze. This seemed an utterly enchanted sea, this lake you could leave to its own devices for a few hours and come back to, and find that it had not stirred, this constant and trustworthy body of water. In the shallows, the dark, water-soaked sticks and twigs, smooth and old, were undulating in clusters on the bottom against the clean ribbed sand, and the track of the mussel was plain. A school of minnows swam by, each minnow with its small individual shadow, doubling the attendance, so clear and sharp in the sunlight. Some of the other campers were in swimming, along the shore, one of them with a cake of soap, and the water felt thin and clear and unsubstantial. Over the years there had been this person with the cake of soap, this cultist, and here he was. There had been no years.

Up to the farmhouse to dinner through the teeming, dusty field, the road under our sneakers was only a two-track road. The middle track was missing, the one with the marks of the hooves and splotches of dried, flaky manure. There had always been three tracks to choose from in choosing which track to walk in; now the choice was narrowed down to two. For a moment I missed terribly the middle alternative. But the way led past the tennis court, and something about the way it lay there in the sun reassured me; the tape had loosened along the backline, the alleys were green with plantains and other weeds, and the net (installed in June and removed in September) sagged in the dry noon, and the whole place steamed with midday heat and hunger and emptiness. There was a choice of pie for dessert, and one was blueberry and one was apple, and the waitresses were the same country girls, there having been no passage of time, only the illusion of it as in a dropped curtain — the waitresses were still fifteen; their hair had been washed, that was the only difference — they had been to the movies and seen the pretty girls with the clean hair.

Summertime, oh summertime, pattern of life indelible, the fade-proof lake, the woods unshatterable, the pasture with the sweetfern and the juniper forever and ever, summer without end; this was the background, and the life along the shore was the design, the cottagers with their innocent and tranquil design, their tiny docks with the flagpole and the American flag floating against the white clouds in the blue sky, the little paths over the roots of the trees leading from camp to camp and the paths leading back to the outhouses and the can of lime for sprinkling, and at the souvenir counters at the store the miniature birch-bark canoes and the postcards that showed things looking a little better than they looked. This was the American family at play, escaping the city heat, wondering whether the newcomers in the camp at the head of the cove were "common" or "nice," wondering whether it was true that the people who drove up for Sunday dinner at the farmhouse were turned away because there wasn't enough chicken.

It seemed to me, as I kept remembering all this, that those times and those summers had been infinitely precious and worth saving. There had been jollity and peace and goodness. The arriving (at the beginning of August) had been so big a business in itself, at the railway station the farm wagon drawn up, the first smell of the pine-laden air, the first glimpse of the smiling farmer, and the great importance of the trunks and your father's enormous authority in such matters, and the feel of the wagon under you for the long ten-mile haul, and at the top of the last long hill catching the first view of the lake after eleven months of not seeing this cherished body of water. The shouts and cries of the other campers when they saw you, and the trunks to be unpacked, to give up their rich burden. (Arriving was less exciting nowadays, when you sneaked up in your car and parked it under a tree near the camp and took out the bags and in five minutes it was all over, no fuss, no loud wonderful fuss about trunks).

Peace and goodness and jollity. The only thing that was wrong now, really, was the sound of the place, an unfamiliar nervous sound of the outboard motors. This was the note that jarred, the one thing that would sometimes break the illusion and set the years moving. In those other summertimes all motors were inboard; and when they were at a little distance, the noise they made was a sedative, an ingredient of summer sleep. They were one-cylinder and two-cylinder engines, and some were make-and-break and some were jump-spark, but they all made a sleepy sound across the lake. The one-lungers throbbed and fluttered, and the twin-cylinder ones purred and purred, and that was a quiet sound too. But now the campers all had outboards. In the daytime, in the hot mornings, these motors made a petulant, irritable sound; at night, in the still evening when the afterglow lit the water, they whined about one's ears like mosquitoes. My boy loved our rented outboard, and his great desire was to achieve singlehanded mastery over it, and authority, and he soon learned the trick of choking it a little (but not too much), and the adjustment of the needle valve. Watching him I would remember the things you could do with the old one-cylinder engines with the heavy flywheel, how you could have it eating out of your hand if you got really close to it spiritually. Motorboats in those days didn't have clutches, and you would make a landing by shutting off the motor at the proper time and coasting in with a dead rudder. But there was a way of reversing them, if you learned the trick, by cutting the switch and putting it on again exactly on the final dying revolution of the flywheel, so that it would kick back against compression and begin reversing. Approaching a dock in a strong following breeze, it was difficult to slow up sufficiently by the ordinary coasting method, and if a boy felt he had complete mastery over his motor, he was tempted to keep it running beyond its time and then reverse it a few feet from the dock. It took a cool nerve, because if you threw the switch a twentieth of a second too soon you could catch the flywheel when it still had speed enough to

10

go up past center, and the boat would leap ahead, charging bull-fashion at the dock.

We had a good week at the camp. The bass were biting well and the sun shone endlessly, day after day. We would be tired at night and lie down in the accumulated heat of the little bedrooms after the long hot day and the breeze would stir almost imperceptibly outside and the smell of the swamp drift in through the rusty screens. Sleep would come easily and in the morning the red squirrel would be on the roof, tapping out his gay routine. I kept remembering everything, lying in bed in the mornings — the small steamboat that had a long rounded stern like the lip of a Ubangi, and how quietly she ran on the moonlight sails, when the older boys played their mandolins and the girls sang and we ate doughnuts dipped in sugar, and how sweet the music was on the water in the shining night, and what it had felt like to think about girls then. After breakfast we would go up to the store and the things were in the same place — the minnows in a bottle, the plugs and spinners disarranged and pawed over by the youngsters from the boys' camp, the Fig Newtons and the Beeman's gum. Outside, the road was tarred and cars stood in front of the store. Inside, all was just as it had always been, except there was more Coca-Cola and not so much Moxie and root beer and birch beer and sarsaparilla. We would walk out with a bottle of pop apiece and sometimes the pop would backfire up our noses and hurt. We explored the streams, quietly, where the turtles slid off the sunny logs and dug their way into the soft bottom; and we lay on the town wharf and fed worms to the tame bass. Everywhere we went I had trouble making out which was I, the one walking at my side, the one walking in my pants.

One afternoon while we were there at that lake a thunderstorm came up. It was like the revival of an old melodrama that I had seen long ago with childish awe. The second-act climax of the drama of the electrical disturbance over a lake in America had not changed in any important respect. This was the big scene, still the big scene. The whole thing was so familiar, the first feeling of oppression and heat and a general air around camp of not wanting to go very far away. In midafternoon (it was all the same) a curious darkening of the sky, and a lull in everything that had made life tick; and then the way the boats suddenly swung the other way at their moorings with the coming of a breeze out of the new quarter, and the premonitory rumble. Then the kettle drum, then the snare, then the bass drum and cymbals, then crackling light against the dark, and the gods grinning and licking their chops in the hills. Afterward the calm, the rain steadily rustling in the calm lake, the return of light and hope and spirits, and the campers running out in joy and relief to go swimming in the rain, their bright cries perpetuating the deathless joke about how they were getting simply drenched, and the children screaming with delight at the new sensation of bathing in the rain, and the joke about getting drenched linking the generations in a strong indestructible chain. And the comedian who waded in carrying an umbrella.

When the others went swimming my son said he was going in, too. He pulled his dripping trunks from the line where they had hung all through the shower and wrung them out. Languidly, and with no thought of going in, I watched him, his hard little body, skinny and bare, saw him wince slightly as he pulled up around his vitals the small, soggy, icy garment. As he buckled the swollen belt, suddenly my groin felt the chill of death.

CONSIDERATIONS

1. In paragraphs 4 and 5, White feels "dizzy" and he gets "a creepy sensation." What causes this reaction?

2. White states three times, "There had been no years" (paragraphs 5 and 6). What is the tone of this sentence, and how does it capture the author's attitude toward his experience? What is the effect of White's repetition?

3. What images of himself does White encounter on this trip? Is there a particular self-image suggested by the final sentence?

4. The title suggests a commonplace, repeated trip. How do your conceptions of the trip and of the lake itself change by the end of the essay?

WRITING SUGGESTIONS

5. Describe the person in your family who looks most like you. Use precise detail to capture both the features that you share and those that are unique. How and why do your similarities please or disturb you?

6. Leaf through an album of pictures of yourself and others, perhaps family members, and write about the effects of looking at old photographs. Do photographic images evoke special reactions? How do the effects resemble or differ from White's reactions? In your answer, consider the role of the medium, photographs, in provoking nostalgia or other emotions.

JOSEPH STEFFAN

Honor Bound

JOSEPH STEFFAN (b. 1964) was a high-ranking senior at the United States Naval Academy in Annapolis when he was discharged in 1987 for homosexuality. He filed a lawsuit and became a leading advocate against the military ban on gay and lesbian service members. He recounted his career and investigation at the academy in *Honor Bound* (1992), from which this selection is taken. Steffan earned a law degree from the University of Connecticut in 1994 and now works as an attorney in Hartford, Connecticut.

I walked into the commandant's outer office and reported to his executive assistant, a junior officer assigned to serve as his aide. He said the commandant would be right with me, and asked me to take a seat. The strange quietness of the hallway seemed to permeate everything, and although the EA's greeting had been cordial, there was an obvious tension in the air. He undoubtedly knew the purpose of this meeting as well, and I began to wonder how long it would take before it leaked to the rest of the brigade.

I tried to keep calm, but it was difficult to ignore the obvious importance of this meeting. What would happen in the next few moments would likely determine, to a very large extent, the rest of my life. My feelings were a strange mixture of fear, anger, and pride, and I was determined that, no matter what, I was going to maintain my sense of dignity.

Finally, the EA signaled that the commandant was ready and led me into his office. The commandant of midshipmen, Captain Howard Habermeyer, was waiting just inside the door as we entered. He greeted me, shaking my hand, and motioned for me to sit as he returned to his desk. The office was relatively opulent by military standards, with dark wood paneling and blue carpeting. Behind the commandant's large wooden desk stood the United States flag and the blue-and-gold flag of the Brigade of Midshipmen. The walls were covered with pictures and plaques, memorabilia from his service as an officer in the submarine service.

Captain Habermeyer was tall, bespectacled, and quite thin, almost to the point of frailty. He and the superintendent had taken over during the previous summer, replacing Captain Chadwick and Admiral Larson, both of whom I had come to know quite well during my previous years. I regretted that they were not here now, and that my fate rested in the hands of two officers who barely knew me. I sometimes wonder if they had been there instead whether it would have changed the outcome at all. Perhaps it would at least have been more difficult for them.

I had first met Captain Habermeyer at a small leadership retreat held for the top incoming stripers of my class. The retreat was relatively informal and was held at an Annapolis hotel. At the time, he impressed me as an intelligent and articulate officer, and we had shared a conversation about his admiration of Japanese culture. It was an interest that had grown through several tours of duty he had in Japan.

I had heard since then that Captain Habermeyer was a stickler for regulations. He played everything exactly by the book. My suspicion was confirmed when the EA remained standing in the doorway as the commandant began to question me about my request. He had apparently been ordered to remain as a witness to the conversation. Despite an outward sense of cordiality, I was beginning to feel like a criminal under interrogation.

As with the previous officers, I refused to discuss the purpose of my request with the commandant, but he continued to question me. He finally stated that no one in the military has an inherent right to meet with anyone above his own commanding officer, which for midshipmen is technically the commandant. If I refused to disclose the purpose of the meeting, he would deny my request. When he again questioned me, I finally answered, "The meeting concerns a situation of which you are already aware."

"You're referring to the NIS investigation presently under way?" he asked.

"Yes, sir."

He responded, "Are you willing to state at this time that you are a homosexual?"

The moment of truth had arrived. In a way, I was surprised that he was even asking the question. Captain Holderby had already basically told him the answer. Was he offering me an out, a chance to deny it, to say that it was all a big misunderstanding? Was he offering me a chance to lie?

I looked him straight in the eye and answered, "Yes sir, I am."

It was a moment I will never forget, one of agony and intense pride. In that one statement, I had given up my dreams, the goals I had spent the last four years of my life laboring to attain. But in exchange, I retained something far more valuable — my honor and my self-esteem.

In many ways, the commandant's words were more than a simple question — they were a challenge to everything I believed in, and to the identity I had struggled to accept. In giving me the opportunity to deny my sexuality, the commandant was challenging that identity. He could just as well have asked, "Are you ashamed enough to deny your true identity in order to graduate?" More than anything I have ever wanted in my entire life, I wanted to be an outstanding midshipman and to graduate from the Naval Academy. And I firmly believe that if I had been willing to lie about my sexuality, to deny my true identity, I would have been allowed to graduate.

I had come to the academy to achieve my potential as an individual.   15
These four years had been filled with trials and lessons from which I learned a great deal about life and about myself. But none of these lessons was more difficult, important, or meaningful than coming to understand and accept my sexuality — in essence, to accept my true identity. By coming out to myself, I gained the strength that can come only from self-acceptance, and it was with that added strength that I had been able to persevere through the many trials and difficulties of life at Annapolis.

The commandant's question was also a challenge to my honor as a midshipman. The Honor Concept at Annapolis is based on the tenet that personal honor is an absolute — you either have honor or you do not. No one can take it from you; it can only be surrendered willingly. And once it is surrendered, once it is compromised, it can never again be fully regained.

I knew that my graduation would mean absolutely nothing if I had to lie to achieve it, especially if that lie was designed to hide the very fact of my own identity. I would have given up my honor, destroying everything it means to be a midshipman. And I would have given up my identity and pride — everything it means to be a person.

The only way to retain my honor and identity, both as a midshipman and a person, was to tell the truth. I was honor bound not simply by the Honor Concept, but by its foundation: the respect for fundamental human dignity. The academy had the power to take away everything tangible that I had attained, but only I had the power to destroy my honor. Even if the academy discharged me for being gay, I could live with the knowledge that I had passed the ultimate test. I was willing to give up everything tangible to retain something intangible but far more meaningful: my honor and my identity. Even the military could not take them away from me now.

Captain Habermeyer said that he could not grant my request to speak with the superintendent because he would eventually sit in judgment over me. A performance board would be scheduled the next day, the first step toward discharge from Annapolis. Although I explained that I still desired to graduate, the commandant assured me that he did not believe the superintendent would allow it.

Before leaving, I looked at the commandant and said, "I'm sorry it   20
had to end this way." He answered, "So am I." I truly believed him, which didn't make the imminent destruction of my life much easier to deal with. It would have been so much easier to have someone to hate, a person to blame for everything that was happening. But there was no one to blame. I couldn't blame myself because I had done what I believed right. There was only a military policy, a rule like countless others that define life in the military, rules that we learn to instinctively enforce and obey.

My perception of what was happening seemed almost detached at times, and I wondered how long it would be before I woke up to realize this was all a horrible dream. In retrospect, I don't doubt that I was suffering from shock, so completely overcome by emotion that I couldn't feel anything at all. I wanted to scream or cry or something, but there was too much to deal with, and I wondered if I would be able to stop once I started.

Not only was the nature of my life changing rapidly, but I was also anticipating how each of my relationships with other people would change. Would my parents and friends reject me as I had feared for so long, or was I not giving them enough credit? In any case, I knew it would be only a short time until the news of my disclosure would leak to the brigade, and I had to be prepared before then. I had heard a story about two male mids who were caught in bed together a year or two before I was inducted. That evening, they were both dragged from their rooms, wrapped in blankets and beaten by other mids in what was called a "blanket party." In a way, I doubted whether anyone would dare do that to me, but I wasn't too excited about the possibility.

There was no doubt in my mind that the story would leak, probably within twenty-four hours. After that, it would spread like wildfire. Annapolis is such a rumor mill that I could expect to hear about five hundred colorful variations of the story within a few hours. I decided that the best way to combat this inevitability was through a controlled release of information, and that release had to start with my closest friends at the academy.

I spent the rest of the afternoon telling six of my friends what was going on. Each of them was shocked and surprised, but they were universally supportive, even more so than I had hoped. I told them I wanted them to hear it from me first, but that they should keep it under wraps for now. I also took the time to go to each of the teachers I had in classes that semester to inform them personally. I felt a need to do this first out of respect for them, and second, to make sure that they knew I was not ashamed to face them. If I was going to leave the academy, I wanted it to be with the same level of pride I had felt as a battalion commander. I didn't want anyone to think I was running away, departing under a cloak of deserved shame. I wanted to show them I was the same person as before — exactly the same.

CONSIDERATIONS

1. How do the descriptive details in paragraphs 1 through 4 evoke the author's experience?

2. After Steffan's meeting with the commandant, why did Steffan tell others about it? What harm did he expect from not speaking out?

3. Do you think the Honor Concept guided Steffan well or ill?

WRITING SUGGESTIONS

4. The current military policy regarding gays and lesbians can be summed up as "Don't ask, don't tell." How does this policy deal with issues of honor and identity confronted by Steffan? What specific policy changes, if any, would you recommend?

5. Steffan carefully defines "honor," an abstract term. Write concretely about an aspect of self-awareness such as self-possession, self-esteem, self-respect, or self-love. When useful, give examples of how abstract ideas are practically expressed. Consider how the meaning of the term might change when used by different generations or different groups in society.

JAMAICA KINCAID

Girl

JAMAICA KINCAID (b. 1949) was born in Antigua in the West Indies, and much of her work draws on her early life on the island. She came to the United States at seventeen and soon began writing fiction and essays. From 1974 to 1995 Kincaid was a staff writer at *The New Yorker* and wrote fiction at the same time, producing a collection of stories, *At the Bottom of the River* (1983), and three novels, *Annie John* (1985), *Lucy* (1990), and *The Autobiography of My Mother* (1996). Kincaid writes about the destructive effects of colonial rule in Antigua in *A Small Place* (1988). The very short story "Girl" is her first published piece of fiction.

Wash the white clothes on Monday and put them on the stone heap; wash the color clothes on Tuesday and put them on the clothesline to dry; don't walk barehead in the hot sun; cook pumpkin fritters in very hot sweet oil; soak your little cloths right after you take them off; when buying cotton to make yourself a nice blouse, be sure that it doesn't have gum on it, because that way it won't hold up well after a wash; soak salt fish overnight before you cook it; is it true that you sing benna[1] in Sunday school?; always eat your food in such a way that it won't turn someone else's stomach; on Sundays try to walk like a lady and not like the slut you are so bent on becoming; don't sing benna in Sunday school; you mustn't speak to wharf-rat boys, not even to give directions; don't eat fruits on the

---

[1] ***benna:*** Calypso music.

street — flies will follow you; *but I don't sing benna on Sundays at all and never in Sunday school;* this is how to sew on a button; this is how to make a buttonhole for the button you have just sewed on; this is how to hem a dress when you see the hem coming down and so to prevent yourself from looking like the slut I know you are so bent on becoming; this is how you iron your father's khaki shirt so that it doesn't have a crease; this is how you iron your father's khaki pants so that they don't have a crease; this is how you grow okra — far from the house, because okra tree harbors red ants; when you are growing dasheen,[2] make sure it gets plenty of water or else it makes your throat itch when you are eating it; this is how you sweep a corner; this is how you sweep a whole house; this is how you sweep a yard; this is how you smile to someone you don't like too much; this is how you smile to someone you don't like at all; this is how you smile to someone you like completely; this is how you set a table for tea; this is how you set a table for dinner; this is how you set a table for dinner with an important guest; this is how you set a table for lunch; this is how you set a table for breakfast; this is how to behave in the presence of men who don't know you very well, and this way they won't recognize immediately the slut I have warned you against becoming; be sure to wash every day, even if it is with your own spit; don't squat down to play marbles — you are not a boy, you know; don't pick people's flowers — you might catch something; don't throw stones at blackbirds, because it might not be a blackbird at all; this is how to make a bread pudding; this is how to make doukona;[3] this is how to make pepper pot;[4] this is how to make a good medicine for a cold; this is how to make a good medicine to throw away a child before it even becomes a child; this is how to catch a fish; this is how to throw back a fish you don't like, and that way something bad won't fall on you; this is how to bully a man; this is how a man bullies you; this is how to love a man, and if this doesn't work there are other ways, and if they don't work don't feel too bad about giving up; this is how to spit up in the air if you feel like it, and this is how to move quick so that it doesn't fall on you; this is how to make ends meet; always squeeze bread to make sure it's fresh; *but what if the baker won't let me feel the bread?;* you mean to say that after all you are really going to be the kind of woman who the baker won't let near the bread?

CONSIDERATIONS

1. "Girl" is a running monologue with no interrupting explanations. Explain who the speakers are and their relationship. How do you know?
2. What kind of warnings and instructions are repeated? What do they tell you about the other speaker? How does the girl answer? Find specific instances of her responses.

[2] *dasheen:* Tropical plant with an edible root.
[3] *doukona:* Spicy pudding made from plantains, a fruit similar in taste and texture to a banana.
[4] *pepper pot:* A stew.

3. What sort of adult do you think this girl will become? Support your answer by referring to details in the story that indicate her probable, or possible, future.

WRITING SUGGESTION

4. Write a brief script of voices inside your head this semester — parents, professors, friends. Include your own voice and responses. Try to vary the voices and attitudes without breaking the monologue.

2

HOME

Family and Groups

THOMAS SIMMONS

Motorcycle Talk

THOMAS SIMMONS (b. 1956) spent his first thirteen years in West Chester, Pennsylvania, where he developed an enduring passion for motorcycles. Simmons graduated from Stanford University and received a Ph.D. in English at the University of California at Berkeley. He has taught writing at the Massachusetts Institute of Technology and at the University of Iowa. "Motorcycle Talk" is taken from *The Unseen Shore: Memories of a Christian Science Childhood* (1991), his memoir about struggling with his religious upbringing. His autobiography continues in his book about learning how to fly, *A Season in the Air* (1993). Simmons's most recent book is *Erotic Reckonings: Mastery and Apprenticeship in the Work of Poets and Lovers* (1994).

My father, who suffered from so many private griefs, was not an easy man to get along with, but in one respect he was magnificent: He was unfailing in his devotion to machines of almost any variety. When he chose to, he could talk to me at length on the virtues of, say, the 1966 Chevrolet four-barrel carburetor or the drawbacks of the Wankel rotary engine. Talking, however, was not his strongest suit: He was a man of action. As he liked to point out, talking would never make an engine run more smoothly.

On weekends sometimes, or on his rare summer days of vacation, he would encourage me in my first and last steps toward automotive literacy. He would allow me to stand beside him as he worked on the car, and

when he needed a simple tool — a crescent wrench or needlenose pliers —
I would be allowed to hand them to him. And when I was twelve, he and
my daring mother bought me a motorcycle.

It was a 50cc Benelli motocross bike — neither new, nor large, nor
powerful, nor expensive. But it gave form and life to my imaginings. No
longer did I have to confine myself wistfully to magazine photos of high-
speed turns and hair-raising rides through rough country. I had the thing
itself — the device that would make these experiences possible, at least to
some degree.

And, although I did not know it at the time, I also had a new kind of
lexicon. The motorcycle was a compendium of gears and springs and
sprockets and cylinder heads and piston rings, which between my father
and me acquired the force of more affectionate words that we could never
seem to use in each other's presence.

Almost immediately the Benelli became a meeting ground, a magnet   5
for the two of us. We would come down to look at it — even if it was too
late in the day for a good ride — and my father would check the tension
of the chain, or examine the spark plug for carbon, or simply bounce the
shock absorbers a few times as he talked. He'd tell me about compression
ratios and ways of down-shifting smoothly through a turn; I'd tell him
about my latest ride, when I leaped two small hummocks or took a spill on
a tight curve.

More rarely, he'd tell the stories of his youth. His favorite, which he
recounted in slightly different versions about four times a year, had to do
with the go-kart he built from scrap parts in his father's basement during
the Depression. It was by any account a masterful performance: He managed to pick up a small, broken gasoline engine for free, and tinkered with
it until it came back to life. The wheels, steering gear, axles, chassis — all
were scrounged for a few cents, or for free, from junkyards and vacant lots
in and around Philadelphia.

Winter was in full swing when my father had his go-kart ready for a
test-drive; snow lay thick on the ground. But he'd built the go-kart in his
father's large basement, and given the weather he felt it made sense to
make a trial run indoors. His engineering skills were topnotch. Assembled from orphaned parts, the go-kart performed like a well-tuned race
car. My father did what any good thirteen-year-old would have done: He
got carried away. He laid on the power coming around the corner of the
basement, lost control, and smashed head-on into the furnace. It was a
great loss for him. The jagged wood and metal cut and bruised him; he
had destroyed his brand-new car. Far worse was the damage to the furnace. In 1933 such damage was almost more than the family finances
could sustain. Furious, my father's father called him names, upbraided
him for his stupidity and irresponsibility, and made him feel worthless.
Years later, as he would tell this story to me, my father would linger over
those words — "stupid," "irresponsible" — as if the pain had never gone
away.

In these moments he and I had a common stake in something. Though he might not know whether I was reading at the eighth-grade level or the twelfth-grade level — or whether my math scores lagged behind those of the rest of the class — he was delighted to see that I knew how to adjust a clutch cable or stop after a low-speed, controlled skid. These skills were a source of genuine adventure for me, and I came to life when he observed my progress.

But this was only part of our rapport with the motorcycle. My father found few occasions to be overtly tender with the family, but he could be tender with a machine. I began to notice this in the countless small adjustments he regularly made. His touch on the cranky carburetor settings for gas and air was gentle, even soothing; at least it seemed to soothe the motorcycle, which ran smoothly under his touch but not under mine.

I found that, from time to time, this tenderness buoyed me up in its   10
wake. If my father was, in his dreams, a flat-track mechanic, then I was his driver: He owed me the best he could give me; that was his job. This dream of his bound us in a metaphor which, at its heart, was not so different from the kind of straightforward love another child might have received from a more accessible father. I did not know this then, not exactly. But I knew, when we both hovered over the Benelli's cylinder head or gearbox, adjusting a cam or replacing a gasket, that he would not have worked on this machine for himself alone.

Yet there was a secret to our new language, a secret that only slowly revealed itself. What we shared through the motorcycle contradicted most of our other encounters in the family. It was almost as if we lived in another world when we came together over this machine, and for a time I hoped that world might be the new one, the ideal on the horizon. I was wrong. The bands of our words were strong, but too narrow to encompass the worlds rising before me.

Almost without knowing it I began to acquire other vocabularies — the tough, subtle speech of girls, the staccato syllables of independence, the wrenching words of love and emptiness. In this I began to leave him behind. He could not talk of these things with me. He remained with his engines; and long after I had ceased to ride it, he would occasionally open the gas jets, prime the carburetor, and take my motorcycle for a spin around the block.

But as it seems that nothing is ever wholly lost, this vocabulary of the garage and the flat-track speed-way has a kind of potency, a place in the scheme of things. When, recently, I had dinner with my father, after not having seen him for nearly a year, we greeted each other with the awkwardness of child cousins: We hardly knew what to say. I had almost given up on the possibility of a prolonged conversation until I happened to mention that my car needed a new clutch. Suddenly we were safe again, as we moved from the clutch to the valves on his souped-up VW and the four-barrel carburetor on the '66 Chevrolet Malibu, still pouring on the power after all these years. We had moved back to the language of our old country. And though one of us had journeyed far and had almost forgotten the idioms, the rusty speech still held, for a time, the words of love.

CONSIDERATIONS

1. The first sentence carries many implications about Simmons and his family. Which suggestions are fully considered in the rest of the essay? Which remain implied?

2. How does the motorcycle change the son's and father's perceptions of each other?

3. By often repeating the story about his go-kart, is the father trying to say something beyond it?

4. Does Simmons suggest both positive and negative links between machines and human beings?

WRITING SUGGESTION

5. In many families, a sport or hobby provides the vocabulary for talk between the generations. Baseball, basketball, tennis, hockey, skiing, photography, camping: Each can become the medium for relationships that would not flow as smoothly without this shared interest. Examine a shared interest that bridges the generation gap in your family (or in another family you know well). As if you were examining the dialect of another tribe, clarify the vocabulary that the family uses to discuss the interest. For instance, does custom allow for praise and criticism from young to old, not just from old to young? Explain what is communicated by this family idiom.

BARBARA DAFOE WHITEHEAD

Women and the Future of Fatherhood

BARBARA DAFOE WHITEHEAD (b. 1944), a social historian, earned her B.A. at the University of Wisconsin and a Ph.D. in American social history from the University of Chicago. Her essays on parenting and family life have appeared in magazines such as *The Atlantic Monthly, Commonweal,* and the *Wilson Quarterly,* where "Women and the Future of Fatherhood" first appeared. Her book, *The Divorce Culture,* will be published in 1997.

Much of our contemporary debate over fatherhood is governed by the assumption that men can solve the fatherhood problem on their own. The organizers of last year's Million Man March asked women to stay home, and the leaders of Promise Keepers and other grass-roots fatherhood movements whose members gather with considerably less fanfare simply do not admit women.

There is a cultural rationale for the exclusion of women. The fatherhood movement sees the task of reinstating responsible fatherhood as an effort to alter today's norms of masculinity and correctly believes that such an effort cannot succeed unless it is voluntarily undertaken and supported by men. There is also a political rationale in defining fatherlessness as a men's issue. In the debate about marriage and parenthood, which women have dominated for at least thirty years, the fatherhood movement gives men a powerful collective voice and presence.

Yet however effective the grass-roots movement is at stirring men's consciences and raising their consciousness, the fatherhood problem will not be solved by men alone. To be sure, by signaling their commitment to accepting responsibility for the rearing of their children, men have taken the essential first step. But what has not yet been acknowledged is that the success of any effort to renew fatherhood as a social fact and a cultural norm also hinges on the attitudes and behavior of women. Men can't be fathers unless the mothers of their children allow it.

Merely to say this is to point to how thoroughly marital disruption has weakened the bond between fathers and children. More than half of all American children are likely to spend at least part of their lives in one-parent homes. Since the vast majority of children in disrupted families live with their mothers, fathers do not share a home or a daily life with their children. It is much more difficult for men to make the kinds of small,

33

routine, instrumental investments in their children that help forge a good relationship. It is hard to fix a flat bike tire or run a bath when you live in another neighborhood or another town. Many a father's instrumental contribution is reduced to the postal or electronic transmission of money, or, all too commonly, to nothing at all. Without regular contact with their children, men often make reduced emotional contributions as well. Fathers must struggle to sustain close emotional ties across time and space, to "be there" emotionally without being there physically. Some may pick up the phone, send a birthday card, or buy a present, but for many fathers, physical absence also becomes emotional absence.

Without marriage, men also lose access to the social and emotional   5 intelligence of women in building relationships. Wives teach men how to care for young children, and they also encourage children to love their fathers. Mothers who do not live with the father of their children are not as likely as married mothers to represent him in positive ways to the children; nor are the relatives who are most likely to have greatest contact with the children — the mother's parents, brothers, and sisters — likely to have a high opinion of the children's father. Many men are able to overcome such obstacles, but only with difficulty. In general, men need marriage in order to be good fathers.

If the future of fatherhood depends on marriage, however, its future is uncertain. Marriage depends on women as well as men, and women are less committed to marriage than ever before in the nation's history. In the past, women were economically dependent on marriage and assumed a disproportionately heavy responsibility for maintaining the bond, even if the underlying relationship was seriously or irretrievably damaged. In the last third of the twentieth century, however, as women have gained more opportunities for paid work and the availability of child care has increased, they have become less dependent on marriage as an economic arrangement. Though it is not easy, it is possible for women to raise children on their own. This has made divorce far more attractive as a remedy for an unsatisfying marriage, and a growing number of women have availed themselves of the option.

Today, marriage and motherhood are coming apart. Remarriage and marriage rates are declining even as the rates of divorce remain stuck at historic highs and childbearing outside marriage becomes more common. Many women see single motherhood as a choice and a right to be exercised if a suitable husband does not come along in time.

The vision of the "first stage" feminism of the 1960s and '70s, which held out the model of the career woman unfettered by husband or children, has been accepted by women only in part. Women want to be fettered by children, even to the point of going through grueling infertility treatments or artificial insemination to achieve motherhood. But they are increasingly ambivalent about the ties that bind them to a husband and about the necessity of marriage as a condition of parenthood. In 1994, a

National Opinion Research survey asked a group of Americans, "Do you agree or disagree: One parent can bring up a child as well as two parents together." Women split 50/50 on the question; men disagreed by more than two to one.

And indeed, women enjoy certain advantages over men in a society marked by high and sustained levels of family breakup. Women do not need marriage to maintain a close bond to their children, and thus to experience the larger sense of social and moral purpose that comes with raising children. As the bearers and nurturers of children and (increasingly) as the sole breadwinners for families, women continue to be engaged in personally rewarding and socially valuable pursuits. They are able to demonstrate their feminine virtues outside marriage.

Men, by contrast, have no positive identity as fathers outside marriage. Indeed, the emblematic absent father today is the infamous "deadbeat dad." In part, this is the result of efforts to stigmatize irresponsible fathers who fail to pay alimony and child support. But this image also reflects the fact that men are heavily dependent on the marriage partnership to fulfill their role as fathers. Even those who keep up their child support payments are deprived of the social importance and sense of larger purpose that comes from providing for children and raising a family. And it is the rare father who can develop the qualities needed to meet the new cultural ideal of the involved and "nurturing" father without the help of a spouse. 10

These differences are reflected in a growing virtue gap. American popular culture today routinely recognizes and praises the achievements of single motherhood, while the widespread failure of men as fathers has resulted in a growing sense of cynicism and despair about men's capacity for virtuous conduct in family life. The enormously popular movie *Waiting to Exhale* captures the essence of this virtue gap with its portrait of steadfast mothers and deadbeat fathers, morally sleazy men and morally unassailable women. And women feel free to vent their anger and frustration with men in ways that would seem outrageous to women if the shoe were on the other foot. In *Operating Instructions* (1993), her memoir of single motherhood, Ann LaMott mordantly observes, "On bad days, I think straight white men are so poorly wired, so emotionally unenlightened and unconscious that you must approach each one as if he were some weird cross between a white supremacist and an incredibly depressing T. S. Eliot poem."

Women's weakening attachment to marriage should not be taken as a lack of interest in marriage or in a husband-wife partnership in child rearing. Rather, it is a sign of women's more exacting emotional standards for husbands and their growing insistence that men play a bigger part in caring for children and the household. Given their double responsibilities as breadwinners and mothers, many working wives find men's need for ego reinforcement and other forms of emotional and physical upkeep irksome and their failure to share housework and child care absolutely infuriating. (Surveys show that husbands perform only one-third of all household tasks even if their wives are working full-time). Why should men be treated like babies? women complain. If men fail to meet their standards, many women are willing to do without them. Poet and polemicist Katha Pollitt captures the prevailing sentiment: "If single women can have sex, their own homes, the respect of friends, and interesting work, they don't need to tell themselves that any marriage is better than none. Why not have a child on one's own? Children are a joy. Many men are not."

For all these reasons, it is important to see the fatherhood problem as part of the larger cultural problem of the decline of marriage as a lasting relationship between men and women. The traditional bargain between men and women has broken down, and a new bargain has not yet been struck. It is impossible to predict what that bargain will look like — or whether there will even be one. However, it is possible to speculate about the talking points that might bring women to the bargaining table. First, a crucial proviso: There must be recognition of the changed social and economic status of women. Rightly or wrongly, many women fear that the fatherhood movement represents an effort to reinstate the status quo ante, to repeal the gains and achievements women have made over the past thirty years and return to the "separate spheres" domestic ideology that put men in the workplace and women in the home. Any effort to rethink marriage must accept the fact that women will continue to work outside the home.

Therefore, a new bargain must be struck over the division of paid work and family work. This does not necessarily mean a 50/50 split in the work load every single day, but it does mean that men must make a more determined and conscientious effort to do more than one-third of the household chores. How each couple arrives at a sense of what is fair will vary, of course, but the goal is to establish some mutual understanding and commitment to an equitable division of tasks.

Another talking point may focus on the differences in the expecta-   15
tions men and women have for marriage and intimacy. Americans have a "best friends" ideal for marriage that includes some desires that might in fact be more easily met by a best friend — someone who doesn't come with all the complicated entanglements of sharing a bed, a bank account, and a bathroom. Nonetheless, high expectations for emotional intimacy in marriage often are confounded by the very different understandings men and women have of intimacy. Much more than men, women seek intimacy and affection through talking and emotional disclosure. Men often prefer sex to talking, and physical disrobing to emotional disclosing. They tend to be less than fully committed to (their own) sexual fidelity, while women view fidelity as a crucial sign of commitment. These are differences that the sexes need to engage with mutual recognition and tolerance.

In renegotiating the marital bargain, it may also be useful to acknowledge the biosocial differences between mothers and fathers rather than to assume an androgynous model for the parental partnership. There can be a high degree of flexibility in parental roles, but men and women are not interchangeable "parental units," particularly in their children's early years. Rather than struggle to establish identical tracks in career and family lives, it may be more realistic to consider how children's needs and well-being might require patterns of paid work and child rearing that are different for mothers and fathers but are nevertheless equitable over the course of a lifetime.

Finally, it may be important to think and talk about marriage in another kind of language than the one that suffuses our current discourse on relationships. The secular language of "intimate relationships" is the language of politics and psychotherapy, and it focuses on individual rights and individual needs. It can be heard most clearly in the personal-ad columns, a kind of masked ball where optimists go in search of partners who respect their rights and meet their emotional needs. These are not unimportant in the achievement of the contemporary ideal of marriage, which emphasizes egalitarianism and emotional fulfillment. But this notion of marriage as a union of two sovereign selves may be inadequate to define a relationship that carries with it the obligations, duties, and sacrifices of parenthood. There has always been tension between marriage as an intimate relationship between a man and a woman and marriage as an institutional arrangement for raising children, and though the language of individual rights plays a part in defining the former, it cannot fully describe the latter. The parental partnership requires some language that acknowledges differences, mutuality, complementarity, and, more than anything else, altruism.

There is a potentially powerful incentive for women to respond to an effort to renegotiate the marriage bargain, and that has to do with their children. Women can be good mothers without being married. But especially with weakened communities that provide little support, children need levels of parental investment that cannot be supplied solely by a good mother, even if she has the best resources at her disposal. These needs are more likely to be met if the child has a father as well as a mother under the same roof. Simply put, even the best mothers cannot be good fathers.

CONSIDERATIONS

1. According to Whitehead, why were women more committed to marriage in the past than they are today? Does she recommend that families return to that situation?

2. What is the "growing virtue gap" that Whitehead observes in contemporary culture?

3. In what ways have women raised the standards for husbands? Do you think there has been a comparable change in men's standards for wives?

WRITING SUGGESTION

4. Whitehead cites some writers who question whether men are even desirable in a family. Do you think fathers provide advantages that independent, emotionally responsive women do not? If you were designing a utopian society, what would you eliminate, preserve, or strengthen in the cultural norm of a family? Explain the reasons for changing one or two current features of parents' roles. Try to show how your changes could lead to an improved cultural norm of marriage.

NANCY FRIDAY

Competition

NANCY FRIDAY (b. 1937) worked as a journalist after attending Wellesley College. She has reexamined woman's identity in several books about the way sexual roles are expressed and enforced in everyday life. Her works consider connections between sexual fantasies and people's real circumstances, as in *Men in Love, Male Sexual Fantasies: The Triumph of Love over Rage* (1981) and *My Secret Garden* (1983). Her most recent book is *The Power of Beauty* (1996). The following excerpt from her autobiography, *My Mother/My Self* (1977), recounts the way that she reacted as an adolescent to the presence of older, more sexually defined and attractive women in her family.

Although I didn't realize it at the time, my mother was getting prettier. My sister was a beauty. My adolescence was the time of our greatest estrangement.

I have a photo of the three of us when I was twelve: my mother, my sister Susie, and I, on a big chintz sofa, each on a separate cushion, leaning away from one another with big spaces in between. I grew up fired with a sense of family spirit, which I loved and needed, with aunts and uncles and cousins under the omnipotent umbrella of my grandfather. "All for one and one for all," he would say at summer reunions, and no one took it more seriously than I. I would have gone to war for any one of them, and believed they would do the same for me. But within our own little nucleus, the three of us didn't touch much.

Now, when I ask her why, my mother sighs and says she supposes it was because that was how she was raised. I remember shrinking from her Elizabeth Arden night-cream kiss, mumbling from under the blanket that yes, I had brushed my teeth. I had not. I had wet the toothbrush in case she felt it, feeling that would get even with her. For what? The further we all get from childhood, the more physically affectionate we try to be with one another. But we are still shy after all these years.

I was a late bloomer, like my mother. But my mother bloomed so late, or had such a penetrating early frost, that she believed it even less than I would in my turn. When she was a freckled sixteen and sitting shyly on her unfortunate hands, her younger sister was already a famous beauty. That is still the relationship between them. Grandmothers both, in their eyes my aunt is still the sleek-haired belle of the ball, immaculately handsome on a horse. My mother's successes do not count. They will argue at 2:00 A.M. over whether one of my aunt's many beaux ever asked my mother out. My mother could never make up a flattering story about herself. I doubt that she so much as heard the nice things men told her once she had grown into the fine-looking woman who smiles at me in family photos. But she always gives in to my aunt, much I'm sure as she gave in to the old self-image after my father died. He — that one splendidly handsome man — may have picked her out from all the rest, but his death just a few years later must have felt like some punishment for having dared to believe for a moment that her father was wrong: Who could possibly want her? She still blushes at a compliment.

I think she was at her prettiest in her early thirties. I was twelve and   5
at my nadir. Her hair had gone a delicate auburn red and she wore it brushed back from her face in soft curls. Seated beside her and Susie, who inherited a raven version of her beautiful hair, I looked like an adopted person. But I had already defended myself against my looks. They were unimportant. There was a distance between me and the mirror commensurate with the growing distance between me and my mother and sister. My success with my made-up persona was proof: I didn't need them. My titles at school, my awards and achievements, so bolstered my image of myself that until writing this book I genuinely believed that I grew up feeling sorry for my sister. What chance had she alongside The Great Achiever and Most Popular Girl in the World? I even worked up some guilt about outshining her. Pure survival instinct? My dazzling smile would divert the most critical observer from comparing me to the cute, petite girls with whom I grew up. I switched the contest: Don't look at my lank hair, my 5'10", don't notice that my right eye wanders bizarrely (though the eye doctor said it was useless to keep me in glasses); watch me tap dance, watch me win the game, let me make you happy! When I describe myself in those days my mother laughs. "Oh, Nancy, you were such a darling little girl." But I wasn't little anymore.

I think my sister, Susie, was born beautiful, a fact that affected my mother and me deeply, though in different ways. I don't think it mattered so much until Susie's adolescence. She turned so lush one ached to look at her. Pictures of Susie then remind me of the young Elizabeth Taylor in *A Place in the Sun*. One has to almost look away from so much beauty. It scared my mother to death. Whatever had gone on between them before came to a head and has never stopped. Their constant friction determined me to get away from this house of women, to be free of women's petty competitions, to live on a bigger scale. I left home eventually but I've never gotten away from feeling how wonderful to be so beautiful your mother can't take her eyes off you, even if only to nag.

I remember an amazing lack of any feeling about my only sibling, with whom I shared a room for years, whose clothes were identical to mine until I was ten. Except for feelings of irritation when she tried to cuddle me when I was four, bursts of anger that erupted into fist fights which I started and won at ten, and after that, indifference, a calculated unawareness that has resulted in a terrible and sad absence of my sister in my life.

My husband says his sister was the only child his father ever paid any attention to: "You have done to Susie what I did to my sister," he says. "You made her invisible." Me, jealous of Susie, who never won a single trophy or had as many friends as I? I must have been insanely jealous.

I only allowed myself to face it twice. Both times happened in that twelfth year, when my usual defenses couldn't take the emotional cross currents of adolescence. When I did slash out it wasn't very glorious, no well-chosen words or contest on the tennis courts. I did it like a thief in the night. Nobody ever guessed it was I who poured the red nail polish down the front of Susie's new white eyelet evening dress the day of her first yacht club dance. When I stole her summer savings and threw her wallet down the sewer, mother blamed Susie for being so careless. I watched my sister accept the criticism with her mother's own resignation, and I felt some relief from the angry emotions that had hold of me.

When Susie went away to boarding school, I made jokes about how   10
glad I was to be rid of her. It was our first separation. Conflicting urges, angers, and envies were coming at me from every direction; I had nothing left over to handle my terrible feelings of loss at her going. It was the summer I was plagued by what I called "my thoughts."

I read every book in the house as a talisman against thinking. I was afraid that if my brain were left idle for even one minute, these "thoughts" would take over. Perhaps I feared they already had. Was my sister's going away the fulfillment of my own murderous wishes against her? I wrote in my first and only diary: "Susie, come home, please come home!!!!!!! I'm sorry, I'm sorry!!!!!!!"

When I outgrew the Nancy Drew books for perfect attendance at Sunday school, and the Girl Scout badges for such merits as selling the most rat poison door to door, I graduated to prizes at the community theater. I won a plastic wake-up radio for the I Speak for Democracy contest. I was captain of the athletic association, president of the student government, and had the lead in the class play, all in the same year. In fact, I wrote the class play. It might have been embarrassing, but no one else wanted these prizes. Scoring home runs and getting straight A's weren't high on the list of priorities among my friends. (The South takes all prizes for raising noncompetitive women.) In the few cases where anyone did give me a run for the money, I had an unbeatable incentive: my grandfather's applause. It was he for whom I ran.

I can't remember ever hearing my grandfather say to my mother, "Well done, Jane." I can't remember my mother ever saying to my sister, "Well done, Susie." And I never gave my mother the chance to say it to me. She was the last to hear of my achievements, and when she did, it was not from me but from her friends. Did she really notice so little that I was leaving her out? Was she so hurt that she pretended not to care? My classmates who won second prize or even no prize at all asked their families to attend the award ceremonies. I, who won first prize, always, did so to the applause of no kin at all. Was I spiting her? I know I was spiting myself. Nothing would have made me happier than to have her there; nothing would induce me to invite her. It is a game I later played with men: "Leave!" I would cry, and when they did, "How could you hurt me so?" I'd implore.

If I deprived her of the chance to praise me, she never criticized me. Criticism was the vehicle by which she could articulate her relationship to my sister. No matter what it was, Susie could never get it right — in my mother's eyes. It continues that way to this day. Difficult as it is to think of my mother as competitive with anyone, how else could she have felt about her beautiful, ripe fourteen-year-old daughter? My mother was coming into her own mature, full bloom but perhaps that only made her more sensitive to the fact that Susie was simultaneously experiencing the same sexual flush. A year later, my mother remarried. Today, only the geography has changed: The argument begins as soon as they enter the same room. But they are often in the same room. They have never been closer.

How often the dinner table becomes the family battleground. When I met Bill he had no table you could sit around in his vast bachelor apartment. The dinner table was where his father waged war; it was the one time the family was together. In Charleston, dinner was served at 2:00. I have this picture of our midday meals: Susie on my right, mother on my left, and me feeling that our cook, Ruth, had set this beautiful table for me alone.

No one else seemed to care about the golden squash, the crisp chicken, the big silver pitcher of iced tea. While I proceeded to eat my way from one end of the table to the other, Susie and mother would begin: "Susie, that lipstick is too dark.... Must you pluck your eyebrows?... Why did you buy high-heeled, open-toe shoes when I told you to get

15

loafers?. . . Those pointy bras make you look a, like a —" But my mother couldn't say the word. At this point one of them would leave the table in tears, while the other shuddered in despair at the sound of the slammed bedroom door. Meanwhile, I pondered my problem of whose house to play at that afternoon. I would finish both their desserts and be gone before Ruth had cleared the table. Am I exaggerating? Did it only happen once a week? Does it matter?

I was lucky to have escaped those devastating battles. "I never had to worry about Nancy," my mother has always said. "She could always take care of herself." It became true. Only my husband has been allowed to see the extent of my needs. But the competitive drive that made me so self-sufficient was fired by more than jealousy of my sister. If my mother wasn't going to acknowledge me, her father would. If she couldn't succeed in his eyes, I would. It's my best explanation for all those years of trophies and presidencies, for my ability to "reach" my grandfather as my mother never could. I not only won what she had wanted all her life — his praise — I learned with the canniness of the young that this great towering man loved to be loved, to be touched. He couldn't allow himself to reach out first to those he loved most, but he couldn't resist an overture of affection.

I greeted his visits with embraces, took the kisses I had won, and sat at his feet like one of his Dalmatians, while my sister stood shyly in the background and my mother waited for his criticism. But I was no more aware of competing with my mother than of being jealous of my sister. Two generations of women in my family have struggled for my grandfather's praise. Perhaps I became his favorite because he sensed I needed it most. The price I paid was that I had to beat my mother and my sister. I am still guilty for that.

In the stereotyping of the sexes, men are granted all the competitive drives, women none. The idea of competitive women evokes disturbing images — the darker, dykey side of femininity, or cartoons of "ladies" in high heels, flailing at each other ineffectively with their handbags. An important step has been left out of our socialization: Mother raises us to win people's love. She gives us no training in the emotions of rivalry that would lose it for us. With no practical experience in the rules that make competition safe, we fear its ferocity. Never having been taught to win, we do not know how to lose. Women are not raised to compete like gentlemen.

CONSIDERATIONS

1. What sort of person was the author as a twelve-year-old? Would you, at that age, have liked or disliked her?

2. What does Friday's mother fear? Identify several things in her life that contribute to those fears. Do Friday's insights into her mother's character seem fair?

3. Explain the difference between "hating to lose" and "loving to win."

WRITING SUGGESTION

4. Among adolescents, how does competitiveness differ for males and females? Are the differences defined more sharply at home or at school?
Write an essay about how your sense of competition differs from the competitiveness you observe in the opposite sex.

SHELBY STEELE

On Being Black and Middle Class

SHELBY STEELE (b. 1946) grew up in Chicago. He earned a
Ph.D. in history from the University of Utah, and he has taught
English at San Jose State University in California. His essays on
race relations have appeared in magazines such as *Harper's*, the
New York Times Magazine, *Commentary*, and *Black World*. His crit-
icisms of both white and black social policies on affirmative action
and other issues are collected in *The Content of Our Character: A
New Vision of Race in America* (1990), which won a National Book
Critics Circle Award.

Not long ago a friend of mine, black like myself, said to me that the
term "black middle class" was actually a contradiction in terms. Race, he
insisted, blurred class distinctions among blacks. If you were black, you
were just black and that was that. When I argued, he let his eyes roll at my
naivete. Then he went on. For us, as black professionals, it was an exercise
in self-flattery, a pathetic pretention, to give meaning to such a distinction. Worse, the very idea of class threatened the unity that was vital to
the black community as a whole. After all, since when had white America
taken note of anything but color when it came to blacks? He then reminded me of an old Malcolm X line that had been popular in the sixties.
Question: What is a black man with a Ph.D.? Answer: A nigger.

For many years I had been on my friend's side of this argument.
Much of my conscious thinking on the old conundrum of race and class
was shaped during my high school and college years in the race-charged
sixties, when the fact of my race took on an almost religious significance.
Progressively, from the mid-sixties on, more and more aspects of my life
found their explanation, their justification, and their motivation in race.
My youthful concerns about career, romance, money, values, and even
styles of dress became a subject [of] consultation with various oracular

sources of racial wisdom. And these ranged from a figure as ennobling as Martin Luther King, Jr., to the underworld elegance of dress I found in jazz clubs on the South Side of Chicago. Everywhere there were signals, and in those days I considered myself so blessed with clarity and direction that I pitied my white classmates who found more embarrassment than guidance in the face of *their* race. In 1968, inflated by my new power, I took a mischievous delight in calling them culturally disadvantaged.

But now, hearing my friend's comment was like hearing a priest from a church I'd grown disenchanted with. I understood him, but my faith was weak. What had sustained me in the sixties sounded monotonous and off the mark in the eighties. For me, race had lost much of its juju, its singular capacity to conjure meaning. And today, when I honestly look at my life and the lives of many other middle-class blacks I know, I can see that race never fully explained our situation in American society. Black though I may be, it is impossible for me to sit in my single-family house with two cars in the driveway and a swing set in the back yard and *not* see the role class has played in my life. And how can my friend, similarly raised and similarly situated, not see it?

Yet despite my certainty I felt a sharp tug of guilt as I tried to explain myself over my friend's skepticism. He is a man of many comedic facial expressions and, as I spoke, his brow lifted in extreme moral alarm as if I were uttering the unspeakable. His clear implication was that I was being elitist and possibly (dare he suggest?) antiblack — crimes for which there might well be no redemption. He pretended to fear for me. I chuckled along with him, but inwardly I did wonder at myself. Though I never doubted the validity of what I was saying, I felt guilty saying it. Why?

After he left (to retrieve his daughter from a dance lesson) I realized   5
that the trap I felt myself in had a tiresome familiarity and, in a sort of slow-motion epiphany, I began to see its outline. It was like the suddenly sharp vision one has at the end of a burdensome marriage when all the long-repressed incompatibilities come undeniably to light.

What became clear to me is that people like myself, my friend, and middle-class blacks generally are caught in a very specific double bind that keeps two equally powerful elements of our identity at odds with each other. The middle-class values by which we were raised — the work ethic, the importance of education, the value of property ownership, of respectability, of "getting ahead," of stable family life, of initiative, of self-reliance, etc. — are, in themselves, raceless and even assimilationist. They urge us toward participation in the American mainstream, toward integration, toward a strong identification with the society — and toward the entire constellation of qualities that are implied in the word "individualism." These values are almost rules for how to prosper in a democratic, free-enterprise society that admires and rewards individual effort. They tell us to work hard for ourselves and our families and to seek our opportunities whenever they appear, inside or outside the confines of whatever ethnic group we may belong to.

But the particular pattern of racial identification that emerged in the sixties and that still prevails today urges middle-class blacks (and all blacks) in the opposite direction. This pattern asks us to see ourselves as an embattled minority, and it urges an adversarial stance toward the mainstream, an emphasis on ethnic consciousness over individualism. It is organized around an implied separatism.

The opposing thrust of these two parts of our identity results in the double bind of middle-class blacks. There is no forward movement on either plane that does not constitute backward movement on the other. This was the familiar trap I felt myself in while talking with my friend. As I spoke about class, his eyes reminded me that I was betraying race. Clearly, the two indispensable parts of my identity were a threat to each other.

Of course when you think about it, class and race are both similar in some ways and also naturally opposed. They are two forms of collective identity with boundaries that intersect. But whether they clash or peacefully coexist has much to do with how they are defined. Being both black and middle class becomes a double bind when class and race are defined in sharply antagonistic terms, so that one must be repressed to appease the other.

But what is the "substance" of these two identities, and how does   10 each establish itself in an individual's overall identity? It seems to me that when we identify with any collective we are basically identifying with images that tell us what it means to be a member of that collective. Identity is not the same thing as the fact of membership in a collective; it is, rather, a form of self-definition, facilitated by images of what we wish our membership in the collective to mean. In this sense, the images we identify with may reflect the aspirations of the collective more than they reflect reality, and their content can vary with shifts in those aspirations.

But the process of identification is usually dialectical. It is just as necessary to say what we are *not* as it is to say what we are — so that finally identification comes about by embracing a polarity of positive and negative images. To identify as middle class, for example, I must have both positive and negative images of what being middle class entails; then I will know what I should and should not be doing in order to be middle class. The same goes for racial identity.

In the racially turbulent sixties the polarity of images that came to define racial identification was very antagonistic to the polarity that defined middle-class identification. One might say that the positive images of one lined up with the negative images of the other, so that to identify with both required either a contortionist's flexibility or a dangerous splitting of the self. The double bind of the black middle class was in place.

The black middle class has always defined its class identity by means of positive images gleaned from middle- and upper-class white society, and by means of negative images of lower-class blacks. This habit goes back to the institution of slavery itself, when "house" slaves both mimicked the whites they served and held themselves above the "field" slaves. But in the sixties the old bourgeois impulse to dissociate from the lower classes (the "we-they" distinction) backfired when racial identity suddenly called for the celebration of this same black lower class. One of the qualities of a double bind is that one feels it more than sees it, and I distinctly remember the tension and strange sense of dishonesty I felt in those days as I moved back and forth like a bigamist between the demands of class and race.

Though my father was born poor, he achieved middle-class standing through much hard work and sacrifice (one of his favorite words) and by identifying fully with solid middle-class values — mainly hard work, family life, property ownership, and education for his children (all four of whom have advanced degrees). In his mind these were not so much values as laws of nature. People who embodied them made up the positive images in his class polarity. The negative images came largely from the blacks he had left behind because they were "going nowhere."

No one in my family remembers how it happened, but as time went   15
on, the negative images congealed into an imaginary character named Sam, who, from the extensive service we put him to, quickly grew to mythic proportions. In our family lore he was sometimes a trickster, sometimes a boob, but always possessed a catalogue of sly faults that gave up graphic images of everything we should not be. On sacrifice: "Sam never thinks about tomorrow. He wants it now or he doesn't care about it." On work: "Sam doesn't favor it too much." On children: "Sam likes to have them but not to raise them." On money: "Sam drinks it up and pisses it out." On fidelity: "Sam has to have two or three women." On clothes: "Sam features loud clothes. He likes to see and be seen." And so on. Sam's persona amounted to a negative instruction manual in class identity.

I don't think that any of us believed Sam's faults were accurate representations of lower-class black life. He was an instrument of self-definition, not of sociological accuracy. It never occurred to us that he looked very much like the white racist stereotype of blacks, or that he might have been a manifestation of our own racial self-hatred. He simply gave us a counterpoint against which to express our aspirations. If self-hatred was a factor, it was not, for us, a matter of hating lower-class blacks but of hating what we did not want to be.

Still, hate or love aside, it is fundamentally true that my middle-class identity involved a dissociation from images of lower-class black life and a corresponding identification with values and patterns of responsibility that are common to the middle class everywhere. These values sent me a clear message: Be both an individual and a responsible citizen; understand that the quality of your life will approximately reflect the quality of effort you put into it; know that individual responsibility is the basis of freedom and that the limitations imposed by fate (whether fair or unfair) are no excuse for passivity.

Whether I live up to these values or not, I know that my acceptance of them is the result of lifelong conditioning. I know also that I share this conditioning with middle-class people of all races and that I can no more easily be free of it than I can be free of my race. Whether all this got started because the black middle class modeled itself on the white middle class is no longer relevant. For the middle-class black, conditioned by these values from birth, the sense of meaning they provide is as immutable as the color of his skin.

In my junior year in college I rode to a debate tournament with three white students and our faculty coach, an elderly English professor. The experience of being the lone black in a group of whites was so familiar to me that I thought nothing of it as our trip began. But then, halfway through the trip, the professor casually turned to me and, in an isn't-the-world-funny sort of tone, said that he had just refused to rent an apartment in a house he owned to a "very nice" black couple because their color would "offend" the white couple who lived downstairs. His eyebrows lifted helplessly over his hawkish nose, suggesting that he too, like me, was a victim of America's racial farce. His look assumed a kind of comradeship: He and I were above this grimy business of race, though for expediency we had occasionally to concede the world its madness.

My vulnerability in this situation came not so much from the professor's blindness to his own racism as from his assumption that I would participate in it, that I would conspire with him against my own race so that he might remain comfortably blind. Why did he think I would be amenable to this? I can only guess that he assumed my middle-class identity was so complete and all-encompassing that I would see his action as nothing more than a trifling concession to the folkways of our land, that I would in fact applaud his decision not to disturb propriety. Blind to both his own racism and to me — one blindness serving the other — he could not recognize that he was asking me to betray my race in the name of my class. 20

His blindness made me feel vulnerable because it threatened to expose my own repressed ambivalence. His comment pressured me to choose between my class identification, which had contributed to my being a college student and a member of the debating team, and my desperate desire to be "black." I could have one but not both; I was double-bound.

Because double binds are repressed there is always an element of terror in them: the terror of bringing to the conscious mind the buried duplicity, self-deception, and pretense involved in serving two masters. This terror is the stuff of vulnerability, and since vulnerability is one of the least tolerable of all human feelings, we usually transform it into an emotion that seems to restore the control of which it has robbed us; most often, that emotion is anger. And so, before the professor had even finished his little story, I had become a furnace of rage. The year was 1967, and I had been primed by endless hours of nap-matching[1] to feel, at least consciously, completely at one with the victim-focused black identity. This identity gave me the license, and the impunity, to unleash upon this professor one of those volcanic eruptions of racial indignation familiar to us from the novels of Richard Wright. Like Cross Damon in *Outsider*, who kills in perfectly righteous anger, I tried to annihilate the man. I punished him not according to the measure of his crime but according to the measure of my vulnerability, a measure set by the cumulative tension of years of repressed terror. Soon I saw that terror in *his* face, as he stared hollow-eyed at the road ahead. My white friends in the back seat, knowing no conflict between their own class and race, were astonished that someone they had taken to be so much like themselves could harbor a rage that for all the world looked murderous.

Though my rage was triggered by the professor's comment, it was deepened and sustained by a complex of need, conflict, and repression in myself of which I had been wholly unaware. Out of my racial vulnerability I had developed the strong need of an identity with which to defend myself. The only such identity available was that of me as victim, him as victimizer. Once in the grip of this paradigm, I began to do far more damage to myself than he had done.

Seeing myself as a victim meant that I clung all the harder to my racial identity, which, in turn, meant that I suppressed my class identity. This cut me off from all the resources my class values might have offered me. In those values, for instance, I might have found the means to a more dispassionate response, the response less of a victim attacked by a victimizer than of an individual offended by a foolish old man. As an individual I might have reported this professor to the college dean. Or I might have calmly tried to reveal his blindness to him, and possibly won a convert. (The flagrancy of his remark suggested a hidden guilt and even self-recognition on which I might have capitalized. Doesn't confession usually signal a willingness to face oneself?) Or I might have simply chuckled and then let my silence serve as an answer to his provocation. Would not my composure, in any form it might take, deflect into his own heart the arrow he'd shot at me?

Instead, my anger, itself the hair-trigger expression of a long-   25
repressed double bind, not only cut me off from the best of my own resources, it also distorted the nature of my true racial problem. The righteousness of this anger and the easy catharsis it brought buoyed the delusion of my victimization and left me as blind as the professor himself.

---

[1]*Nap-matching*: Slang for measuring one's black identification.

CONSIDERATIONS

1. In paragraph 6, Steele lists specific values that define the middle class. Would you add to or challenge any items on his list? What items would define a lower class? An upper class?

2. How, if at all, did the imaginary Sam differ from a racist image? From an advertising image?

3. Steele criticizes his younger reaction to an insult from his college debate coach. How do you regard his response? Do you think the alternatives he names are preferable?

4. Do you think Steele was most powerfully influenced by race, class, or family? Choose one and support your choice.

WRITING SUGGESTION

5. In your family or social group, what puts you in conflict with another good part of yourself? What two identities or allegiances can turn into a double bind? Perhaps your religious or ethnic upbringing, your athletic ability, your family's expectations for you, or your desire to travel aimlessly for a while threatens some other value or goal you uphold. Explain the double bind that can operate in your situation.

ALICE WALKER

Everyday Use

ALICE WALKER (b. 1944), one of America's leading contemporary writers, was raised in a Georgia sharecropper's family as the
youngest of eight children. After graduating from Sarah
Lawrence College, she became active in the civil rights movement
and in feminism. Her work as a poet, essayist, and fiction writer
includes five novels, among them *The Color Purple* (1982), winner
of both the Pulitzer Prize and the American Book Award.
Walker's most recent collection of essays is *The Same River Twice:
Honoring the Difficult* (1996). The following short story is taken
from *In Love and Trouble: Stories of Black Women* (1973).

for your grandmama

I will wait for her in the yard that Maggie and I made so clean and
wavy yesterday afternoon. A yard like this is more comfortable than most
people know. It is not just a yard. It is like an extended living room. When
the hard clay is swept clean as a floor and the fine sand around the edges
lined with tiny, irregular grooves, anyone can come and sit and look up
into the elm tree and wait for the breezes that never come inside the
house.

Maggie will be nervous until after her sister goes: She will stand
hopelessly in corners, homely and ashamed of the burn scars down her
arms and legs, eying her sister with a mixture of envy and awe. She thinks
her sister has held life always in the palm of one hand, that "no" is a word
the world never learned to say to her.

You've no doubt seen those TV shows where the child who has
"made it" is confronted, as a surprise, by her own mother and father, tot-
tering in weakly from backstage. (A pleasant surprise, of course: What
would they do if parent and child came on the show only to curse out and
insult each other?) On TV mother and child embrace and smile into each
other's faces. Sometimes the mother and father weep, the child wraps
them in her arms and leans across the table to tell how she would not have
made it without their help. I have seen these programs.

Sometimes I dream a dream in which Dee and I are suddenly
brought together on a TV program of this sort. Out of a dark and soft-
seated limousine I am ushered into a bright room filled with many people.
There I meet a smiling, gray, sporty man like Johnny Carson who shakes

my hand and tells me what a fine girl I have. Then we are on the stage and
Dee is embracing me with tears in her eyes. She pins on my dress a large
orchid, even though she has told me once that she thinks orchids are tacky
flowers.

In real life I am a large, big-boned woman with rough, man-working   5
hands. In the winter I wear flannel nightgowns to bed and overalls during
the day. I can kill and clean a hog as mercilessly as a man. My fat keeps me
hot in zero weather. I can work outside all day, breaking ice to get water
for washing; I can eat pork liver cooked over the open fire minutes after it
comes steaming from the hog. One winter I knocked a bull calf straight in
the brain between the eyes with a sledge hammer and had the meat hung
up to chill before nightfall. But of course all this does not show on television. I am the way my daughter would want me to be: a hundred pounds
lighter, my skin like an uncooked barley pancake. My hair glistens in the
hot bright lights. Johnny Carson has much to do to keep up with my
quick and witty tongue.

But that is a mistake. I know even before I wake up. Who ever knew
a Johnson with a quick tongue? Who can even imagine me looking a
strange white man in the eye? It seems to me I have talked to them always
with one foot raised in flight, with my head turned in whichever way is
farthest from them. Dee, though. She would always look anyone in the
eye. Hesitation was no part of her nature.

"How do I look, Mama?" Maggie says, showing just enough of her
thin body enveloped in pink skirt and red blouse for me to know she's
there, almost hidden by the door.

"Come out into the yard," I say.

Have you ever seen a lame animal, perhaps a dog run over by some
careless person rich enough to own a car, sidle up to someone who is ignorant enough to be kind to him? That is the way my Maggie walks. She
has been like this, chin on chest, eyes on ground, feet in shuffle, ever since
the fire that burned the other house to the ground.

Dee is lighter than Maggie, with nicer hair and a fuller figure. She's   10
a woman now, though sometimes I forget. How long ago was it that the
other house burned? Ten, twelve years? Sometimes I can still hear the
flames and feel Maggie's arms sticking to me, her hair smoking and her
dress falling off her in little black papery flakes. Her eyes seemed
stretched open, blazed open by the flames reflected in them. And Dee. I
see her standing off under the sweet gum tree she used to dig gum out of;
a look of concentration on her face as she watched the last dingy gray
board of the house fall in toward the red-hot brick chimney. Why don't
you do a dance around the ashes? I'd wanted to ask her. She had hated the
house that much.

I used to think she hated Maggie, too. But that was before we raised
the money, the church and me, to send her to Augusta to school. She used
to read to us without pity; forcing words, lies, other folks' habits, whole

lives upon us two, sitting trapped and ignorant underneath her voice. She washed us in a river of make-believe, burned us with a lot of knowledge we didn't necessarily need to know. Pressed us to her with the serious way she read, to shove us away at just the moment, like dimwits, we seemed about to understand.

Dee wanted nice things. A yellow organdy dress to wear to her graduation from high school; black pumps to match a green suit she'd made from an old suit somebody gave me. She was determined to stare down any disaster in her efforts. Her eyelids would not flicker for minutes at a time. Often I fought off the temptation to shake her. At sixteen she had a style of her own: and knew what style was.

I never had an education myself. After second grade the school was closed down. Don't ask me why: In 1927 colored asked fewer questions than they do now. Sometimes Maggie reads to me. She stumbles along good-naturedly but can't see well. She knows she is not bright. Like good looks and money, quickness passed her by. She will marry John Thomas (who has mossy teeth in an earnest face) and then I'll be free to sit here and I guess just sing church songs to myself. Although I never was a good singer. Never could carry a tune. I was always better at a man's job. I used to love to milk till I was hooked in the side in '49. Cows are soothing and slow and don't bother you, unless you try to milk them the wrong way.

I have deliberately turned my back on the house. It is three rooms, just like the one that burned, except the roof is tin; they don't make shingle roofs any more. There are no real windows, just some holes cut in the sides, like the portholes in a ship, but not round and not square, with rawhide holding the shutters up on the outside. This house is in a pasture, too, like the other one. No doubt when Dee sees it she will want to tear it down. She wrote me once that no matter where we "choose" to live, she will manage to come see us. But she will never bring her friends. Maggie and I thought about this and Maggie asked me, "Mama, when did Dee ever *have* any friends?"

She had a few. Furtive boys in pink shirts hanging about on washday 15 after school. Nervous girls who never laughed. Impressed with her they worshiped the well-turned phrase, the cute shape, the scalding humor that erupted like bubbles in lye. She read to them.

When she was courting Jimmy T she didn't have much time to pay to us, but turned all her faultfinding power on him. He *flew* to marry a cheap city girl from a family of ignorant flashy people. She hardly had time to recompose herself.

When she comes I will meet — but there they are!

Maggie attempts to make a dash for the house, in her shuffling way, but I stay her with my hand. "Come back here," I say. And she stops and tries to dig a well in the sand with her toe.

It is hard to see them clearly through the strong sun. But even the first glimpse of leg out of the car tells me it is Dee. Her feet were always neat-looking, as if God himself had shaped them with a certain style. From the other side of the car comes a short, stocky man. Hair is all over his head a foot long and hanging from his chin like a kinky mule tail. I hear Maggie suck in her breath. "Uhnnnh," is what it sounds like. Like when you see the wriggling end of a snake just in front of your foot on the road. "Uhnnnh."

Dee next. A dress down to the ground, in this hot weather. A dress   20
so loud it hurts my eyes. There are yellows and oranges enough to throw back the light of the sun. I feel my whole face warming from the heat waves it throws out. Earrings gold, too, and hanging down to her shoulders. Bracelets dangling and making noises when she moves her arm up to shake the folds of the dress out of her armpits. The dress is loose and flows, and as she walks closer, I like it. I hear Maggie go "Uhnnnh" again. It is her sister's hair. It stands straight up like the wool on a sheep. It is black as night and around the edges are two long pigtails that rope about like small lizards disappearing behind her ears.

"Wa-su-zo-Tean-o!" she says, coming on in that gliding way the dress makes her move. The short stocky fellow with the hair to his navel is all grinning and he follows up with "Asalamalakim, my mother and sister!" He moves to hug Maggie but she falls back, right up against the back of my chair. I feel her trembling there and when I look up I see the perspiration falling off her chin.

"Don't get up," says Dee. Since I am stout it takes something of a push. You can see me trying to move a second or two before I make it. She turns, showing white heels through her sandals, and goes back to the car. Out she peeks next with a Polaroid. She stoops down quickly and lines up picture after picture of me sitting there in front of the house with Maggie cowering behind me. She never takes a shot without making sure the house is included. When a cow comes nibbling around the edge of the yard she snaps it and me and Maggie *and* the house. Then she puts the Polaroid in the back seat of the car, and comes up and kisses me on the forehead.

Meanwhile Asalamalakim is going through motions with Maggie's hand. Maggie's hand is as limp as a fish, and probably as cold, despite the sweat, and she keeps trying to pull it back. It looks like Asalamalakim wants to shake hands but wants to do it fancy. Or maybe he don't know how people shake hands. Anyhow, he soon gives up on Maggie.

"Well," I say. "Dee."

"No, Mama," she says. "Not 'Dee,' Wangero Leewanika Kemanjo!"   25
"What happened to 'Dee'?" I wanted to know.

"She's dead," Wangero said. "I couldn't bear it any longer, being named after the people who oppress me."

"You know as well as me you was named after your aunt Dicie," I said. Dicie is my sister. She named Dee. We called her "Big Dee" after Dee was born.

"But who was *she* named after?" asked Wangero.

"I guess after Grandma Dee," I said.   30

"And who was she named after?" asked Wangero.

"Her mother," I said, and saw Wangero was getting tired. "That's about as far back as I can trace it," I said. Though, in fact, I probably could have carried it back beyond the Civil War through the branches.

"Well," said Asalamalakim, "there you are."

"Uhnnnh," I heard Maggie say.

"There I was not," I said, "before 'Dicie' cropped up in our family,   35
so why should I try to trace it that far back?"

He just stood there grinning, looking down on me like somebody inspecting a Model A car. Every once in a while he and Wangero sent eye signals over my head.

"How do you pronounce this name?" I asked.

"You don't have to call me by it if you don't want to," said Wangero.

"Why shouldn't I?" I asked. "If that's what you want us to call you, we'll call you."

"I know it might sound awkward at first," said Wangero.   40

"I'll get used to it," I said. "Ream it out again."

Well, soon we got the name out of the way. Asalamalakim had a name twice as long and three times as hard. After I tripped over it two or three times he told me to just call him Hakim-a-barber. I wanted to ask him was he a barber, but I didn't really think he was, so I didn't ask.

"You must belong to those beef-cattle peoples down the road," I said. They said "Asalamalakim" when they met you, too, but they didn't shake hands. Always too busy: feeding the cattle, fixing the fences, putting up salt-lick shelters, throwing down hay. When the white folks poisoned some of the herd the men stayed up all night with rifles in their hands. I walked a mile and a half just to see the sight.

Hakim-a-barber said, "I accept some of their doctrines, but farming and raising cattle is not my style." (They didn't tell me, and I didn't ask, whether Wangero (Dee) had really gone and married him.)

We sat down to eat and right away he said he didn't eat collards and   45
pork was unclean. Wangero, though, went on through the chitlins and corn bread, the greens and everything else. She talked a blue streak over the sweet potatoes. Everything delighted her. Even the fact that we still used the benches her daddy made for the table when we couldn't afford to buy chairs.

"Oh, Mama!" she cried. Then turned to Hakim-a-barber. "I never knew how lovely these benches are. You can feel the rump prints," she said, running her hands underneath her and along the bench. Then she gave a sigh and her hand closed over Grandma Dee's butter dish. "That's it!" she said. "I knew there was something I wanted to ask you if I could have." She jumped up from the table and went over in the corner where the churn stood, the milk in it clabber by now. She looked at the churn and looked at it.

"This churn top is what I need," she said. "Didn't Uncle Buddy whittle it out of a tree you all used to have?"

"Yes," I said.

"Uh huh," she said happily. "And I want the dasher, too."

"Uncle Buddy whittle that, too?" asked the barber.   50

Dee (Wangero) looked up at me.

"Aunt Dee's first husband whittled the dash," said Maggie so low you almost couldn't hear her. "His name was Henry, but they called him Stash."

"Maggie's brain is like an elephant's," Wangero said, laughing. "I can use the churn top as a centerpiece for the alcove table," she said, sliding a plate over the churn, "and I'll think of something artistic to do with the dasher."

When she finished wrapping the dasher the handle stuck out. I took it for a moment in my hands. You didn't even have to look close to see where hands pushing the dasher up and down to make butter had left a kind of sink in the wood. In fact, there were a lot of small sinks; you could see where thumbs and fingers had sunk into the wood. It was beautiful light yellow wood, from a tree that grew in the yard where Big Dee and Stash had lived.

After dinner Dee (Wangero) went to the trunk at the foot of my bed   55
and started rifling through it. Maggie hung back in the kitchen over the dishpan. Out came Wangero with two quilts. They had been pieced by Grandma Dee and then Big Dee and me had hung them on the quilt frames on the front porch and quilted them. One was in the Lone Star pattern. The other was Walk Around the Mountain. In both of them were scraps of dresses Grandma Dee had worn fifty and more years ago. Bits and pieces of Grandpa Jarrell's Paisley shirts. And one teeny faded blue piece, about the size of a penny matchbox, that was from Great Grandpa Ezra's uniform that he wore in the Civil War.

"Mama," Wangero said sweet as a bird. "Can I have these old quilts?"

I heard something fall in the kitchen, and a minute later the kitchen door slammed.

"Why don't you take one or two of the others?" I asked. "These old things was just done by me and Big Dee from some tops your grandma pieced before she died."

"No," said Wangero. "I don't want those. They are stitched around the borders by machine."

"That'll make them last better," I said.   60

"That's not the point," said Wangero. "These are all pieces of dresses Grandma used to wear. She did all this stitching by hand. Imagine!" She held the quilts securely in her arms, stroking them.

"Some of the pieces, like those lavender ones, come from old clothes her mother handed down to her," I said, moving up to touch the quilts. Dee (Wangero) moved back just enough so that I couldn't reach the quilts. They already belonged to her.

"Imagine!" she breathed again, clutching them closely to her bosom.

"The truth is," I said, "I promised to give them quilts to Maggie, for when she marries John Thomas."

She gasped like a bee had stung her.   65

"Maggie can't appreciate these quilts!" she said. "She'd probably be backward enough to put them to everyday use."

"I reckon she would," I said. "God knows I been saving 'em for long enough with nobody using 'em. I hope she will!" I didn't want to bring up how I had offered Dee (Wangero) a quilt when she went away to college. Then she had told me they were old-fashioned, out of style.

"But they're *priceless!*" she was saying now, furiously; for she has a temper. "Maggie would put them on the bed and in five years they'd be in rags. Less than that!"

"She can always make some more," I said. "Maggie knows how to quilt."

Dee (Wangero) looked at me with hatred. "You just will not under-   70
stand. The point is these quilts, *these* quilts!"

"Well," I said, stumped. "What would *you* do with them?"

"Hang them," she said. As if that was the only thing you *could* do with quilts.

Maggie by now was standing in the door. I could almost hear the sound her feet made as they scraped over each other.

"She can have them, Mama," she said, like somebody used to never winning anything, or having anything reserved for her. "I can 'member Grandma Dee without the quilts."

I looked at her hard. She had filled her bottom lip with checkerberry   75
snuff and it gave her face a kind of dopey, hangdog look. It was Grandma Dee and Big Dee who taught her how to quilt herself. She stood there with her scarred hands hidden in the folds of her skirt. She looked at her sister with something like fear but she wasn't mad at her. This was Maggie's portion. This was the way she knew God to work.

When I looked at her like that something hit me in the top of my head and ran down to the soles of my feet. Just like when I'm in church and the spirit of God touches me and I get happy and shout. I did something I never had done before: hugged Maggie to me, then dragged her on into the room, snatched the quilts out of Miss Wangero's hands and dumped them into Maggie's lap. Maggie just sat there on my bed with her mouth open.

"Take one or two of the others," I said to Dee.

But she turned without a word and went out to Hakim-a-barber.

"You just don't understand," she said, as Maggie and I came out to the car.

"What don't I understand?" I wanted to know.

"Your heritage," she said. And then she turned to Maggie, kissed her, and said, "You ought to try to make something of yourself, too, Maggie. It's really a new day for us. But from the way you and Mama still live you'd never know it."

She put on some sunglasses that hid everything above the tip of her nose and her chin.

Maggie smiled; maybe at the sunglasses. But a real smile, not scared. After we watched the car dust settle I asked Maggie to bring me a dip of snuff. And then the two of us sat there just enjoying, until it was time to go in the house and go to bed.

CONSIDERATIONS

1. Mama says, "I was always better at a man's job." How does her mannishness affect our sympathy with or detachment from her as the narrator?

2. How does Mama's decision about the quilts add to the meaning of the story's title?

3. What two kinds of heritage come into conflict in this story?

WRITING SUGGESTIONS

4. Analyze the conflict of generations between Mama and Dee. How does each generation appear in the eyes of the other?

5. Do young people (adolescents through twenty-somethings) need to identify with or be liberated from their group identities? What strengths and vulnerabilities draw you close to your heritage — or pull you farther away? Discuss one connection to your ethnic, racial, or religious heritage that you have embraced or rejected. Explain why you made the choice you did.

3

RELATIONSHIPS

Friends and Lovers

BARBARA EHRENREICH

In Praise of "Best Friends"

BARBARA EHRENREICH (b. 1941) graduated from Reed College
and received her Ph.D. at Rockefeller University. Her commen-
taries on social history, popular culture, and contemporary issues
have been published in magazines such as *Mother Jones*, the *Nation*, *The New Republic*, and *Ms.*, where this article first appeared in
1987. Ehrenreich's book-length critiques of American society include *The Hearts of Men: American Dreams and the Flight from
Commitment* (1983). Her most recent collection of essays is *The
Snarling Citizen* (1995).

All the politicians, these days, are "profamily," but I've never heard
of one who was "profriendship." This is too bad and possibly short-
sighted. After all, most of us would never survive our families if we didn't
have our friends.

I'm especially concerned about the fine old institution of "best
friends." I realized that it was on shaky ground a few months ago, when
the occasion arose to introduce my own best friend (we'll call her Joan) at
a somewhat intimidating gathering. I got as far as saying, "I am very
proud to introduce my best friend, Joan . . ." when suddenly I wasn't
proud at all. I was blushing. "Best friend," I realized as soon as I heard the
words out loud, sounds like something left over from sixth-grade cliques:
the kind of thing where if Sandy saw you talking to Stephanie at recess,
she might tell you after school that she wasn't going to be your best friend

anymore, and so forth. Why couldn't I have just said "my good friend Joan" or something *grown-up* like that?

But Joan is not just any friend, or even a "good friend"; she is my best friend. We have celebrated each other's triumphs together, nursed each other through savage breakups with the various men in our lives, discussed the Great Issues of Our Time, and cackled insanely over things that were, objectively speaking, not even funny. We have quarreled and made up; we've lived in the same house and we've lived thousands of miles apart. We've learned to say hard things, like "You really upset me when . . ." and even "I love you." Yet, for all this, our relationship has no earthly weight or status. I can't even say the name for it without sounding profoundly silly.

Why is best friendship, particularly between women, so undervalued and unrecognized? Partly, no doubt, because women themselves have always been so undervalued and unrecognized. In the Western tradition, male best friendships are the stuff of history and high drama. Reread Homer, for example, and you'll realize that Troy did not fall because Paris, that spoiled Trojan prince, loved Helen, but because Achilles so loved Patroclus. It was Patroclus's death, at the hands of the Trojans, that made Achilles snap out of his sulk long enough to slay the Trojans' greatest warrior and guarantee victory to the Greeks. Did Helen have a best friend, or any friend at all? We'll never know, because the only best friendships that have survived in history and legend are man-on-man: Alexander and Hephaestion, Orestes and Pylades, Heracles and Iolas.

Christianity did not improve the status of female friendship. "Every woman ought to be filled with shame at the thought that she is a woman," declaimed one of the early church fathers, Clement of Alexandria, and when two women got together, the shame presumably doubled. Male friendship was still supposed to be a breeding ground for all kinds of upstanding traits — honor, altruism, courage, faith, loyalty. Consider Arthur's friendship with Lancelot, which easily survived the latter's dalliance with Queen Guinevere. But when two women got together, the best you could hope for, apparently, was bitchiness, and the worst was witchcraft.

Yet, without the slightest encouragement from history, women have persisted in finding best friends. According to recent feminist scholarship, the nineteenth century seems to have been a heyday of female best friendship. In fact, feminism might never have gotten off the ground at all if it hadn't been for the enduring bond between Elizabeth Cady Stanton, the theoretician of the movement, and Susan B. Anthony, the movement's first great pragmatist.

And they are only the most famous best friends. According to Lillian Faderman's book *Surpassing the Love of Men*, there were thousands of anonymous female couples who wrote passionate letters to each other, exchanged promises and tokens of love, and suffered through the separations occasioned by marriage and migration. Feminist scholars have debated whether these great best friendships were actually lesbian, sexual relationships — a question I find both deeply fascinating (if these were lesbian relationships, were the women involved conscious of what a bold and subversive step they had taken?) and somewhat beside the point. What matters is that these women honored their friendships, and sought ways to give them the kind of coherence and meaning that the larger society reserved only for marriage.

In the twentieth century, female best friendship was largely eclipsed by the new ideal of the "companionate marriage." At least in the middle-class culture that celebrated "togetherness," your *husband* was now supposed to be your best friend, as well, of course, as being your lover, provider, coparent, housemate, and principal heir. My own theory (profamily politicians please take note) is that these expectations have done more damage to the institution of marriage than no-fault divorce and the sexual revolution combined. No man can be all things to even one woman. And the foolish idea that one could has left untold thousands of women not only divorced, but what is in the long run far worse — friendless.

Yet even feminism, when it came back to life in the early seventies, did not rehabilitate the institution of female best friendship. Lesbian relationships took priority, for the good and obvious reason that they had been not only neglected, but driven underground. But in our zeal to bring lesbian relationships safely out of the closet, we sometimes ended up shoving best friendships further out of sight. "Best friends?" a politically ever-so-correct friend once snapped at me, in reference to Joan, "why aren't you lovers?" In the same vein, the radical feminist theoretician Shulamith Firestone wrote that after the gender revolution, there would be no asexual friendships. The coming feminist Utopia, I realized sadly, was going to be a pretty lonely place for some of us.

Then, almost before we could get out of our jeans and into our corporate clone clothes, female friendship came back into fashion — but in the vastly attenuated form of "networking." Suddenly we were supposed to have dozens of women friends, hundreds if time and the phone bill allow, but each with a defined function: mentors, contacts, connections, allies, even pretty ones who might be able to introduce us, now and then, to their leftover boyfriends. The voluminous literature on corporate success for women is full of advice on friends: whom to avoid ("turkeys" and whiners), whom to cultivate (winners and potential clients), and how to tell when a friend is moving from the latter category into the former. This is an advance, because it means we are finally realizing that women are important enough to be valued friends and that friendship among women is valuable enough to write and talk about. But in the pushy new dress-for-success world, there's less room than ever for best friendships that last through thick and thin, through skidding as well as climbing.

Hence my campaign to save the institution of female best friendship. I am not asking you to vote for anyone, to pray to anyone, or even to send me money. I'm just suggesting that we all begin to give a little more space, and a little more respect, to the best friendships in our lives. To this end, I propose three rules:

1. Best friendships should be given social visibility. If you are inviting Pat over for dinner, you would naturally think of inviting her husband, Ed. Why not Pat's best friend, Jill? Well, you may be thinking, how childish! They don't have to go everywhere together. Of course they don't, but neither do Pat and Ed. In many settings, including your next dinner party or potluck, Pat and Jill may be the combination that makes the most sense and has the most fun.

2. Best friends take time and nurturance, even when that means taking time and nurturance away from other major relationships. Everyone knows that marriages require "work." (A ghastly concept, that. "Working on a marriage" has always sounded to me like something on the order of lawn maintenance.) Friendships require effort, too, and best friendships require our very best efforts. It should be possible to say to husband Ed or whomever, "I'm sorry I can't spend the evening with you because I need to put in some quality time with Jill." He will only be offended if he is a slave to heterosexual couple-ism — in which case you shouldn't have married him in the first place.

3. Best friendship is more important than any work-related benefit that may accrue from it, and should be treated accordingly. Maybe your best friend will help you get that promotion, transfer, or new contract. That's all well and good, but the real question is: Will that promotion, transfer, or whatever help your best friendship? If it's a transfer to San Diego, and your best friend's in Cincinnati, it may not be worth it. For example, as a writer who has collaborated with many friends, including "Joan," I am often accosted by strangers exclaiming, "It's just amazing that you got through that book [article, or other project] together and you're still friends!" The truth is, in nine cases out of ten, that the friendship was always far more important than the book. If a project isn't going to strengthen my friendship — and might even threaten it — I'd rather not start.

When I was thinking through this column — out loud of course,   15
with a very good friend on the phone — she sniffed, "So what exactly do you want — formal, legalized friendships, with best-friend licenses and showers and property settlements in case you get in a fight over the sweaters you've been borrowing from each other for the past ten years?" No, of course not, because the beauty of best friendship, as opposed to, say, marriage, is that it's a totally grass-roots, creative effort that requires no help at all from the powers-that-be. Besides, it would be too compli-

cated. In contrast to marriage — and even to sixth-grade cliques — there's no rule that says you can have only one "best" friend.

CONSIDERATIONS

1. According to Ehrenreich, why would a name for "best friendship" improve its status in society? What other significant relationships lack names that confer positive status?

2. According to the author, society respects friendships between men but denigrates those shared by women. Do you agree? Without using examples from literature, provide contemporary publicly known illustrations that support or dispute her point.

3. What gains and losses to friendship does Ehrenreich attribute to women's greater participation in careers?

WRITING SUGGESTION

4. Of the three rules Ehrenreich proposes to upgrade friendships, the third might cause the most difficulties, especially for young people facing choices about education and careers. Are you prepared to follow such a rule? Have you already had to break this rule in your choice of a college? Explain your outlook on separating from a friend.

PATRICIA WILLIAMS

My Best White Friend

PATRICIA WILLIAMS (b. 1951) graduated from Wellesley College and received her law degree from Harvard University. As a professor of law at Columbia University she teaches and writes about social issues, particularly the rights of women and minorities. Her essays are published in *The Alchemy of Race and Rights* (1992) and *The Rooster's Egg* (1995). The following account of a friendship appeared first in *The New Yorker* in 1996.

Cinderella revisited.

My best white friend is giving me advice on how to get myself up like a trophy-wife-in-waiting. We are obliged to attend a gala fund-raiser for an organization on whose board we both sit. I'm not a wife of any sort at all, and she says she knows why: I'm prickly as all getout, I dress down instead of up, and my hair is "a complete disaster." My best white friend, who is already a trophy wife of considerable social and philanthropic standing, is pressing me to borrow one of her Real Designer gowns and a couple of those heavy gold bracelets that are definitely not something you can buy on the street.

I tell her she's missing the point. Cinderella wasn't an over-thirty black professional with an attitude. What sort of Master of the Universe is going to go for that?

"You're not a *racist*, are you?" she asks.

"How could I be?" I reply, with wounded indignation. "What, being the American Dream personified and all."

"Then let's get busy and make you *up*," she says soothingly, break-   5
ing out the little pots of powder, paint, and polish.

From the first exfoliant to the last of the cucumber rinse, we fight about my man troubles. From powder base through lip varnish, we fight about hers.

You see, part of the problem is that white knights just don't play the same part in my mythical landscape of desire. If poor Cinderella had been black, it would have been a whole different story. I tell my best white friend the kind of stories my mother raised me on: about slave girls who worked their fingers to the bone for their evil half sisters, the "legitimate" daughters of their mutual father, the master of the manse, the owner of them all; about scullery maids whose oil-and-ashes complexions would not wash clean even after multiple waves of the wand. These were the ones who harbored impossible dreams of love for lost mates who had been sold down rivers of tears into oblivion. These were the ones who became runaways.

"Just think about it," I say. "The human drama is compact enough so that when my mother was little she knew women who had been slaves, including a couple of runaways. Cinderellas who had burned their masters' beds and then fled for their lives. It doesn't take too much, even across the ages, to read between those lines. Women who invented their own endings, even when they didn't get to live happily or very long thereafter."

My best white friend says, "Get a grip. It's just a party."

I've called my best white friend my best white friend ever since she   10
started calling me her best black friend. I am her only black friend, as far as I know, a circumstance for which she blames "the class thing." At her end of the social ladder, I am *my* only black friend — a circumstance for which I blame "the race thing."

"People should stop putting so much emphasis on color — it doesn't matter whether you're black or white or blue or green," she says from beneath an avocado mask.

Lucky for you, I think, even as my own pores are expanding or contracting — I forget which — beneath a cool neon-green sheath.

In fact, I have been looking forward to the makeover. M.B.W.F. has a masseuse and a manicurist and colors in her palette like Après Sun and Burnt Straw, which she swears will match my skin tones more or less.

"Why don't they just call it Racial Envy?" I ask, holding up a tube of Deep Copper Kiss.

"Now, now, we're all sisters under the makeup," she says cheerfully.   15

"When ever will we be sisters without?" I grumble.

I've come this far because she's convinced me that my usual slapdash routine is the equivalent of being "unmade"; and being unmade, she underscores, is a most exclamatory form of unsophistication. "Even Strom Thurmond wears a little pancake when he's in public."

M.B.W.F. is somewhat given to hyperbole, but it *is* awfully hard to bear, the thought of making less of a fashion statement than old Strom. I do draw the line, though. She has a long history of nips, tucks, and liposuction. Once, I tried to suggest how appalled I was, but I'm not good at being graceful when I have a really strong opinion roiling up inside. She dismissed me sweetly: "You can afford to disapprove. You are aging *so* very nicely."

There was the slightest pause as I tried to suppress the anxious rise in my voice: "You think I'm aging?"

Very gently, she proceeded to point out the flawed and falling features that give me away to the carefully trained eye, the insistent voyeur.   20
There were the pores. And those puffs beneath my eyes. No, not there — those are the bags under my eyes. The bags aren't so bad, according to her — no deep wrinkling just yet. But keep going — the puffs are just below the bags. Therein lies the facial decay that gives my age away.

I had never noticed them before, but for a while after that those puffs just dominated my face. I couldn't look at myself for their explosive insolence — the body's betrayal, obscuring every other feature.

I got over it the day we were standing in line by a news rack at the Food Emporium. Gazing at a photo of Princess Diana looking radiantly, elegantly melancholic on the cover of some women's magazine, M.B.W.F. snapped, "God! Bulimia must work!"

This is not the first time M.B.W.F. has shepherded me to social doom. The last time, it was a very glitzy cocktail party where husband material supposedly abounded. I had a long, businesslike conversation with a man she introduced me to, who, I realized as we talked, grew more and more fascinated by me. At first, I was only conscious of winning him over; then I remember becoming aware that there was something funny about his fierce infatuation. I was *surprising* him, I slowly realized. Finally, he came clean: He said that he had never before had a conversation like this with a black person. "I think I'm in love," he blurted in a voice bubbling with fear.

"I think not," I consoled him. "It's just the power of your undone expectations, in combination with my being a basically likable person. It's throwing you for a loop. That and the Scotch, which, as you ought to know, is inherently depoliticizing."

I remember telling M.B.W.F. about him afterward. She had always   25
thought of him as "that perfect Southern gentleman." The flip side of the Southern gentleman is the kind master, I pointed out. "Bad luck," she said. "It's true, though — he's the one man I wouldn't want to be owned by, if I were you."

My best white friend doesn't believe that race is a big social problem anymore. "It's all economics," she insists. "It's how you came to be my *friend*" — for once, she does not qualify me as black — "the fact that we were both in college together." I feel compelled to remind her that affirmative action is how both of us ended up in the formerly all-male bastion we attended.

The odd thing is, we took most of the same classes. She ended up musically proficient, gifted in the art of interior design, fluent in the mother tongue, whatever it might be, of the honored visiting diplomat of the moment. She actively aspired, she says, to be "a cunning little meringue of a male prize."

"You," she says to me, "were always more like Gladys Knight."

"Come again?" I say.

"Ethnic woman warrior, always on that midnight train to someplace   30
else, intent on becoming the highest-paid Aunt Jemima in history."

"Ackh," I cough, a sudden strangulation of unmade thoughts fluttering in my windpipe.

The night after the cocktail party, I dreamed that I was in a bedroom with a tall, faceless man. I was his breeding slave. I was trying to be very, very good, so that I might one day earn my freedom. He did not trust me. I was always trying to hide some essential part of myself from him, which I would preserve and take with me on that promised day when I was permitted to leave; he felt it as an innate wickedness in me, a darkness that he could not penetrate, a dangerous secret that must be wrested from me. I tried everything I knew to please him; I walked a tightrope of anxious servitude and survivalist withholding. But it was not good enough. One morning, he just reached for a sword and sliced me in half, to see for himself what was inside. A casual flick, and I lay dead on the floor in two dark, unyielding halves; in exasperated disgust, he stepped over my remains and rushed from the room, already late for other business, leaving the cleanup for another slave.

"You didn't dream that!" M.B.W.F. says in disbelief.

"I did so."

"You're making it up," she says. "People don't really have dreams   35
like that."

"*I* do. Aren't I a people, too?"

"That's amazing! Tell me another."

"O.K., here's a fairy tale for you," I say, and tell her I dreamed I was being held by Sam Malone, the silly, womanizing bartender on *Cheers*. He was tall, broad-chested, good-looking, unbelievably strong. My head, my face were pressed against his chest. We were whispering our love for each other. I was moved deeply, my heart was banging, he held me tight and told me that he loved me. I told him that I loved him, too. We kissed so that heaven and earth moved in my heart; I wanted to make love to him fiercely. He put a simple thick gold band on my finger. I turned and, my voice cracking with emotion and barely audible, said, "What's this?" He asked me to marry him. I told him yes, I loved him, yes, yes, I loved him. He told me he loved me, too. I held out my hand and admired the ring in awe. I was the luckiest woman on earth.

Suddenly Diane Chambers, Sam's paramour on *Cheers*, burst through the door. She was her perky, petulant self, bouncing blond hair and black-green eyes like tarnished copper beads, like lumps of melted metal — eyes that looked carved yet soft, almost brimming. She turned those soft-hard eyes on me and said, "Oh no, Sam, not tonight — you promised!"

And with that I realized that I was to be consigned to a small room   40 on the other side of the house. Diane followed me as I left, profusely apologetic with explanations: She was sorry, and she didn't mind him being with me once or twice a month, but this was getting ridiculous. I realized that I was Sam's part-time mistress — a member of the household somehow, but having no rights.

Then Diane went back into the master bedroom and Sam came in to apologize, to say that there had been a mixup, that it was just this once, that he'd make it up to me, that he was sorry. And, of course, I forgave him, for there was nothing I wanted more than to relive the moment when he held me tightly and our love was a miracle and I was the only woman he wanted in the world, forever.

"Have you thought of going into therapy?" she jokes.

"As a matter of fact, I have," I say, sighing and rubbing my temples. "On average, we black women have bigger, better problems than any other women alive. We bear the burden of being seen as pretenders to the thrones of both femininity and masculinity, endlessly mocked by the ambiguously gendered crown-of-thorns imagery of 'queen' — Madame Queen, snap queen, welfare queen, quota queen, Queenie Queen, *Queen* Queen Queen. We black women are figured more as stand-ins for men, sort of like reverse drag queens: women pretending to be women but more male than men — bare-breasted, sweat-glistened, plow-pulling, sole supporters of their families. Arnold Schwarzenegger and Sylvester Stallone meet Sojourner Truth, the *Real* Real Thing, the Ace-of-Spades Gender Card Herself, Thelma and Louise knocked up by Wesley Snipes, the ultimate hard-drinking, tobacco-growing-and-aspitting, nut-crushing ball-buster of all time. . . . I mean, think about it — how'd you like to go to the ball dressed like a walking cultural pathology? Wouldn't it make you just a wee bit tense?"

"But," she sputters, "but — you always seem so *strong!*"

We have just about completed our toilette. She looks at my hair as 45 though it were a rude construction of mud and twigs, bright glass beads, and flashy bits of tinfoil. I look at hers for what it is — the high-tech product of many hours of steam rollers, shine enhancers, body spritzers, perms, and about eighteen hundred watts of blow-dried effort. We gaze at each other with the deep disapproval of one gazing into a mirror. It is inconceivable to both of us that we have been friends for as long as we have. We shake our heads in sympathetic unison and sigh.

One last thing: It seems we have forgotten about shoes. It turns out that my feet are much too big to fit into any of her sequined little evening slippers, so I wear my own sensible square-soled pumps. My prosaic feet, like overgrown roots, peek out from beneath the satiny folds of the perfect dress. She looks radiant; I feel dubious. Our chariot and her husband await. As we climb into the limousine, her husband lights up a cigar and holds forth on the reemerging popularity of same. My friend responds charmingly with a remarkably detailed production history of the Biedermeier humidor.

I do not envy her. I do not resent her. I do not hold my breath.

CONSIDERATIONS

1. Williams describes herself as a person "with an attitude." What is the author's tone or attitude in this essay? Choose three adjectives that fit, and explain your choice.

2. How do Williams's romantic dreams compare to the classic Cinderella fantasy?

3. What do you think are the strengths of this friendship? What might change if the friends were of the same color?

WRITING SUGGESTIONS

4. Do you think Williams is one of the "women who invented their own endings" (paragraph 8)? Using specific details from the essay to support your view, try to account for the differences between her romantic fantasies and the person she seems to be.

5. Parents often maintain fairy-tale expectations for their sons' and daughters' romantic lives, thinking that they will be magically awakened to adult life like Sleeping Beauty. Have you had to struggle against this or another fairy tale imposed by parents? Analyze the main features of the active myth, and explain how it is imposed on your life.

SCOTT RUSSELL SANDERS

The Men We Carry
in Our Minds

SCOTT RUSSELL SANDERS (b. 1945), a fiction writer and essayist, graduated from Brown University and received a Ph.D. in English from Cambridge University in England. He teaches at Indiana University, and his writings appear in magazines such as *Harper's*, *Georgia Review*, and *Science Fiction*. His personal essays are published in *Writing from the Center* (1996), *Staying Put: Making a Home in a Restless World* (1993), and *The Paradise of Bombs* (1987), which includes the following selection.

"This must be a hard time for women," I say to my friend Anneke. "They have so many paths to choose from, and so many voices calling them."

"I think it's a lot harder for men," she replies.

"How do you figure that?"

"The women I know feel excited, innocent, like crusaders in a just cause. The men I know are eaten up with guilt."

We are sitting at the kitchen table drinking sassafras tea, our hands wrapped around the mugs because this April morning is cool and drizzly. "Like a Dutch morning," Anneke told me earlier. She is Dutch herself, a writer and midwife and peacemaker, with the round face and sad eyes of a woman in a Vermeer painting who might be waiting for the rain to stop, for a door to open. She leans over to sniff a sprig of lilac, pale lavender, that rises from a vase of cobalt blue.

"Women feel such pressure to be everything, do everything," I say. "Career, kids, art, politics. Have their babies and get back to the office a week later. It's as if they're trying to overcome a million years' worth of evolution in one lifetime."

"But we help one another. We don't try to lumber on alone, like so many wounded grizzly bears, the way men do." Anneke sips her tea. I gave her the mug with the owls on it, for wisdom. "And we have this deep-down sense that we're in the *right* — we've been held back, passed over, used — while men feel they're in the wrong. Men are the ones who've been discredited, who have to search their souls."

I search my soul. I discover guilty feelings aplenty — toward the poor, the Vietnamese, Native Americans, the whales, an endless list of debts — a guilt in each case that is as bright and unambiguous as a neon sign. But toward women I feel something more confused, a snarl of shame, envy, wary tenderness, and amazement. This muddle troubles me. To hide my unease I say, "You're right, it's tough being a man these days."

"Don't laugh." Anneke frowns at me, mournful-eyed, through the sassafras steam. "I wouldn't be a man for anything. It's much easier being the victim. All the victim has to do is break free. The persecutor has to live with his past."

How deep is that past? I find myself wondering after Anneke has   10
left. How much of an inheritance do I have to throw off? Is it just the beliefs I breathed in as a child? Do I have to scour memory back through father and grandfather? Through St. Paul? Beyond Stonehenge and into the twilit caves? I'm convinced the past we must contend with is deeper even than speech. When I think back on my childhood, on how I learned to see men and women, I have a sense of ancient, dizzying depths. The back roads of Tennessee and Ohio where I grew up were probably closer, in their sexual patterns, to the campsites of Stone Age hunters than to the genderless cities of the future into which we are rushing.

The first men, besides my father, I remember seeing were black convicts and white guards, in the cottonfield across the road from our farm on the outskirts of Memphis. I must have been three or four. The prisoners wore dingy gray-and-black zebra suits, heavy as canvas, sodden with sweat. Hatless, stooped, they chopped weeds in the fierce heat, row after row, breathing the acrid dust of boll-weevil poison. The overseers wore dazzling white shirts and broad shadowy hats. The oiled barrels of their shotguns flashed in the sunlight. Their faces in memory are utterly blank. Of course those men, white and black, have become for me an emblem of racial hatred. But they have also come to stand for the twin poles of my early vision of manhood — the brute toiling animal and the boss.

When I was a boy, the men I knew labored with their bodies. They were marginal farmers, just scraping by, or welders, steelworkers, carpenters; they swept floors, dug ditches, mined coal, or drove trucks, their forearms ropy with muscle; they trained horses, stoked furnaces, built tires, stood on assembly lines wrestling parts onto cars and refrigerators. They got up before light, worked all day long whatever the weather, and when they came home at night they looked as though somebody had been whipping them. In the evenings and on weekends they worked on their own places, tilling gardens that were lumpy with clay, fixing broken-down cars, hammering on houses that were always too drafty, too leaky, too small.

The bodies of the men I knew were twisted and maimed in ways visible and invisible. The nails of their hands were black and split, the hands tattooed with scars. Some had lost fingers. Heavy lifting had given many of them finicky backs and guts weak from hernias. Racing against conveyor belts had given them ulcers. Their ankles and knees ached from years of standing on concrete. Anyone who had worked for long around machines was hard of hearing. They squinted, and the skin of their faces was creased like the leather of old work gloves. There were times, studying them, when I dreaded growing up. Most of them coughed, from dust or cigarettes, and most of them drank cheap wine or whiskey, so their eyes looked bloodshot and bruised. The fathers of my friends always seemed older than the mothers. Men wore out sooner. Only women lived into old age.

As a boy I also knew another sort of men, who did not sweat and break down like mules. They were soldiers, and so far as I could tell they scarcely worked at all. During my early school years we lived on a military base, an arsenal in Ohio, and every day I saw GIs in the guardshacks, on the stoops of barracks, at the wheels of olive drab Chevrolets. The chief fact of their lives was boredom. Long after I left the arsenal I came to recognize the sour smell the soldiers gave off as that of souls in limbo. They were all waiting — for wars, for transfers, for leaves, for promotions, for the end of their hitch — like so many braves waiting for the hunt to begin. Unlike the warriors of older tribes, however, they would have no say about when the battle would start or how it would be waged. Their waiting was broken only when they practiced for war. They fired guns at targets, drove tanks across the churned-up fields of the military reservation, set off bombs in the wrecks of old fighter planes. I knew this was all play. But I also felt certain that when the hour for killing arrived, they would kill. When the real shooting started, many of them would die. This was what soldiers were *for*, just as a hammer was for driving nails.

Warriors and toilers: Those seemed, in my boyhood vision, to be   15
the chief destinies for men. They weren't the only destinies, as I learned from having a few male teachers, from reading books, and from watching television. But the men on television — the politicians, the astronauts, the generals, the savvy lawyers, the philosophical doctors, the bosses who gave orders to both soldiers and laborers — seemed as remote and unreal to me as the figures in tapestries. I could no more imagine growing up to become one of these cool, potent creatures than I could imagine becoming a prince.

A nearer and more hopeful example was that of my father, who had escaped from a red-dirt farm to a tire factory, and from the assembly line to the front office. Eventually he dressed in a white shirt and tie. He carried himself as if he had been born to work with his mind. But his body, remembering the earlier years of slogging work, began to give out on him in his fifties, and it quit on him entirely before he turned sixty-five. Even such a partial escape from man's fate as he had accomplished did not seem possible for most of the boys I knew. They joined the army, stood in line for jobs in the smoky plants, helped build highways. They were bound to work as their fathers had worked, killing themselves or preparing to kill others.

A scholarship enabled me not only to attend college, a rare enough feat in my circle, but even to study in a university meant for the children of the rich. Here I met for the first time young men who had assumed from birth that they would lead lives of comfort and power. And for the first time I met women who told me that men were guilty of having kept all the joys and privileges of the earth for themselves. I was baffled. What privileges? What joys? I thought about the maimed, dismal lives of most of the men back home. What had they stolen from their wives and daughters? The right to go five days a week, twelve months a year, for thirty or forty years to a steel mill or a coal mine? The right to drop bombs and die in war? The right to feel every leak in the roof, every gap in the fence, every cough in the engine, as a wound they must mend? The right to feel, when the lay-off comes or the plant shuts down, not only afraid but ashamed?

I was slow to understand the deep grievances of women. This was because, as a boy, I had envied them. Before college, the only people I had ever known who were interested in art or music or literature, the only ones who read books, the only ones who ever seemed to enjoy a sense of ease and grace were the mothers and daughters. Like the menfolk, they fretted about money, they scrimped and made-do. But, when the pay stopped coming in, they were not the ones who had failed. Nor did they have to go to war, and that seemed to me a blessed fact. By comparison with the narrow, ironclad days of fathers, there was an expansiveness, I thought, in the days of mothers. They went to see neighbors, to shop in town, to run errands at school, at the library, at church. No doubt, had I looked harder at their lives, I would have envied them less. It was not my fate to become a woman, so it was easier for me to see the graces. Few of them held jobs outside the home, and those who did filled thankless roles as clerks and waitresses. I didn't see, then, what a prison a house could be, since houses seemed to me brighter, handsomer places than any factory. I did not realize — because such things were never spoken of — how often women suffered from men's bullying. I did learn about the wretchedness of abandoned wives, single mothers, widows; but I also learned about the wretchedness of lone men. Even then I could see how exhausting it was for a mother to cater all day to the needs of young children. But if I had been asked, as a boy, to choose between tending a baby and tending a machine, I think I would have chosen the baby. (Having now tended both, I know I would choose the baby.)

So I was baffled when the women at college accused me and my sex of having cornered the world's pleasures. I think something like my bafflement has been felt by other boys (and by girls as well) who grew up in dirt-poor farm country, in mining country, in black ghettos, in Hispanic barrios, in the shadows of factories, in Third World nations — any place where the fate of men is as grim and bleak as the fate of women. Toilers and warriors. I realize now how ancient these identities are, how deep the tug they exert on men, the undertow of a thousand generations. The miseries I saw, as a boy, in the lives of nearly all men I continue to see in the lives of many — the body-breaking toil, the tedium, the call to be tough, the humiliating powerlessness, the battle for a living and for territory.

When the women I met at college thought about the joys and privi-   20
leges of men, they did not carry in their minds the sort of men I had
known in my childhood. They thought of their fathers, who were bankers,
physicians, architects, stockbrokers, the big wheels of the big cities. These
fathers rode the train to work or drove cars that cost more than any of my
childhood houses. They were attended from morning to night by female
helpers, wives, and nurses and secretaries. They were never laid off, never
short of cash at month's end, never lined up for welfare. These fathers
made decisions that mattered. They ran the world.

The daughters of such men wanted to share in this power, this
glory. So did I. They yearned for a say over their future, for jobs worthy
of their abilities, for the right to live at peace, unmolested, whole. Yes, I
thought, yes yes. The difference between me and these daughters was that
they saw me, because of my sex, as destined from birth to become like
their fathers, and therefore as an enemy to their desires. But I knew better. I wasn't an enemy, in fact or in feeling. I was an ally. If I had known,
then, how to tell them so, would they have believed me? Would they
now?

CONSIDERATIONS

1. In their conversation, Anneke points out to the author that men have
   "been discredited." For what, and by whom? Evaluate her allegation.

2. As a boy, what did Sanders envy in women? What is his adult view of
   women?

3. Reconsider the title of the essay. Does the word "carry" acquire added
   meaning by the end of the essay?

WRITING SUGGESTIONS

4. Is contemporary life a "hard time" for women or for men? Or for both?
   Continue the discussion between Anneke and Sanders. Explain one or two
   of the preconceptions or prejudicial attitudes about the other sex that com-
   plicate relations between young men and women.

5. Sanders considers *class* more important than other cultural determinants,
   such as gender, race, and family. Compare and contrast his views with
   those of Barbara Dafoe Whitehead, Shelby Steele, and Patricia Williams
   (pp. 33, 43, 62). As you examine the writers' views, develop your own opinion about which category wields the strongest influence on peoples' lives.

MARC FEIGEN FASTEAU

Friendships Among Men

MARC FEIGEN FASTEAU (b. 1942) is a lawyer who specializes in
sex discrimination cases. He lectures widely on the topic of sexual
stereotypes, and his articles have appeared in feminist magazines,
such as *Ms.*, as well as journals for scientists. His book *The Male
Machine* (1974) is a study of the masculine stereotype in our society. In the following selection from that book, Fasteau argues that
men remain unemotional and impersonal even in their friendships.

There is a long-standing myth in our society that the great friendships are between men. Forged through shared experience, male friendship is portrayed as the most unselfish, if not the highest, form of human
relationship. The more traditionally masculine the shared experience
from which it springs, the stronger and more profound the friendship is
supposed to be. Going to war, weathering crises together at school or
work, playing on the same athletic team, are some of the classic experiences out of which friendships between men are believed to grow.

By and large, men do prefer the company of other men, not only in
their structured time but in the time they fill with optional, nonobligatory
activity. They prefer to play games, drink, and talk, as well as work and
fight together. Yet something is missing. Despite the time men spend together, their contact rarely goes beyond the external, a limitation which
tends to make their friendships shallow and unsatisfying.

My own childhood memories are of doing things with my friends —
playing games or sports, building walkie-talkies, going camping. Other
people and my relationships to them were never legitimate subjects for attention. If someone liked me, it was an opaque, mysterious occurrence
that bore no analysis. When I was slighted, I felt hurt. But relationships
with people just happened. I certainly had feelings about my friends, but I
can't remember a single instance of trying consciously to sort them out
until I was well into college.

For most men this kind of shying away from the personal continues
into adult life. In conversations with each other, we hardly ever use ourselves as reference points. We talk about almost everything except how we
ourselves are affected by people and events. Everything is discussed as
though it were taking place out there somewhere, as though we had no
more felt response to it than to the weather. Topics that can be treated in
this detached, objective way become conversational mainstays. The few

subjects which are fundamentally personal are shaped into discussions of abstract general questions. Even in an exchange about their reactions to liberated women — a topic of intensely personal interest — the tendency will be to talk in general, theoretical terms. Work, at least its objective aspects, is always a safe subject. Men also spend an incredible amount of time rehashing the great public issues of the day. Until early 1973, Vietnam was the workhorse topic. Then came Watergate. It doesn't seem to matter that we've all had a hundred similar conversations. We plunge in for another round, trying to come up with a new angle as much to impress the others with what we know as to keep from being bored stiff.

Games play a central role in situations organized by men. I remember a weekend some years ago at the country house of a law-school classmate as a blur of softball, football, croquet, poker, and a dice-and-board game called Combat, with swimming thrown in on the side. As soon as one game ended, another began. Taken one at a time, these "activities" were fun, but the impression was inescapable that the host, and most of his guests, would do anything to stave off a lull in which they would be together without some impersonal focus for their attention. A snapshot of almost any men's club would show the same thing, 90 percent of the men engaged in some activity — ranging from backgammon to watching the tube — other than, or at least as an aid to, conversation.[1]

My composite memory of evenings spent with a friend at college and later when we shared an apartment in Washington is of conversations punctuated by silences during which we would internally pass over any personal or emotional thoughts which had arisen and come back to the permitted track. When I couldn't get my mind off personal matters, I said very little. Talks with my father have always had the same tone. Respect for privacy was the rationale for our diffidence. His questions to me about how things were going at school or at work were asked as discreetly as he would have asked a friend about someone's commitment to a hospital for the criminally insane. Our conversations, when they touched these matters at all, to say nothing of more sensitive matters, would veer quickly back to safe topics of general interest. In our popular literature, the archetypal male hero embodying this personal muteness is the cowboy. The classic mold for the character was set in 1902 by Owen Wister's novel *The Virginian* where the author spelled out, with an explicitness that was never again necessary, the characteristics of his protagonist. Here's how it goes when two close friends the Virginian hasn't seen in some time take him out for a drink:

> All of them had seen rough days together, and they felt guilty with emotion.
>
> "It's hot weather," said Wiggin.

---

[1]Women may use games as a reason for getting together — bridge clubs, for example. But the show is more for the rest of the world — to indicate that they are doing *something* — and the games themselves are not the only means of communication. [Fasteau's note]

"Hotter in Box Elder," said McLean. "My kid has started teething."

Words ran dry again. They shifted their positions, looked in their glasses, read the labels on the bottles. They dropped a word now and then to the proprietor about his trade, and his ornaments.

One of the Virginian's duties is to assist at the hanging of an old friend as a horse thief. Afterward, for the first time in the book, he is visibly upset. The narrator puts his arm around the hero's shoulders and describes the Virginian's reaction:

I had the sense to keep silent, and presently he shook my hand, not looking at me as he did so. He was always very shy of demonstration.

And, for explanation of such reticence, "As all men know, he also knew that many things should be done in this world in silence, and that talking about them is a mistake."

There are exceptions, but they only prove the rule.

One is the drunken confidence. "Bob, ole boy, I gotta tell ya — being divorced isn't so hot. . . . [and see, I'm too drunk to be held responsible for blurting it out]." Here, drink becomes an excuse for exchanging confidences and a device for periodically loosening the restraint against expressing a need for sympathy and support from other men — which may explain its importance as a male ritual. Marijuana fills a similar need.

Another exception is talking to a stranger — who may be either 10 someone the speaker doesn't know or someone who isn't in the same social or business world. (Several black friends told me that they have been on the receiving end of personal confidences from white acquaintances that they were sure had not been shared with white friends.) In either case, men are willing to talk about themselves only to other men with whom they do not have to compete or whom they will not have to confront socially later.

Finally, there is the way men depend on women to facilitate certain conversations. The women in a mixed group are usually the ones who make the first personal reference, about themselves or others present. The men can then join in without having the onus for initiating a discussion of "personalities." Collectively, the men can "blame" the conversation on the women. They can also feel in these conversations that since they are talking "to" the women instead of "to" the men, they can be excused for deviating from the masculine norm. When the women leave, the tone and subject invariably shift away from the personal.

The effect of these constraints is to make it extraordinarily difficult for men to really get to know each other. A psychotherapist who has conducted a lengthy series of encounter groups for men summed it up:

With saddening regularity [the members of these groups] described how much they wanted to have closer, more satisfying relationships

with other men: "I'd settle for having one really close man friend. I supposedly have some close men friends now. We play golf or go for a
drink. We complain about our jobs and our wives. I care about them
and they care about me. We even have some physical contact — I mean
we may even give a hug on a big occasion. But it's not enough."

The sources of this stifling ban on self-disclosure, the reasons why men
hide from each other, lie in the taboos and imperatives of the masculine
stereotype.

To begin with, men are supposed to be functional, to spend their
time working or otherwise solving or thinking about how to solve problems. Personal reaction, how one feels about something, is considered
dysfunctional, at best an irrelevant distraction from the expected objectivity. Only weak men, and women, talk about — i.e., "give in" to — their
feelings. "I group my friends in two ways," said a business executive:

> those who have made it and don't complain and those who haven't
> made it. And only the latter spend time talking to their wives about
> their problems and how bad their boss is and all that. The ones who
> concentrate more on communicating . . . are those who have realized
> that they aren't going to make it and therefore they have changed the
> focus of attention.

In a world which tells men they have to choose between expressiveness
and manly strength, this characterization may be accurate. Most of the
men who talk personally to other men *are* those whose problems have
gotten the best of them, who simply can't help it. Men not driven to despair don't talk about themselves, so the idea that self-disclosure and expressiveness are associated with problems and weakness becomes a self-
fulfilling prophecy.

Obsessive competitiveness also limits the range of communication
in male friendships. Competition is the principal mode by which men relate to each other — at one level because they don't know how else to
make contact, but more basically because it is the way to demonstrate, to
themselves and others, the key masculine qualities of unwavering tough-
ness and the ability to dominate and control. The result is that they inject
competition into situations which don't call for it.

In conversations, you must show that you know more about the sub-   15
ject than the other man, or at least as much as he does. For example, I
have often engaged in a contest that could be called My Theory Tops
Yours, disguised as a serious exchange of ideas. The proof that it wasn't
serious was that I was willing to participate even when I was sure that the
participants, including myself, had nothing fresh to say. Convincing the
other person — victory — is the main objective, with control of the floor
an important tactic. Men tend to lecture at each other, insist that the dis-

cussion follow their train of thought, and are often unwilling to listen. As one member of a men's rap group said,

> When I was talking I used to feel that I had to be driving to a point, that it had to be rational and organized, that I had to persuade at all times, rather than exchange thoughts and ideas.

Even in casual conversation some men hold back unless they are absolutely sure of what they are saying. They don't want to have to change a position once they've taken it. It's "just like a woman" to change your mind, and, more important, it is inconsistent with the approved masculine posture of total independence.

Competition was at the heart of one of my closest friendships, now defunct. There was a good deal of mutual liking and respect. We went out of our way to spend time with each other and wanted to work together. We both had "prospects" as "bright young men" and the same "liberal but tough" point of view. We recognized this about each other, and this recognition was the basis of our respect and of our sense of equality. That we saw each other as equals was important — our friendship was confirmed by the reflection of one in the other. But our constant and all-encompassing competition made this equality precarious and fragile. One way or another, everything counted in the measuring process. We fought out our tennis matches as though our lives depended on it. At poker, the two of us would often play on for hours after the others had left. These *mano a mano* poker marathons seem in retrospect especially revealing of the competitiveness of the relationship: Playing for small stakes, the essence of the game is in outwitting, psychologically beating down the other player — the other skills involved are negligible. Winning is the only pleasure, one that evaporates quickly, a truth that struck me in inchoate form every time our game broke up at four A.M. and I walked out the door with my five-dollar winnings, a headache, and a sense of time wasted. Still, I did the same thing the next time. It was what we did together, and somehow it counted. Losing at tennis could be balanced by winning at poker; at another level, his moving up in the federal government by my getting on the *Harvard Law Review.*

This competitiveness feeds the most basic obstacle to openness between men, the inability to admit to being vulnerable. Real men, we learn early, are not supposed to have doubts, hopes and ambitions which may not be realized, things they don't (or even especially do) like about themselves, fears, and disappointments. Such feelings and concerns, of course, are part of everyone's inner life, but a man must keep quiet about them. If others know how you really feel, you can be hurt, and that in itself is incompatible with manhood. The inhibiting effect of this imperative is not limited to disclosures of major personal problems. Often men do not share even ordinary uncertainties and half-formulated plans of daily life with their friends. And when they do, they are careful to suggest that they already know how to proceed — that they are not really asking for help or understanding but simply for particular bits of information. Either way, any doubts they have are presented as external, carefully characterized as having to do with the issue as distinct from the speaker. They are especially guarded about expressing concern or asking a question that would invite personal comment. It is almost impossible for men to simply exchange thoughts about matters involving them personally in a comfortable, noncrisis atmosphere. If a friend tells you of his concern that he and a colleague are always disagreeing, for example, he is likely to quickly supply his own explanation — something like "different professional backgrounds." The effect is to rule out observations or suggestions that do not fit within this already reconnoitered protective structure. You don't suggest, even if you believe it is true, that in fact the disagreements arise because he presents his ideas in a way which tends to provoke a hostile reaction. It would catch him off guard; it would be something he hadn't already thought of and accepted about himself and, for that reason, no matter how constructive and well-intentioned you might be, it would put you in control for the moment. He doesn't want that; he is afraid of losing your respect. So, sensing he feels that way, because you would yourself, you say something else. There is no real give-and-take.

It is hard for men to get angry at each other honestly. Anger between friends often means that one has hurt the other. Since the straightforward expression of anger in these situations involves an admission of vulnerability, it is safer to stew silently or find an "objective" excuse for retaliation. Either way, trust is not fully restored.

Men even try not to let it show when they feel good. We may report the reasons for our happiness, if they have to do with concrete accomplishments, but we try to do it with straight face, as if to say, "Here's what happened, but it hasn't affected my grown-up unemotional equilibrium, and I am not asking for any kind of response." Happiness is a precarious, "childish" feeling, easy to shoot down. Others may find the event that triggers it trivial or incomprehensible, or even threatening to their own self-esteem — in the sense that if one man is up, another man is down. So we tend not to take the risk of expressing it.

What is particularly difficult for men is seeking or accepting help   20 from friends. I, for one, learned early that dependence was unacceptable. When I was eight, I went to a summer camp I disliked. My parents visited me in the middle of the summer and, when it was time for them to leave, I wanted to go with them. They refused, and I yelled and screamed and was miserably unhappy for the rest of the day. That evening an older camper comforted me, sitting by my bed as I cried, patting me on the back soothingly and saying whatever it is that one says at times like that. He was in some way clumsy or funny-looking, and a few days later I joined a group of kids in cruelly making fun of him, an act which upset me, when I thought about it, for years. I can only explain it in terms of my feeling, as early as the age of eight, that by needing and accepting his help and comfort I had compromised myself, and took it out on him.

"You can't express dependence when you feel it," a corporate executive said, "because it's a kind of absolute. If you are loyal 90 percent of the time and disloyal 10 percent, would you be considered loyal? Well, the same happens with independence: You are either dependent or independent; you can't be both." "Feelings of dependence," another explained, "are identified with weakness or 'untoughness' and our culture doesn't accept those things in men." The result is that we either go it alone or "act out certain games or rituals to provoke the desired reaction in the other and have our needs satisfied without having to ask for anything."

Somewhat less obviously, the expression of affection also runs into emotional barriers growing out of the masculine stereotype. When I was in college, I was suddenly quite moved while attending a friend's wedding. The surge of feeling made me uncomfortable and self-conscious. There was nothing inherently difficult or, apart from the fact of being moved by a moment of tenderness, "unmasculine" about my reaction. I just did not know how to deal with or communicate what I felt. "I consider myself a sentimentalist," one man said, "and I think I am quite able to express my feelings. But the other day my wife described a friend of mine to some people as my best friend and I felt embarrassed when I heard her say it."

A major source of these inhibitions is the fear of being, of being thought, homosexual. Nothing is more frightening to a heterosexual man in our society. It threatens, at one stroke, to take away every vestige of his claim to a masculine identity — something like knocking out the foundation of a building — and to expose him to the ostracism, ranging from polite tolerance to violent revulsion, of his friends and colleagues. A man can be labeled as homosexual not just because of an overt sexual act but because of almost any sign of behavior which does not fit the masculine stereotype. The touching of another man, other than shaking hands, or, under emotional stress, an arm around the shoulder, is taboo. Women may kiss each other when they meet; men are uncomfortable when hugged even by close friends. Onlookers might misinterpret what they saw, and more important, what would we think of ourselves if we feel a twinge of sexual pleasure from the embrace.

Direct verbal expressions of affection or tenderness are also something that only homosexuals and women engage in. Between "real" men affection has to be disguised in gruff, "you old son-of-a-bitch" style. Paradoxically, in some instances, terms of endearment between men can be used as a ritual badge of manhood, dangerous medicine safe only for the strong. The flirting with homosexuality that characterizes the initiation rites of many fraternities and men's clubs serves this purpose. Claude Brown wrote about black life in New York City in the 1950s:

The term ["baby"] had a hip ring to it. . . . It was like saying, "Man look at me. I've got masculinity to spare. . . . I can say 'baby' to another cat and he can say 'baby' to me, and we can say it with strength in our voices." If you could say it, this meant that you really had to be sure of yourself, sure of your masculinity.

Fear of homosexuality does more than inhibit the physical display of affection. One of the major recurring themes in the men's groups led by psychotherapist Don Clark was:

A large segment of my feelings about other men are unknown or distorted because I am afraid they might have something to do with homosexuality. Now I'm lonely for other men and I don't know how to find what I want with them.

As Clark observes, "The specter of homosexuality seems to be the dragon at the gateway to self-awareness, understanding, and acceptance of male-male needs. If a man tries to pretend the dragon is not there by turning a blind eye to erotic feelings for all other males, he also blinds himself to the rich variety of feelings that are related."

The few situations in which men do acknowledge strong feelings of 25 affection and dependence toward other men are exceptions which prove the rule. With "cop couples," for example, or combat soldier "buddies," intimacy and dependence are forced on the men by their work — they have to ride in the patrol car or be in the same foxhole with somebody — and the jobs themselves have such highly masculine images that the man can get away with behavior that would be suspect under any other conditions.

Furthermore, even these combat-buddy relationships, when looked at closely, turn out not to be particularly intimate or personal. Margaret Mead has written:

During the last war English observers were confused by the apparent contradiction between American soldiers' emphasis on the buddy, so grievously exemplified in the breakdowns that followed a buddy's death, and the results of detailed inquiry which showed how transitory these buddy relationships were. It was found that men actually accepted their buddies as derivatives from their outfit, and from accidents of association, rather than because of any special personality characteristics capable of ripening into friendship.

One effect of the fear of appearing to be homosexual is to reinforce the practice that two men rarely get together alone without a reason. I once called a friend to suggest that we have dinner together. "O.K.," he said. "What's up?" I felt uncomfortable telling him that I just wanted to talk, that there was no other reason for the invitation.

Men get together to conduct business, to drink, to play games and sports, to re-establish contact after long absences, to participate in hetero-sexual social occasions — circumstances in which neither person is responsible for actually wanting to see the other. Men are particularly comfortable seeing each other in groups. The group situation defuses any possible assumptions about the intensity of feelings between particular men and provides the safety of numbers — "All the guys are here." It makes personal communication, which requires a level of trust and mutual understanding not generally shared by all members of a group, more difficult and offers an excuse for avoiding this dangerous territory. And it provides what is most sought after in men's friendships: mutual reassurance of masculinity.

CONSIDERATIONS

1. Are the first two paragraphs contradictory? If male friendships are superficial, why are they widely regarded as models of great friendship? Explain the author's point in paragraphs 1 and 2, adding whatever you think is needed to clarify his argument.

2. According to the author, what are the satisfactions that games provide that make them more important to men than to women? Do you agree?

3. What example does the author give of society's archetypal male hero? Can you substitute a more up-to-date popular image of admired masculinity? (Pick a type, not an individual.) Is your example similar to or different from Fasteau's type of hero?

4. What does Fasteau say are the barriers to better friendships among men? Do you regard them as mainly social or mainly personal barriers? Does Fasteau suggest how the barriers can be overcome?

WRITING SUGGESTION

5. Fasteau and Barbara Ehrenreich (p. 58) assume that friendship has very different meaning and value for men and for women. To what extent would you support, reject, update, or modify this assumption?

DIANE ACKERMAN

The Chemistry of Love

DIANE ACKERMAN (b. 1948), a poet and natural history writer, earned a doctorate in English from Cornell University. Her collections of verse include *Jaguar of Sweet Laughter* (1991). As a staff contributor to *The New Yorker*, Ackerman writes about various roles of nature in human experience. Her *Natural History of the Senses* (1990) examines each of the five senses. The following essay is excerpted from *A Natural History of Love* (1994).

Oxytocin, a hormone that encourages labor and the contractions during childbirth, seems to play an important role in mother love. The sound of a crying baby makes its mother's body secrete more oxytocin, which in turn erects her nipples and helps the milk to flow. As the baby nurses, even more oxytocin is released, making the mother want to nuzzle and hug it. It's been called the "cuddle chemical" by zoologists who have artificially raised the oxytocin level in goats and other animals and produced similar behavior. Oxytocin has many functions, some of them beneficial for the mother. The baby feels warm and safe as it nurses, and its digestive and respiratory systems run smoothly. The baby's nursing, which also coaxes the oxytocin level to rise in the mother, results, too, in contractions of the uterus that stop bleeding and detach the placenta. So mother and baby find themselves swept away in a chemical dance of love, interdependency, and survival.

Later in life, oxytocin seems to play an equally important role in romantic love, as a hormone that encourages cuddling between lovers and increases pleasure during lovemaking. The hormone stimulates the smooth muscles and sensitizes the nerves, and snowballs during sexual arousal — the more intense the arousal, the more oxytocin is produced. As arousal builds, oxytocin is thought to cause the nerves in the genitals to fire spontaneously, bringing on orgasm. Unlike other hormones, oxytocin arousal can be generated both by physical and emotional cues — a certain look, voice, or gesture is enough — and can become conditioned to one's personal love history. The lover's smell or touch may trigger the production of oxytocin. So might a richly woven and redolent sexual fantasy. Women are more responsive to oxytocin's emotional effects, probably because of the important role it plays in mothering. Indeed, women who have gone through natural childbirth sometimes report that they felt an orgasmic sense of pleasure during delivery. Some nonorgasmic women have found it easier to achieve orgasm after they've been through childbirth; the secretion of oxytocin during delivery and nursing melts their sexual blockage. This hormonal outpouring may help explain why women more than men prefer to continue embracing after sex. A woman may yearn to feel close and connected, tightly coiled around the mainspring of the man's heart. In evolutionary terms, she hopes the man will be staying around for a while, long enough to protect her and the child he just fathered.

Men's oxytocin levels quintuple during orgasm. But a Stanford University study showed that women have even higher levels of oxytocin than men do during sex, and that it takes more oxytocin for women to achieve orgasm. Drenched in this spa of the chemical, women are able to have more multiple orgasms than men, as well as full body orgasms. Mothers have told me during their baby's first year or so they were surprised to find themselves "in love" with it, "turned on" by it, involved with it in "the best romance ever." Because the same hormone controls a woman's pleasure during orgasm, childbirth, cuddling, and nursing her baby, it makes perfect sense that she should feel this way. The brain may have an excess of gray matter, but in some things it's economical. It likes to reuse convenient pathways and chemicals for many purposes. Why plow fresh paths through the snow of existence when old paths already lead part of the way there?

"The meeting of two personalities is like the contact of two chemical substances," Carl Jung wrote, "if there is any reaction, both are transformed." When two people find each other attractive, their bodies quiver with a gush of PEA (phenylethylamine), a molecule that speeds up the flow of information between nerve cells. An amphetaminelike chemical, PEA whips the brain into a frenzy of excitement, which is why lovers feel euphoric, rejuvenated, optimistic, and energized, happy to sit up talking all night or making love for hours on end. Because "speed" is addictive, even the body's naturally made speed, some people become what Michael Liebowitz and Donald Klein of the New York State Psychiatric Institute refer to as "attraction junkies," needing a romantic relationship to feel excited by life. The craving catapults them from high to low in an exhilarating, exhausting cycle of thrill and depression. Driven by a chemical hunger, they choose unsuitable partners, or quickly misconstrue a potential partner's feelings. Sliding down the slippery chute of their longing, they fall head over heels into a sea of all-consuming, passionate love. Soon the relationship crumbles, or they find themselves rejected. In either case, tortured by lovesick despair, they plummet into a savage depression, which they try to cure by falling in love again. Liebowitz and Klein think that this roller coaster is fueled by a chemical imbalance in the brain, a craving for PEA. When they gave some attraction junkies MAO inhibitors — antidepressants that work by disabling certain enzymes that can subdue PEA and other neurotransmitters — they were amazed to find how quickly the therapy worked. No longer craving PEA, the patients were able to choose partners more calmly and realistically. Other studies with humans seem to confirm these findings. Researchers have also found that injecting mice, rhesus monkeys, and other animals with PEA produces noises of pleasure, courting behavior, and addiction (they keep pressing a lever to get more PEA). All this strongly suggests that when we fall in love the brain drenches itself in PEA, a chemical that makes us feel pleasure, rampant excitement, and well-being. A sweet fix, love.

The body uses PEA for more than infatuation. The same chemical soars in thrill-seeking of any kind, because it keeps one alert, confident, and ready to try something new. That may help explain a fascinating phenomenon: People are more likely to fall in love when they're in danger. Wartime romances are legendary. I am part of a "baby boom" produced by such an event. Love thrives especially well in exotic locales. When the senses are heightened because of stress, novelty, or fear, it's much easier to become a mystic or feel ecstasy or fall in love. Danger makes one receptive to romance. Danger is an aphrodisiac. To test this, researchers asked single men to cross a suspension bridge. The bridge was safe, but frightening. Some men met women on the bridge. Other men encountered the same women — but not on the bridge — in a safer setting such as a campus or an office.

The men who met the women on the trembling bridge were much more likely to ask them out on dates.

While the chemical sleigh ride of infatuation carries one at a fast clip over uneven terrain, lives become blended, people mate and genes mix, and babies are born. Then the infatuation subsides and a new group of chemicals takes over, the morphinelike opiates of the mind, which calm and reassure. The sweet blistering rage of infatuation gives way to a narcotic peacefulness, a sense of security and belonging. Being in love is a state of chaotic equilibrium. Its rewards of intimacy, warmth, empathy, dependability, and shared experiences trigger the production of that mental comfort food, the endorphins. The feeling is less steep than falling in love, but it's steadier and more addictive. The longer two people have been married, the more likely it is they'll stay married. And couples who have three or more children tend to be lifelong spouses. Stability, friendship, familiarity, and affection are rewards the body clings to. As much as we love being happily unsettled, not to mention dizzied by infatuation, such a state is stressful. On the other hand, it also feels magnificent to rest, to be free of anxiety or fretting, and to enjoy one's life with a devoted companion who is as comfortable as a childhood playmate, as predictable if at times irksome as a sibling, as attentive as a parent, and also affectionate and loving: a longtime spouse. This is a tonic that is hard to give up, even if the relationship isn't perfect, and one is tempted by rejuvenating affairs. Shared events, including shared stresses and crises, are rivets that draw couples closer together. Soon they are fastened by so many it becomes difficult to pull free. It takes a vast amount of courage to leap off a slowly moving ship and grab a lifebuoy drifting past, not knowing exactly where it's headed or if it will keep one afloat. As the "other women" embroiled with long-married men discover, the men are unlikely to divorce, no matter how mundane their marriages, what they may promise, or how passionately in love they genuinely feel.

CONSIDERATIONS

1. Ackerman lists several functions researchers have noted for oxytocin. How does she explain its many unrelated or contradictory functions?

2. Ackerman says, "When the senses are heightened . . . it is much easier . . . to fall in love" (paragraph 5). Do you agree? Some might argue that novelty, fear, and danger can also deaden the senses — that fear, for example, retards love. Explain where you stand on this question and whether or not Ackerman's arguments about PEA ring true.

3. Find phrases and sentences that help you recognize Ackerman's purpose in identifying love chemicals. Does she achieve this purpose?

WRITING SUGGESTION

4. Since the love chemicals affect our good feelings, should we sometimes use supplemental doses? For instance, in recent years the hormone melatonin has been widely sold to help people fall asleep. How do the love chemicals differ, if at all, from taking vitamins or antidepressants, which also supply the body's natural chemicals? Explain what you would consider and decide if given the choice.

RAYMOND CARVER

What We Talk About
When We Talk About Love

RAYMOND CARVER (1938–1988), acclaimed for his poetry and short stories about hardscrabble contemporary lives, wrote about people under heavy social and emotional constraints. After graduating from California State University at Humboldt, Carver studied at the Writers' Workshop at the University of Iowa. While teaching writing he published several volumes of poems and stories, including *What We Talk About When We Talk About Love* (1981). In the title story of that collection four people half-drunkenly discuss the peculiarities of loves they have known and witnessed.

My friend Mel McGinnis was talking. Mel McGinnis is a cardiologist, and sometimes that gives him the right.

The four of us were sitting around his kitchen table drinking gin. Sunlight filled the kitchen from the big windows behind the sink. There were Mel and me and his second wife, Teresa — Terri, we called her — and my wife, Laura. We lived in Albuquerque then. But we were all from somewhere else.

There was an ice bucket on the table. The gin and the tonic water kept going around, and we somehow got on the subject of love. Mel thought real love was nothing less than spiritual love. He said he'd spent five years in a seminary before quitting to go to medical school. He said he still looked back on those years in the seminary as the most important years in his life.

Terri said the man she lived with before she lived with Mel loved her so much he tried to kill her. Then Terri said, "He beat me up one night. He dragged me around the living room by my ankles. He kept saying, 'I love you, I love you, you bitch.' He went on dragging me around the living room. My head kept knocking on things." Terri looked around the table. "What do you do with love like that?"

She was a bone-thin woman with a pretty face, dark eyes, and brown hair that hung down her back. She liked necklaces made of turquoise, and long pendant earrings.

"My God, don't be silly. That's not love, and you know it," Mel said. "I don't know what you'd call it, but I sure know you wouldn't call it love."

5

"Say what you want to, but I know it was," Terri said. "It may sound crazy to you, but it's true just the same. People are different, Mel. Sure, sometimes he may have acted crazy. Okay. But he loved me. In his own way maybe, but he loved me. There was love there, Mel. Don't say there wasn't."

Mel let out his breath. He held his glass and turned to Laura and me. "The man threatened to kill me," Mel said. He finished his drink and reached for the gin bottle. "Terri's a romantic. Terri's of the kick-me-so-I'll-know-you-love-me school. Terri, hon, don't look that way." Mel reached across the table and touched Terri's cheek with his fingers. He grinned at her.

"Now he wants to make up," Terri said.

"Make up what?" Mel said. "What is there to make up? I know what   10
I know. That's all."

"How'd we get started on this subject, anyway?" Terri said. She raised her glass and drank from it. "Mel always has love on his mind," she said. "Don't you, honey?" She smiled, and I thought that was the last of it.

"I just wouldn't call Ed's behavior love. That's all I'm saying, honey," Mel said. "What about you guys?" Mel said to Laura and me. "Does that sound like love to you?"

"I'm the wrong person to ask," I said. "I didn't even know the man. I've only heard his name mentioned in passing. I wouldn't know. You'd have to know the particulars. But I think what you're saying is that love is an absolute."

Mel said, "The kind of love I'm talking about is. The kind of love I'm talking about, you don't try to kill people."

Laura said, "I don't know anything about Ed, or anything about the   15
situation. But who can judge anyone else's situation?"

I touched the back of Laura's hand. She gave me a quick smile. I picked up Laura's hand. It was warm, the nails polished, perfectly manicured. I encircled the broad wrist with my fingers, and I held her.

"When I left, he drank rat poison," Terri said. She clasped her arms with her hands. "They took him to the hospital in Santa Fe. That's where we lived then, about ten miles out. They saved his life. But his gums went crazy from it. I mean they pulled away from his teeth. After that, his teeth stood out like fangs. My God," Terri said. She waited a minute, then let go of her arms and picked up her glass.

"What people won't do!" Laura said.

"He's out of the action now," Mel said. "He's dead."

Mel handed me the saucer of limes. I took a section, squeezed it   20
over my drink, and stirred the ice cubes with my finger.

"It gets worse," Terri said. "He shot himself in the mouth. But he bungled it. Poor Ed," she said. Terri shook her head.

"Poor Ed nothing," Mel said. "He was dangerous."

Mel was forty-five years old. He was tall and rangy with curly soft hair. His face and arms were brown from the tennis he played. When he was sober, his gestures, all his movements, were precise, very careful.

"He did love me though, Mel. Grant me that," Terri said. "That's all I'm asking. He didn't love me the way you love me. I'm not saying that. But he loved me. You can grant me that, can't you?"

"What do you mean, he bungled it?" I said.   25

Laura leaned forward with her glass. She put her elbows on the table and held her glass in both hands. She glanced from Mel to Terri and waited with a look of bewilderment on her open face, as if amazed that such things happened to people you were friendly with.

"How'd he bungle it when he killed himself?" I said.

"I'll tell you what happened," Mel said. "He took his twenty-two pistol he'd bought to threaten Terri and me with. Oh, I'm serious, the man was always threatening. You should have seen the way we lived in those days. Like fugitives. I even bought a gun myself. Can you believe it? A guy like me? But I did. I bought one for self-defense and carried it in the glove compartment. Sometimes I'd have to leave the apartment in the middle of the night. To go to the hospital, you know? Terri and I weren't married then, and my first wife had the house and kids, the dog, everything, and Terri and I were living in this apartment here. Sometimes, as I say, I'd get a call in the middle of the night and have to go into the hospital at two or three in the morning. It'd be dark out there in the parking lot, and I'd break into a sweat before I could even get to my car. I never knew if he was going to come up out of the shrubbery or from behind a car and start shooting. I mean, the man was crazy. He was capable of wiring a bomb, anything. He used to call my service at all hours and say he needed to talk to the doctor, and when I'd return the call, he'd say, 'Son of a bitch, your days are numbered.' Little things like that. It was scary, I'm telling you."

"I still feel sorry for him," Terri said.

"It sounds like a nightmare," Laura said. "But what exactly hap-   30
pened after he shot himself?"

Laura is a legal secretary. We'd met in a professional capacity. Before we knew it, it was a courtship. She's thirty-five, three years younger than I am. In addition to being in love, we like each other and enjoy one another's company. She's easy to be with.

"What happened?" Laura said.

Mel said, "He shot himself in the mouth in his room. Someone heard the shot and told the manager. They came in with a passkey, saw what had happened, and called an ambulance. I happened to be there when they brought him in, alive but past recall. The man lived for three days. His head swelled up to twice the size of a normal head. I'd never seen anything like it, and I hope I never do again. Terri wanted to go in and sit with him when she found out about it. We had a fight over it. I didn't think she should see him like that. I didn't think she should see him, and I still don't."

"Who won the fight?" Laura said.

"I was in the room with him when he died," Terri said. "He never   35
came up out of it. But I sat with him. He didn't have anyone else."

"He was dangerous," Mel said. "If you call that love, you can have it."

"It was love," Terri said. "Sure, it's abnormal in most people's eyes. But he was willing to die for it. He did die for it."

"I sure as hell wouldn't call it love," Mel said. "I mean, no one knows what he did it for. I've seen a lot of suicides, and I couldn't say anyone ever knew what they did it for."

Mel put his hands behind his neck and tilted his chair back. "I'm not interested in that kind of love," he said. "If that's love, you can have it."

Terri said, "We were afraid. Mel even made a will out and wrote to   40
his brother in California who used to be a Green Beret. Mel told him who to look for if something happened to him."

Terri drank from her glass. She said, "But Mel's right — we lived like fugitives. We were afraid. Mel was, weren't you, honey? I even called the police at one point, but they were no help. They said they couldn't do anything until Ed actually did something. Isn't that a laugh?" Terri said.

She poured the last of the gin into her glass and waggled the bottle. Mel got up from the table and went to the cupboard. He took down another bottle.

"Well, Nick and I know what love is," Laura said. "For us, I mean," Laura said. She bumped my knee with her knee. "You're supposed to say something now," Laura said, and turned her smile on me.

For an answer, I took Laura's hand and raised it to my lips. I made a big production out of kissing her hand. Everyone was amused.

"We're lucky," I said.   45

"You guys," Terri said. "Stop that now. You're making me sick. You're still on the honeymoon, for God's sake. You're still gaga, for crying out loud. Just wait. How long have you been together now? How long has it been? A year? Longer than a year?"

"Going on a year and a half," Laura said, flushed and smiling.

"Oh, now," Terri said. "Wait awhile."

She held her drink and gazed at Laura.

"I'm only kidding," Terri said.   50

Mel opened the gin and went around the table with the bottle.

"Here, you guys," he said. "Let's have a toast. I want to propose a toast. A toast to love. To true love," Mel said.

We touched glasses.

"To love," we said.

Outside in the backyard, one of the dogs began to bark. The leaves   55
of the aspen that leaned past the window ticked against the glass. The af-

ternoon sun was like a presence in this room, the spacious light of ease and generosity. We could have been anywhere, somewhere enchanted. We raised our glasses again and grinned at each other like children who had agreed on something forbidden.

"I'll tell you what real love is," Mel said. "I mean, I'll give you a good example. And then you can draw your own conclusions." He poured more gin into his glass. He added an ice cube and a sliver of lime. We waited and sipped our drinks. Laura and I touched knees again. I put a hand on her warm thigh and left it there.

"What do any of us really know about love?" Mel said. "It seems to me we're just beginners at love. We say we love each other and we do, I don't doubt it. I love Terri and Terri loves me, and you guys love each other too. You know the kind of love I'm talking about now. Physical love, that impulse that drives you to someone special, as well as love of the other person's being, his or her essence, as it were. Carnal love and, well, call it sentimental love, the day-to-day caring about the other person. But sometimes I have a hard time accounting for the fact that I must have loved my first wife too. But I did, I know I did. So I suppose I am like Terri in that regard. Terri and Ed." He thought about it and then he went on. "There was a time when I thought I loved my first wife more than life itself. But now I hate her guts. I do. How do you explain that? What happened to that love? What happened to it, is what I'd like to know. I wish someone could tell me. Then there's Ed. Okay, we're back to Ed. He loves Terri so much he tries to kill her and he winds up killing himself." Mel stopped talking and swallowed from his glass. "You guys have been together eighteen months and you love each other. It shows all over you. You glow with it. But you both loved other people before you met each other. You've both been married before, just like us. And you probably loved other people before that too, even. Terri and I have been together five years, been married for four. And the terrible thing, the terrible thing is, but the good thing too, the saving grace, you might say, is that if something happened to one of us — excuse me for saying this — but if something happened to one of us tomorrow, I think the other one, the other person, would grieve for a while, you know, but then the surviving party would go out and love again, have someone else soon enough. All this, all of this love we're talking about, it would just be a memory. Maybe not even a memory. Am I wrong? Am I way off base? Because I want you to set me straight if you think I'm wrong. I want to know. I mean, I don't know anything, and I'm the first one to admit it."

"Mel, for God's sake," Terri said. She reached out and took hold of his wrist. "Are you getting drunk? Honey? Are you drunk?"

"Honey, I'm just talking," Mel said. "All right? I don't have to be drunk to say what I think. I mean, we're all just talking, right?" Mel said. He fixed his eyes on her.

"Sweetie, I'm not criticizing," Terri said.

She picked up her glass.

"I'm not on call today," Mel said. "Let me remind you of that. I am not on call," he said.

"Mel, we love you," Laura said.

Mel looked at Laura. He looked at her as if he could not place her, as if she was not the woman she was.

"Love you too, Laura," Mel said. "And you, Nick, love you too. You know something?" Mel said. "You guys are our pals," Mel said.   65

He picked up his glass.

Mel said, "I was going to tell you about something. I mean, I was going to prove a point. You see, this happened a few months ago, but it's still going on right now, and it ought to make us feel ashamed when we talk like we know what we're talking about when we talk about love."

"Come on now," Terri said. "Don't talk like you're drunk if you're not drunk."

"Just shut up for once in your life," Mel said very quietly. "Will you do me a favor and do that for a minute? So as I was saying, there's this old couple who had this car wreck out on the interstate. A kid hit them and they were all torn to shit and nobody was giving them much chance to pull through."

Terri looked at us and then back at Mel. She seemed anxious, or   70
maybe that's too strong a word.

Mel was handing the bottle around the table.

"I was on call that night," Mel said. "It was May or maybe it was June. Terri and I had just sat down to dinner when the hospital called. There'd been this thing out on the interstate. Drunk kid, teenager, plowed his dad's pickup into this camper with this old couple in it. They were up in their mid-seventies, that couple. The kid — eighteen, nineteen, something — he was DOA. Taken the steering wheel through his sternum. The old couple, they were alive, you understand. I mean, just barely. But they had everything. Multiple fractures, internal injuries, hemorrhaging, contusions, lacerations, the works, and they each of them had themselves concussions. They were in a bad way, believe me. And, of course, their age was two strikes against them. I'd say she was worse off than he was. Ruptured spleen along with everything else. Both kneecaps broken. But they'd been wearing their seatbelts and, God knows, that's what saved them for the time being."

"Folks, this is an advertisement for the National Safety Council," Terri said. "This is your spokesman, Dr. Melvin R. McGinnis, talking." Terri laughed. "Mel," she said, "sometimes you're too much. But I love you, hon," she said.

"Honey, I love you," Mel said.

He leaned across the table. Terri met him halfway. They kissed.   75

"Terri's right," Mel said as he settled himself again. "Get those seatbelts on. But seriously, they were in some shape, those oldsters. By the time I got down there, the kid was dead, as I said. He was off in a corner, laid out on a gurney. I took one look at the old couple and told the ER nurse to get me a neurologist and an orthopedic man and a couple of surgeons down there right away."

He drank from his glass. "I'll try to keep this short," he said. "So we took the two of them up to the OR and worked like fuck on them most of the night. They had these incredible reserves, those two. You see that once in a while. So we did everything that could be done, and toward morning we're giving them a fifty-fifty chance, maybe less than that for her. So here they are, still alive the next morning. So, okay, we move them into the ICU, which is where they both kept plugging away at it for two weeks, hitting it better and better on all the scopes. So we transfer them out to their own room."

Mel stopped talking. "Here," he said, "let's drink this cheapo gin the hell up. Then we're going to dinner, right? Terri and I know a new place. That's where we'll go, to this new place we know about. But we're not going until we finish up this cut-rate, lousy gin."

Terri said, "We haven't actually eaten there yet. But it looks good. From the outside, you know."

"I like food," Mel said. "If I had it to do all over again, I'd be a chef, you know? Right? Terri?" Mel said. 80

He laughed. He fingered the ice in his glass.

"Terri knows," he said. "Terri can tell you. But let me say this. If I could come back again in a different life, a different time and all, you know what? I'd like to come back as a knight. You were pretty safe wearing all that armor. It was all right being a knight until gunpowder and muskets and pistols came along."

"Mel would like to ride a horse and carry a lance," Terri said.

"Carry a woman's scarf with you everywhere," Laura said.

"Or just a woman," Mel said. 85

"Shame on you," Laura said.

Terri said, "Suppose you came back as a serf. The serfs didn't have it so good in those days," Terri said.

"The serfs never had it good," Mel said. "But I guess even the knights were vessels to someone. Isn't that the way it worked? But then everyone is always a vessel to someone. Isn't that right? Terri? But what I liked about knights, besides their ladies, was that they had that suit of armor, you know, and they couldn't get hurt very easy. No cars in those days, you know? No drunk teenagers to tear into your ass."

"Vassals," Terri said.

"What?" Mel said. 90

"Vassals," Terri said. "They were called vassals, not vessels."

"Vassals, vessels," Mel said, "what the fuck's the difference? You knew what I meant anyway. All right," Mel said. "So I'm not educated. I learned my stuff. I'm a heart surgeon, sure, but I'm just a mechanic. I go in and fuck around and fix things. Shit," Mel said.

"Modesty doesn't become you," Terri said.

"He's just a humble sawbones," I said. "But sometimes they suffocated in all that armor, Mel. They'd even have heart attacks if it got too hot and they were too tired and worn out. I read somewhere that they'd fall off their horses and not be able to get up because they were too tired to stand with all that armor on them. They got trampled by their own horses sometimes."

"That's terrible," Mel said. "That's a terrible thing, Nicky. I guess they'd just lay there and wait until somebody came along and made a shish kebab out of them."

"Some other vessel," Terri said.

"That's right," Mel said. "Some vassal would come along and spear the bastard in the name of love. Or whatever the fuck it was they fought over in those days."

"Same things we fight over these days," Terri said.

Laura said, "Nothing's changed."

The color was still high in Laura's cheeks. Her eyes were bright. She brought her glass to her lips.

Mel poured himself another drink. He looked at the label closely as if studying a long row of numbers. Then he slowly put the bottle down on the table and slowly reached for the tonic water.

"What about the old couple?" Laura said. "You didn't finish that story you started."

Laura was having a hard time lighting her cigarette. Her matches kept going out.

The sunshine inside the room was different now, changing, getting thinner. But the leaves outside the window were still shimmering, and I stared at the pattern they made on the panes and on the Formica counter. They weren't the same patterns, of course.

"What about the old couple?" I said.

"Older but wiser," Terri said.

Mel stared at her.

Terri said, "Go on with your story, hon. I was only kidding. Then what happened?"

"Terri, sometimes," Mel said.

"Please, Mel," Terri said. "Don't always be so serious, sweetie. Can't you take a joke?"

"Where's the joke?" Mel said.

He held his glass and gazed steadily at his wife.

"What happened?" Laura said.

Mel fastened his eyes on Laura. He said, "Laura, if I didn't have Terri and if I didn't love her so much, and if Nick wasn't my best friend, I'd fall in love with you. I'd carry you off, honey," he said.

"Tell your story," Terri said. "Then we'll go to that new place, okay?"

"Okay?" Mel said. "Where was I?" he said. He stared at the table and then he began again.

"I dropped in to see each of them every day, sometimes twice a day if I was up doing other calls anyway. Casts and bandages, head to foot, the both of them. You know, you've seen it in the movies. That's just the way they looked, just like in the movies. Little eye-holes and nose-holes and mouth-holes. And she had to have her legs slung up on top of it. Well, the husband was very depressed for the longest while. Even after he found out that his wife was going to pull through, he was still very depressed. Not about the accident, though. I mean, the accident was one thing, but it wasn't everything. I'd get up to his mouth-hole, you know, and he'd say no, it wasn't the accident exactly but it was because he couldn't see her through his eye-holes. He said that was what was making him feel so bad. Can you imagine? I'm telling you, the man's heart was breaking because he couldn't turn his goddamn head and *see* his goddamn wife."

Mel looked around the table and shook his head at what he was going to say.

"I mean, it was killing the old fart just because he couldn't *look* at the fucking woman."

We all looked at Mel.   120

"Do you see what I'm saying?" he said.

Maybe we were a little drunk by then. I know it was hard keeping things in focus. The light was draining out of the room, going back through the window where it had come from. Yet nobody made a move to get up from the table to turn on the overhead light.

"Listen," Mel said. "Let's finish this fucking gin. There's about enough left here for one shooter all around. Then let's go eat. Let's go to the new place."

"He's depressed," Terri said. "Mel, why don't you take a pill?"

Mel shook his head. "I've taken everything there is."   125

"We all need a pill now and then," I said.

"Some people are born needing them," Terri said.

She was using her finger to rub at something on the table. Then she stopped rubbing.

"I think I want to call my kids," Mel said. "Is that all right with everybody? I'll call my kids," he said.

Terri said, "What if Marjorie answers the phone? You guys, you've   130
heard us on the subject of Marjorie? Honey, you know you don't want to talk to Marjorie. It'll make you feel even worse."

"I don't want to talk to Marjorie," Mel said. "But I want to talk to my kids."

"There isn't a day goes by that Mel doesn't say he wishes she'd get married again. Or else die," Terri said. "For one thing," Terri said, "She's bankrupting us. Mel says it's just to spite him that she won't get married again. She has a boyfriend who lives with her and the kids, so Mel is supporting the boyfriend too."

"She's allergic to bees," Mel said. "If I'm not praying she'll get married again, I'm praying she'll get herself stung to death by a swarm of fucking bees."

"Shame on you," Laura said.

"Bzzzzzzz," Mel said, turning his fingers into bees and buzzing them   135
at Terri's throat. Then he let his hands drop all the way to his sides.

"She's vicious," Mel said. "Sometimes I think I'll go up there dressed like a beekeeper. You know, that hat that's like a helmet with the plate that comes down over your face, the big gloves, and the padded coat? I'll knock on the door and let loose a hive of bees in the house. But first I'd make sure the kids were out, of course."

He crossed one leg over the other. It seemed to take him a lot of time to do it. Then he put both feet on the floor and leaned forward, elbows on the table, his chin cupped in his hands.

"Maybe I won't call the kids, after all. Maybe it isn't such a hot idea. Maybe we'll just go eat. How does that sound?"

"Sounds fine to me," I said. "Eat or not eat. Or keep drinking. I could head right out into the sunset."

"What does that mean, honey?" Laura said.   140

"It just means what I said," I said. "It means I could just keep going. That's all it means."

"I could eat something myself," Laura said. "I don't think I've ever been so hungry in my life. Is there something to nibble on?"

"I'll put out some cheese and crackers," Terri said.

But Terri just sat there. She did not get up to get anything.

Mel turned his glass over. He spilled it out on the table.   145

"Gin's gone," Mel said.

Terri said, "Now what?"

I could hear my heart beating. I could hear everyone's heart. I could hear the human noise we sat there making, not one of us moving, not even when the room went dark.

CONSIDERATIONS

1. Think of three adjectives that together summarize Mel's character in the first half of the story. Would you change the adjectives to fit his character at the end of the story?

2. What aspect of love is especially troubling to Mel? What bearing does it have on his earlier intention to become a priest and his present vocation as a cardiologist?

3. Why does Mel's language become more vulgar as he tells his story about the old people? What is agitating him?

4. Mel categorizes love as "carnal" or "sentimental." Does his example of true love fit either category? How would you define it?

WRITING SUGGESTION

5. Our commonly used expressions about love indicate that love is not just an emotion: It is also a whole set of ideas and beliefs about that emotion. Is love something to "work on"? Is it something to "share"? Is it "communication"? or a "commitment"? Is it a "feeling"? or a "trip"? Consider the assumptions and implications surrounding the concept of love that is current among a group of people you know. Examine the specific words, gestures, and reactions that indicate their assumed view of love.

4

LESSONS

Language and Learning

JOAN DIDION

On Keeping a Notebook

JOAN DIDION (b. 1934) was raised in California and graduated from the University of California at Berkeley. Her career in journalism has included work as an editor and columnist for magazines such as *Vogue* and *The Saturday Evening Post*. Her essays are collected in *Slouching Towards Bethlehem* (1969), *The White Album* (1979), and *After Henry* (1992). Didion has reported on international issues in *Salvador* (1983) and *Miami* (1987), and with her husband she has coauthored several screenplays. Her most recent novel is *The Last Thing He Wanted* (1996). A prolific and versatile author, Didion examines her earliest, most fundamental reasons for writing in the following essay.

"'That woman Estelle,'" the note reads, "'is partly the reason why George Sharp and I are separated today.' *Dirty crepe-de-Chine wrapper, hotel bar, Wilmington RR, 9:45 A.M. August Monday morning.*"

Since the note is in my notebook, it presumably has some meaning to me. I study it for a long while. At first I have only the most general notion of what I was doing on an August Monday morning in the bar of the hotel across from the Pennsylvania Railroad station in Wilmington, Delaware (waiting for a train? missing one? 1960? 1961? why Wilmington?), but I do remember being there. The woman in the dirty crepe-de-Chine wrapper had come down from her room for a beer, and the bartender had heard before the reason why George Sharp and she were separated today. "Sure," he said, and went on mopping the floor. "You

97

told me." At the other end of the bar is a girl. She is talking, pointedly, not to the man beside her but to a cat lying in the triangle of sunlight cast through the open door. She is wearing a plaid silk dress from Peck & Peck, and the hem is coming down.

Here is what it is: The girl has been on the Eastern Shore, and now she is going back to the city, leaving the man beside her, and all she can see ahead are the viscous summer sidewalks and the 3 A.M. long-distance calls that will make her lie awake and then sleep drugged through all the steaming mornings left in August (1960? 1961?). Because she must go directly from the train to lunch in New York, she wishes that she had a safety pin for the hem of the plaid silk dress, and she also wishes that she could forget about the hem and the lunch and stay in the cool bar that smells of disinfectant and malt and make friends with the woman in the crepe-de-Chine wrapper. She is afflicted by a little self-pity, and she wants to compare Estelles. That is what that was all about.

Why did I write it down? In order to remember, of course, but exactly what was it I wanted to remember? How much of it actually happened? Did any of it? Why do I keep a notebook at all? It is easy to deceive oneself on all those scores. The impulse to write things down is a peculiarly compulsive one, inexplicable to those who do not share it, useful only accidentally, only secondarily, in the way that any compulsion tries to justify itself. I suppose that it begins or does not begin in the cradle. Although I have felt compelled to write things down since I was five years old, I doubt that my daughter ever will, for she is a singularly blessed and accepting child, delighted with life exactly as life presents itself to her, unafraid to go to sleep and unafraid to wake up. Keepers of private notebooks are a different breed altogether, lonely and resistant rearrangers of things, anxious malcontents, children afflicted apparently at birth with some presentiment of loss.

My first notebook was a Big Five tablet, given to me by my mother   5 with the sensible suggestion that I stop whining and learn to amuse myself by writing down my thoughts. She returned the tablet to me a few years ago; the first entry is an account of a woman who believed herself to be freezing to death in the Arctic night, only to find, when day broke, that she had stumbled onto the Sahara Desert, where she would die of the heat before lunch. I have no idea what turn of a five-year-old's mind could have prompted so insistently "ironic" and exotic a story, but it does reveal a certain predilection for the extreme which has dogged me into adult life; perhaps if I were analytically inclined I would find it a truer story than any I might have told about Donald Johnson's birthday party or the day my cousin Brenda put Kitty Litter in the aquarium.

So the point of my keeping a notebook has never been, nor is it now, to have an accurate factual record of what I have been doing or thinking. That would be a different impulse entirely, an instinct for reality which I sometimes envy but do not possess. At no point have I ever been able successfully to keep a diary; my approach to daily life ranges from the grossly negligent to the merely absent, and on those few occasions when I have tried dutifully to record a day's events, boredom has so overcome me that the results are mysterious at best. What is this business about "shopping, typing piece, dinner with E, depressed"? Shopping for what? Typing what piece? Who is E? Was this "E" depressed, or was I depressed? Who cares?

In fact I have abandoned altogether that kind of pointless entry; instead I tell what some would call lies. "That's simply not true," the members of my family frequently tell me when they come up against my memory of a shared event. "The party was *not* for you, the spider was *not* a black widow, *it wasn't that way at all.*" Very likely they are right, for not only have I always had trouble distinguishing between what happened and what merely might have happened, but I remain unconvinced that the distinction, for my purposes, matters. The cracked crab that I recall having for lunch the day my father came home from Detroit in 1945 must certainly be embroidery, worked into the day's pattern to lend verisimilitude; I was ten years old and would not now remember the cracked crab. The day's events did not turn on cracked crab. And yet it is precisely that fictitious crab that makes me see the afternoon all over again, a home movie run all too often, the father bearing gifts, the child weeping, an exercise in family love and guilt. Or that is what it was to me. Similarly, perhaps it never did snow that August in Vermont; perhaps there never were flurries in the night wind, and maybe no one else felt the ground hardening and summer already dead even as we pretended to bask in it, but that was how it felt to me, and it might as well have snowed, could have snowed, did snow.

How it felt to me: That is getting closer to the truth about a notebook. I sometimes delude myself about why I keep a notebook, imagine that some thrifty virtue derives from preserving everything observed. See enough and write it down, I tell myself, and then some morning when the world seems drained of wonder, some day when I am only going through the motions of doing what I am supposed to do, which is write — on that bankrupt morning I will simply open my notebook and there it will all be, a forgotten account with accumulated interest, paid passage back to the world out there: dialogue overheard in hotels and elevators and at the hatcheck counter in Pavillon (one middle-aged man shows his hat check to another and says, "That's my old football number"); impressions of Bettina Aptheker and Benjamin Sonnenberg and Teddy ("Mr. Acapulco") Stauffer; careful *aperçus* about tennis bums and failed fashion models and Greek shipping heiresses, one of whom taught me a significant lesson (a lesson I could have learned from F. Scott Fitzgerald, but perhaps we all must meet the very rich for ourselves) by asking, when I arrived to interview her in her orchid-filled sitting room on the second day of a paralyzing New York blizzard, whether it was snowing outside.

I imagine, in other words, that the notebook is about other people. But of course it is not. I have no real business with what one stranger said to another at the hatcheck counter in Pavillon; in fact I suspect that the line "That's my old football number" touched not my own imagination at all, but merely some memory of something once read, probably "The Eighty-Yard Run." Nor is my concern with a woman in a dirty crepe-de-Chine wrapper in a Wilmington bar. My stake is always, of course, in the unmentioned girl in the plaid silk dress. *Remember what it was to be me:* That is always the point.

It is a difficult point to admit. We are brought up in the ethic that   10
others, any others, all others, are by definition more interesting than our-selves; taught to be diffident, just this side of self-effacing. ("You're the least important person in the room and don't forget it," Jessica Mitford's governess would hiss in her ear on the advent of any social occasion; I copied that into my notebook because it is only recently that I have been able to enter a room without hearing some such phrase in my inner ear.) Only the very young and the very old may recount their dreams at break-fast, dwell upon self, interrupt with memories of beach picnics and fa-vorite Liberty lawn dresses and the rainbow trout in a creek near Col-orado Springs. The rest of us are expected, rightly, to affect absorption in other people's favorite dresses, other people's trout.

And so we do. But our notebooks give us away, for however duti-fully we record what we see around us, the common denominator of all we see is always, transparently, shamelessly, the implacable "I." We are not talking here about the kind of notebook that is patently for public consumption, a structural conceit for binding together a series of graceful *pensées;*[1] we are talking about something private, about bits of the mind's string too short to use, an indiscriminate and erratic assemblage with meaning only for its maker.

And sometimes even the maker has difficulty with the meaning. There does not seem to be, for example, any point in my knowing for the rest of my life that, during 1964, 720 tons of soot fell on every square mile of New York City, yet there it is in my notebook, labeled "FACT." Nor do I really need to remember that Ambrose Bierce liked to spell Leland Stanford's name "£eland $tanford" or that "smart women al-most always wear black in Cuba," a fashion hint without much potential for practical application. And does not the relevance of these notes seem marginal at best?:

> In the basement museum of the Inyo County Courthouse in Indepen-dence, California, sign pinned to a mandarin coat: "This MANDARIN COAT was often worn by Mrs. Minnie S. Brooks when giving lectures on her TEAPOT COLLECTION."

[1] *pensées:* In French, connected thoughts or philosophical reflections.

Redhead getting out of car in front of Beverly Wilshire Hotel, chinchilla stole, Vuitton bags with tags reading:

> MRS LOU FOX
> HOTEL SAHARA
> VEGAS

Well, perhaps not entirely marginal. As a matter of fact, Mrs. Minnie S. Brooks and her MANDARIN COAT pull me back into my own childhood, for although I never knew Mrs. Brooks and did not visit Inyo County until I was thirty, I grew up in just such a world, in houses cluttered with Indian relics and bits of gold ore and ambergris and the souvenirs my Aunt Mercy Farnsworth brought back from the Orient. It is a long way from that world to Mrs. Lou Fox's world, where we all live now, and is it not just as well to remember that? Might not Mrs. Minnie S. Brooks help me to remember what I am? Might not Mrs. Lou Fox help me to remember what I am not?

But sometimes the point is harder to discern. What exactly did I have in mind when I noted down that it cost the father of someone I know $650 a month to light the place on the Hudson in which he lived before the Crash? What use was I planning to make of this line by Jimmy Hoffa: "I may have my faults, but being wrong ain't one of them"? And although I think it interesting to know where the girls who travel with the Syndicate have their hair done when they find themselves on the West Coast, will I ever make suitable use of it? Might I not be better off just passing it on to John O'Hara? What is a recipe for sauerkraut doing in my notebook? What kind of magpie keeps this notebook? *"He was born the night the Titanic went down."* That seems a nice enough line, and I even recall who said it, but is it not really a better line in life than it could ever be in fiction?

But of course that is exactly it: not that I should ever use the line, but that I should remember the woman who said it and the afternoon I heard it. We were on her terrace by the sea, and we were finishing the wine left from lunch, trying to get what sun there was, a California winter sun. The woman whose husband was born the night the *Titanic* went down wanted to rent her house, wanted to go back to her children in Paris. I remember wishing that I could afford the house, which cost $1,000 a month. "Someday you will," she said lazily. "Someday it all comes." There in the sun on her terrace it seemed easy to believe in someday, but later I had a low-grade afternoon hangover and ran over a black snake on the way to the supermarket and was flooded with inexplicable fear when I heard the checkout clerk explaining to the man ahead of me why she was finally divorcing her husband. "He left me no choice," she said over and over as she punched the register. "He has a little seven-month-old baby by her, he left me no choice." I would like to believe that my dread then was for the human condition, but of course it was for me, because I wanted a baby and did not then have one and because I wanted to own the house that cost $1,000 a month to rent and because I had a hangover.

It all comes back. Perhaps it is difficult to see the value in having one's self back in that kind of mood, but I do see it; I think we are well advised to keep on nodding terms with the people we used to be whether we find them attractive company or not. Otherwise they turn up unannounced and surprise us, come hammering on the mind's door at 4 A.M. of a bad night and demand to know who deserted them, who betrayed them, who is going to make amends. We forget all too soon the things we thought we could never forget. We forget the loves and the betrayals alike, forget what we whispered and what we screamed, forget who we were. I have already lost touch with a couple of people I used to be; one of them, a seventeen-year-old, presents little threat, although it would be of some interest to me to know again what it feels like to sit on a river levee drinking vodka-and-orange-juice and listening to Les Paul and Mary Ford and their echoes sing "How High the Moon" on the car radio. (You see I still have the scenes, but I no longer perceive myself among those present, no longer could even improvise the dialogue.) The other one, a twenty-three-year-old, bothers me more. She was always a good deal of trouble, and I suspect she will reappear when I least want to see her, skirts too long, shy to the point of aggravation, always the injured party, full of recriminations and little hurts and stories I do not want to hear again, at once saddening me and angering me with her vulnerability and ignorance, an apparition all the more insistent for being so long banished.

It is a good idea, then, to keep in touch, and I suppose that keeping in touch is what notebooks are all about. And we are all on our own when it comes to keeping those lines open to ourselves: Your notebook will never help me, nor mine you. "*So what's new in the whiskey business?*" What could that possibly mean to you? To me it means a blonde in a Pucci bathing suit sitting with a couple of fat men by the pool at the Beverly Hills Hotel. Another man approaches, and they all regard one another in silence for a while. "So what's new in the whiskey business?" one of the fat men finally says by way of welcome, and the blonde stands up, arches one foot and dips it in the pool, looking all the while at the cabaña where Baby Pignatari is talking on the telephone. That is all there is to that, except that several years later I saw the blonde coming out of Saks Fifth Avenue in New York with her California complexion and a voluminous mink coat. In the harsh wind that day she looked old and irrevocably tired to me, and even the skins in the mink coat were not worked the way they were doing them that year, not the way she would have wanted them done, and there is the point of the story. For a while after that I did not like to look in the mirror, and my eyes would skim the newspapers and pick out only the deaths, the cancer victims, the premature coronaries, the suicides, and I stopped riding the Lexington Avenue IRT because I noticed for the first time that all the strangers I had seen for years — the man with the seeing-eye dog, the spinster who read the classified pages every day, the fat girl who always got off with me at Grand Central — looked older than they once had.

It all comes back. Even that recipe for sauerkraut: Even that brings it back. I was on Fire Island when I first made that sauerkraut, and it was raining, and we drank a lot of bourbon and ate the sauerkraut and went to bed at ten, and I listened to the rain and the Atlantic and felt safe. I made the sauerkraut again last night and it did not make me feel any safer, but that is, as they say, another story.

CONSIDERATIONS

1. How does Didion contrast the purposes of a diary and of a notebook? Why does she consider herself unsuited to diary-keeping?

2. How does Didion's style illustrate her statement of purpose for writing?

3. Didion says, "I have already lost touch with a couple of people I used to be" (paragraph 16) and names two such people. Has she really lost touch with them?

WRITING SUGGESTION

4. Explain the reasons you once had for starting a diary, notebook, or journal. Include enough details to illustrate your motives and interests at that time. If you have never kept one, try to imagine why you might want to now.

RICHARD RODRIGUEZ

Public and Private Language

RICHARD RODRIGUEZ (b. 1944) grew up in San Francisco, where
as the child of Spanish-speaking Mexican Americans he received
his education in a language that was not spoken at home. His attraction to English and to English-speaking culture became his
avenue to a promising future. He received a Ph.D. in English
from the University of California at Berkeley and remained there
as a teacher, until he decided to write about the conflicting aspirations that divided him between two cultures. This selection from
his autobiography, *Hunger of Memory* (1982), recounts the origin
of his adult views about bilingualism. Rodriguez has continued his
memoir in *Days of Obligation: An Argument with My Mexican Father* (1992).

Supporters of bilingual education today imply that students like me
miss a great deal by not being taught in their family's language. What
they seem not to recognize is that, as a socially disadvantaged child, I considered Spanish to be a private language. What I needed to learn in school
was that I had the right — and the obligation — to speak the public language of *los gringos*.[1] The odd truth is that my first-grade classmates could
have become bilingual, in the conventional sense of that word, more easily
than I. Had they been taught (as upper-middle-class children are often
taught early) a second language like Spanish or French, they could have
regarded it simply as that: another public language. In my case such bilingualism could not have been so quickly achieved. What I did not believe
was that I could speak a single public language.

Without question, it would have pleased me to hear my teachers address me in Spanish when I entered the classroom. I would have felt much
less afraid. I would have trusted them and responded with ease. But I
would have delayed — for how long postponed? — having to learn the
language of public society. I would have evaded — and for how long could
I have afforded to delay? — learning the great lesson of school, that I had
a public identity.

Fortunately, my teachers were unsentimental about their responsibility. What they understood was that I needed to speak a public lan-

[1] *los gringos:* Foreigners.

guage. So their voices would search me out, asking me questions. Each time I'd hear them, I'd look up in surprise to see a nun's face frowning at me. I'd mumble, not really meaning to answer. The nun would persist, "Richard, stand up. Don't look at the floor. Speak up. Speak to the entire class, not just to me!" but I couldn't believe that the English language was mine to use. (In part, I did not want to believe it.) I continued to mumble. I resisted the teacher's demands. (Did I somehow suspect that once I learned public language my pleasing family life would be changed?) Silent, waiting for the bell to sound, I remained dazed, diffident, afraid.

Because I wrongly imagined that English was intrinsically a public language and Spanish an intrinsically private one, I easily noted the difference between classroom language and the language of home. At school, words were directed to a general audience of listeners. ("Boys and girls.") Words were meaningfully ordered. And the point was not self-expression alone but to make oneself understood by many others. The teacher quizzed: "Boys and girls, why do we use that word in this sentence? Could we think of a better word to use there? Would the sentence change its meaning if the words were differently arranged? And wasn't there a better way of saying much the same thing?" (I couldn't say. I wouldn't try to say.)

Three months. Five. Half a year passed. Unsmiling, ever watchful, 5 my teachers noted my silence. They began to connect my behavior with the difficult progress my older sister and brother were making. Until one Saturday morning three nuns arrived at the house to talk to our parents. Stiffly, they sat on the blue living room sofa. From the doorway of another room, spying the visitors, I noted the incongruity — the clash of two worlds, the faces and voices of school intruding upon the familiar setting of home. I overheard one voice gently wondering, "Do your children speak only Spanish at home, Mrs. Rodriguez?" While another voice added, "That Richard especially seems so timid and shy."

That Rich-heard!

With great tact the visitors continued, "Is it possible for you and your husband to encourage your children to practice their English when they are home?" Of course, my parents complied. What would they not do for their children's well-being? And how could they have questioned the Church's authority which those women represented? In an instant, they agreed to give up the language (the sounds) that had revealed and accentuated our family's closeness. The moment after the visitors left, the change was observed. "*Ahora,* speak to us *en inglés,*"[2] my father and mother united to tell us.

At first, it seemed a kind of game. After dinner each night, the family gathered to practice "our" English. (It was still then *inglés,* a language foreign to us, so we felt drawn as strangers to it.) Laughing, we would try

---

[2]"*Now,* speak to us *in English.*"

to define words we could not pronounce. We played with strange English sounds, often overanglicizing our pronunciations. And we filled the smiling gaps of our sentences with familiar Spanish sounds. But that was cheating, somebody shouted. Everyone laughed. In school, meanwhile, like my brother and sister, I was required to attend a daily tutoring session. I needed a full year of special attention. I also needed my teachers to keep my attention from straying in class by calling out, *Rich-heard* — their English voices slowly prying loose my ties to my other name, its three notes, *Ri-car-do*. Most of all I needed to hear my mother and father speak to me in a moment of seriousness in broken — suddenly heartbreaking — English. The scene was inevitable: One Saturday morning I entered the kitchen where my parents were talking in Spanish. I did not realize that they were talking in Spanish however until, at the moment they saw me, I heard their voices change to speak English. Those *gringo* sounds they uttered startled me. Pushed me away. In that moment of trivial misunderstanding and profound insight, I felt my throat twisted by unsounded grief. I turned quickly and left the room. But I had no place to escape to with Spanish. (The spell was broken.) My brother and sisters were speaking English in another part of the house.

Again and again in the days following, increasingly angry, I was obliged to hear my mother and father: "Speak to us *en inglés*." (*Speak.*) Only then did I determine to learn classroom English. Weeks after, it happened: One day in school I had my hand raised to volunteer an answer. I spoke out in a loud voice. And I did not think it remarkable when the entire class understood. That day, I moved very far from the disadvantaged child I had been only days earlier. The belief, that calming assurance that I belonged in public, had at last taken hold.

Shortly after, I stopped hearing the high and loud sounds of *los gringos*. A more and more confident speaker of English, I didn't trouble to listen to *how* strangers sounded, speaking to me. And there simply were too many English-speaking people in my day for me to hear American accents anymore. Conversations quickened. Listening to persons whose voices sounded eccentrically pitched, I usually noted their sounds for an initial few seconds before I concentrated on *what* they were saying. Conversations became content-full. Transparent. Hearing someone's *tone* of voice — angry or questioning or sarcastic or happy or sad — I didn't distinguish it from the words it expressed. Sound and word were thus tightly wedded. At the end of a day, I was often bemused, always relieved, to realize how "silent," though crowded with words, my day in public had been. (This public silence measured and quickened the change in my life.)

At last, seven years old, I came to believe what had been technically true since my birth: I was an American citizen.

But the special feeling of closeness at home was diminished by then. Gone was the desperate, urgent, intense feeling of being at home; rare was the experience of feeling myself individualized by family intimates. We remained a loving family, but one greatly changed. No longer so close; no longer bound tight by the pleasing and troubling knowledge of our public separateness. Neither my older brother nor sister rushed home after school anymore. Nor did I. When I arrived home there would often be neighborhood kids in the house. Or the house would be empty of sounds.

Following the dramatic Americanization of their children, even my parents grew more publicly confident. Especially my mother. She learned the names of all the people on our block. And she decided we needed to have a telephone installed in the house. My father continued to use the word *gringo*. But it was no longer charged with the old bitterness or distrust. (Stripped of any emotional content, the word simply became a name for those Americans not of Hispanic descent.) Hearing him, sometimes, I wasn't sure if he was pronouncing the Spanish word *gringo* or saying gringo in English.

Matching the silence I started hearing in public was a new quiet at home. The family's quiet was partly due to the fact that, as we children learned more and more English, we shared fewer and fewer words with our parents. Sentences needed to be spoken slowly when a child addressed his mother or father. (Often the parent wouldn't understand.) The child would need to repeat himself. (Still the parent misunderstood.) The young voice, frustrated, would end up saying, "Never mind" — the subject was closed. Dinners would be noisy with the clinking of knives and forks against dishes. My mother would smile softly between her remarks; my father at the other end of the table would chew and chew at his food, while he stared over the heads of his children.

My *mother!* My *father!* After English became my primary language, I no longer knew what words to use in addressing my parents. The old Spanish words (those tender accents of sound) I had used earlier — *mamá* and *papá* — I couldn't use anymore. They would have been too painful reminders of how much had changed in my life. On the other hand, the words I heard neighborhood kids call *their* parents seemed equally unsatisfactory. *Mother* and *Father; Ma, Papa, Pa, Dad, Pop* (how I hated the all-American sound of that last word especially) — all these terms I felt were unsuitable, not really terms of address for *my* parents. As a result, I never used them at home. Whenever I'd speak to my parents, I would try to get their attention with eye contact alone. In public conversations, I'd refer to "my parents" or "my mother and father."   15

My mother and father, for their part, responded differently, as their children spoke to them less and less. She grew restless, seemed troubled and anxious at the scarcity of words exchanged in the house. It was she who would question me about my day when I came home from school. She smiled at the small talk. She pried at the edges of my sentences to get me to say something more. (What?) She'd join conversations she overheard, but her intrusions often stopped her children's talking. By contrast, my father seemed reconciled to the new quiet. Though his English improved somewhat, he retired into silence. At dinner he spoke very little.

One night his children and even his wife helplessly giggled at his garbled English pronunciation of the Catholic Grace before Meals. Thereafter he made his wife recite the prayer at the start of each meal, even on formal occasions, when there were guests in the house. Hers became the public voice of the family. On official business, it was she, not my father, one would usually hear on the phone or in stores, talking to strangers. His children grew so accustomed to his silence that, years later, they would speak routinely of his shyness. (My mother would often try to explain: Both his parents died when he was eight. He was raised by an uncle who treated him like little more than a menial servant. He was never encouraged to speak. He grew up alone. A man of few words.) But my father was not shy, I realized, when I'd watch him speaking Spanish with relatives. Using Spanish, he was quickly effusive. Especially when talking with other men, his voice would spark, flicker, flare alive with sounds. In Spanish, he expressed ideas and feelings he rarely revealed in English. With firm Spanish sounds, he conveyed confidence and authority English would never allow him.

The silence at home, however, was finally more than a literal silence. Fewer words passed between parent and child, but more profound was the silence that resulted from my inattention to sounds. At about the time I no longer bothered to listen with care to the sounds of English in public, I grew careless about listening to the sounds family members made when they spoke. Most of the time I heard someone speaking at home and didn't distinguish his sounds from the words people uttered in public. I didn't even pay much attention to my parents' accented and ungrammatical speech. At least not at home. Only when I was with them in public would I grow alert to their accents. Though, even then, their sounds caused me less and less concern. For I was increasingly confident of my own public identity.

Today I hear bilingual educators say that children lose a degree of "individuality" by becoming assimilated into public society. (Bilingual schooling was popularized in the seventies, that decade when middle-class ethnics began to resist the process of assimilation — the American melting pot.) But the bilingualists simplistically scorn the value and necessity of assimilation. They do not seem to realize that there are *two* ways a person is individualized. So they do not realize that while one suffers a diminished sense of *private* individuality by becoming assimilated into public society, such assimilation makes possible the achievement of *public* individuality.

CONSIDERATIONS

1. How does Rodriguez regard his childhood teachers? Distinguish between his childhood and his adult perspectives.

2. How does the English language change his parents' lives? How does Rodriguez respond to those changes?

3. Rodriguez differentiates between *private* and *public* individuality, but he does not explicitly define either concept. Has he defined them implicitly? Explain his terms, adding your understanding of what they mean.

WRITING SUGGESTION

4. Should schools offer bilingual education to children of minority groups? Or perhaps to all children? (For instance, in Canada, all children learn both English and French.) Consider positive and negative effects of having a single public language in a multicultural society.

MAYA ANGELOU

Graduation

MAYA ANGELOU (b. 1928) was raised by her grandmother, who ran a small store for blacks in the town of Stamps, Arkansas. She survived a childhood that seemed certain to defeat her, and as she once told an interviewer: "One would say of my life — born loser — had to be; from a broken family, raped at eight, unwed mother at sixteen." During her adult life, she became a dancer, an actress, a poet, a television writer and producer, and a coordinator in Martin Luther King's Southern Christian Leadership Conference. She is most widely known for her autobiographical books, beginning with *I Know Why the Caged Bird Sings* (1970), from which this selection is taken. Her memoirs continue through *All God's Children Need Traveling Shoes* (1986). Angelou's most recent book is a collection of essays, *Wouldn't Take Nothing for My Journey Now* (1993).

The children in Stamps trembled visibly with anticipation. Some adults were excited too, but to be certain the whole young population had come down with graduation epidemic. Large classes were graduating from both the grammar school and the high school. Even those who were years removed from their own day of glorious release were anxious to help with preparations as a kind of dry run. The junior students who were moving into the vacating classes' chairs were tradition-bound to show their talents for leadership and management. They strutted through the school and around the campus exerting pressure on the lower grades. Their authority was so new that occasionally if they pressed a little too hard it had to be overlooked. After all, next term was coming, and it never hurt a sixth grader to have a play sister in the eighth grade, or a tenth-year student to be able to call a twelfth grader Bubba. So all was endured in a spirit of shared understanding. But the graduating classes themselves were the nobility. Like travelers with exotic destinations on their minds, the graduates were remarkably forgetful. They came to school without their books, or tablets, or even pencils. Volunteers fell over themselves to secure replacements for the missing equipment. When accepted, the willing workers might or might not be thanked, and it was of no importance to the pregraduation rites. Even teachers were respectful of the now quiet and aging seniors, and tended to speak to them, if not as equals, as beings only slightly lower than themselves. After tests were returned and grades given, the student body, which acted like an extended family, knew who did well, who excelled, and what piteous ones had failed.

Unlike the white school, Lafayette County Training School distinguished itself by having neither lawn, nor hedges, nor tennis court, nor climbing ivy. Its two buildings (main classrooms, the grade school, and home economics) were set on a dirt hill with no fence to limit either its boundaries or those of bordering farms. There was a large expanse to the left of the school which was used alternately as a baseball diamond or a basketball court. Rusty hoops on the swaying poles represented the permanent recreational equipment, although bats and balls could be borrowed from the P.E. teacher if the borrower was qualified and if the diamond wasn't occupied.

Over this rocky area relieved by a few shady tall persimmon trees the graduating class walked. The girls often held hands and no longer bothered to speak to the lower students. There was a sadness about them, as if this old world was not their home and they were bound for higher ground. The boys, on the other hand, had become more friendly, more outgoing. A decided change from the closed attitude they projected while studying for finals. Now they seemed not ready to give up the old school, the familiar paths and classrooms. Only a small percentage would be continuing on to college — one of the South's A & M (agricultural and mechanical) schools, which trained Negro youths to be carpenters, farmers, handymen, masons, maids, cooks, and baby nurses. Their future rode heavily on their shoulders, and blinded them to the collective joy that had pervaded the lives of the boys and girls in the grammar school graduating class.

Parents who could afford it had ordered new shoes and ready-made clothes for themselves from Sears and Roebuck or Montgomery Ward. They also engaged the best seamstresses to make the floating graduating dresses and to cut down secondhand pants which would be pressed to a military slickness for the important event.

Oh, it was important, all right. Whitefolks would attend the ceremony, and two or three would speak of God and home, and the Southern way of life, and Mrs. Parsons, the principal's wife, would play the graduation march while the lower-grade graduates paraded down the aisles and took their seats below the platform. The high school seniors would wait in empty classrooms to make their dramatic entrance.

In the Store I was the person of the moment. The birthday girl. The center. Bailey[1] had graduated the year before, although to do so he had had to forfeit all pleasures to make up for his time lost in Baton Rouge.

My class was wearing butter-yellow piqué dresses, and Momma launched out on mine. She smocked the yoke into tiny crisscrossing puckers, then shirred the rest of the bodice. Her dark fingers ducked in and out of the lemony cloth as she embroidered raised daisies around the hem. Before she considered herself finished she had added a crocheted cuff on the puff sleeves, and a pointy crocheted collar.

I was going to be lovely. A walking model of all the various styles of fine hand sewing and it didn't worry me that I was only twelve years old and merely graduating from the eighth grade. Besides, many teachers in Arkansas Negro schools had only that diploma and were licensed to impart wisdom.

The days had become longer and more noticeable. The faded beige of former times had been replaced with strong and sure colors. I began to see my classmates' clothes, their skin tones, and the dust that waved off pussy willows. Clouds that lazed across the sky were objects of great concern to me. Their shiftier shapes might have held a message that in my new happiness and with a little bit of time I'd soon decipher. During that period I looked at the arch of heaven so religiously my neck kept a steady ache. I had taken to smiling more often, and my jaws hurt from the unaccustomed activity. Between the two physical sore spots, I suppose I could have been uncomfortable, but that was not the case. As a member of the winning team (the graduating class of 1940) I had outdistanced unpleasant sensations by miles. I was headed for the freedom of open fields.

Youth and social approval allied themselves with me and we trammeled memories of slights and insults. The wind of our swift passage remodeled my features. Lost tears were pounded to mud and then to dust. Years of withdrawal were brushed aside and left behind, as hanging ropes of parasitic moss.   10

My work alone had awarded me a top place and I was going to be one of the first called in the graduating ceremonies. On the classroom blackboard, as well as on the bulletin board in the auditorium, there were blue stars and white stars and red stars. No absences, no tardinesses, and my academic work was among the best of the year. I could say the preamble to the Constitution even faster than Bailey. We timed ourselves often: "WethepeopleoftheUnitedStatesinordertoformamoreperfectunion . . ." I had memorized the Presidents of the United States from Washington to Roosevelt in chronological as well as alphabetical order.

My hair pleased me too. Gradually the black mass had lengthened and thickened, so that it kept at last to its braided pattern, and I didn't have to yank my scalp off when I tried to comb it.

[1]The author's brother. The children help out in their grandmother's store.

Louise and I had rehearsed the exercises until we tired out our-selves. Henry Reed was class valedictorian. He was a small, very black boy with hooded eyes, a long, broad nose, and an oddly shaped head. I had ad-mired him for years because each term he and I vied for the best grades in our class. Most often he bested me, but instead of being disappointed I was pleased that we shared top places between us. Like many Southern Black children, he lived with his grandmother, who was as strict as Momma and as kind as she knew how to be. He was courteous, respectful, and soft-spoken to elders, but on the playground he chose to play the roughest games. I admired him. Anyone, I reckoned, sufficiently afraid or sufficiently dull could be polite. But to be able to operate at top level with both adults and children was admirable.

His valedictory speech was entitled "To Be or Not to Be." The rigid tenth-grade teacher had helped him to write it. He'd been working on the dramatic stresses for months.

The weeks until graduation were filled with heady activities. A group   15 of small children were to be presented in a play about buttercups and daisies and bunny rabbits. They could be heard throughout the building practicing their hops and their little songs that sounded like silver bells. The older girls (nongraduates, of course) were assigned the task of making refresh-ments for the night's festivities. A tangy scent of ginger, cinnamon, nutmeg, and chocolate wafted around the home economics building as the budding cooks made samples for themselves and their teachers.

In every corner of the workshop, axes and saws split fresh timber as the woodshop boys made sets and stage scenery. Only the graduates were left out of the general bustle. We were free to sit in the library at the back of the building or look in quite detachedly, naturally, on the measures being taken for our event.

Even the minister preached on graduation the Sunday before. His subject was "Let your light so shine that men will see your good works and praise your Father, Who is in Heaven." Although the sermon was purported to be addressed to us, he used the occasion to speak to backslid-ers, gamblers, and general ne'er-do-wells. But since he had called our names at the beginning of the service we were mollified.

Among Negroes the tradition was to give presents to children going only from one grade to another. How much more important this was when the person was graduating at the top of the class. Uncle Willie and Momma had sent away for a Mickey Mouse watch like Bailey's. Louise gave me four embroidered handkerchiefs. (I gave her three crocheted doilies.) Mrs. Sneed, the minister's wife, made me an underskirt to wear for graduation, and nearly every customer gave me a nickel or maybe even a dime with the instruction "Keep on moving to higher ground," or some such encouragement.

Amazingly the great day finally dawned and I was out of bed before I knew it. I threw open the back door to see it more clearly, but Momma said, "Sister, come away from that door and put your robe on."

I hoped the memory of that morning would never leave me. Sun-   20
light was itself still young, and the day had none of the insistence maturity
would bring it in a few hours. In my robe and barefoot in the backyard,
under cover of going to see about my new beans, I gave myself up to the
gentle warmth and thanked God that no matter what evil I had done in
my life He had allowed me to live to see this day. Somewhere in my fatal-
ism I had expected to die, accidentally, and never have the chance to walk
up the stairs in the auditorium and gracefully receive my hard-earned
diploma. Out of God's merciful bosom I had won reprieve.

Bailey came out in his robe and gave me a box wrapped in Christmas
paper. He said he had saved his money for months to pay for it. It felt like
a box of chocolates, but I knew Bailey wouldn't save money to buy candy
when we had all we could want under our noses.

He was as proud of the gift as I. It was a soft-leather-bound copy of
a collection of poems by Edgar Allan Poe, or, as Bailey and I called him,
"Eap." I turned to "Annabel Lee" and we walked up and down the garden
rows, the cool dirt between our toes, reciting the beautifully sad lines.

Momma made a Sunday breakfast although it was only Friday. After
we finished the blessing, I opened my eyes to find the watch on my plate.
It was a dream of a day. Everything went smoothly and to my credit. I
didn't have to be reminded or scolded for anything. Near evening I was
too jittery to attend to chores, so Bailey volunteered to do all before his
bath.

Days before, we had made a sign for the Store and as we turned out
the lights Momma hung the cardboard over the doorknob. It read clearly:
CLOSED. GRADUATION.

My dress fitted perfectly and everyone said that I looked like a sun-   25
beam in it. On the hill, going toward the school, Bailey walked behind
with Uncle Willie, who muttered, "Go on, Ju." He wanted him to walk
ahead with us because it embarrassed him to have to walk so slowly. Bailey
said he'd let the ladies walk together, and the men would bring up the
rear. We all laughed, nicely.

Little children dashed by out of the dark like fireflies. Their
crepepaper dresses and butterfly wings were not made for running and we
heard more than one rip, dryly, and the regretful "uh uh" that followed.

The school blazed without gaiety. The windows seemed cold and
unfriendly from the lower hill. A sense of ill-fated timing crept over me,
and if Momma hadn't reached for my hand I would have drifted back to
Bailey and Uncle Willie, and possibly beyond. She made a few slow jokes
about my feet getting cold, and tugged me along to the now-strange
building.

Around the front steps, assurance came back. There were my fellow
"greats," the graduating class. Hair brushed back, legs oiled, new dresses
and pressed pleats, fresh pocket handkerchiefs and little handbags, all
homesewn. Oh, we were up to snuff, all right. I joined my comrades and
didn't even see my family go in to find seats in the crowded auditorium.

The school band struck up a march and all classes filed in as had been rehearsed. We stood in front of our seats, as assigned, and on a signal from the choir director, we sat. No sooner had this been accomplished than the band started to play the national anthem. We rose again and sang the song, after which we recited the pledge of allegiance. We remained standing for a brief minute before the choir director and the principal signaled to us, rather desperately I thought, to take our seats. The command was so unusual that our carefully rehearsed and smooth-running machine was thrown off. For a full minute we fumbled for our chairs and bumped into each other awkwardly. Habits change or solidify under pressure, so in our state of nervous tension we had been ready to follow our usual assembly pattern: the American National Anthem, then the pledge of allegiance, then the song every Black person I knew called the Negro National Anthem. All done in the same key, with the same passion and most often standing on the same foot.

Finding my seat at last, I was overcome with a presentiment of 30 worse things to come. Something unrehearsed, unplanned, was going to happen, and we were going to be made to look bad. I distinctly remember being explicit in the choice of pronoun. It was "we," the graduating class, the unit, that concerned me then.

The principal welcomed "parents and friends" and asked the Baptist minister to lead us in prayer. His invocation was brief and punchy, and for a second I thought we were getting back on the high road to right action. When the principal came back to the dais, however, his voice had changed. Sounds always affected me profoundly and the principal's voice was one of my favorites. During assembly it melted and lowed weakly into the audience. It had not been in my plan to listen to him, but my curiosity was piqued and I straightened up to give him my attention.

He was talking about Booker T. Washington, our "late great leader," who said we can be as close as the fingers on the hand, etc. . . . Then he said a few vague things about friendship and the friendship of kindly people to those less fortunate than themselves. With that his voice nearly faded, thin, away. Like a river diminishing to a stream and then to a trickle. But he cleared his throat and said, "Our speaker tonight, who is also our friend, came from Texarkana to deliver the commencement address, but due to the irregularity of the train schedule, he's going to, as they say, 'speak and run.'" He said that we understood and wanted the man to know that we were most grateful for the time he was able to give us and then something about how we were willing always to adjust to another's program, and without more ado — "I give you Mr. Edward Donleavy."

Not one but two white men came through the door offstage. The shorter one walked to the speaker's platform, and the tall one moved over to the center seat and sat down. But that was our principal's seat, and already occupied. The dislodged gentleman bounced around for a long breath or two before the Baptist minister gave him his chair, then with more dignity than the situation deserved, the minister walked off the stage.

Donleavy looked at the audience once (on reflection, I'm sure that he wanted only to reassure himself that we were really there), adjusted his glasses, and began to read from a sheaf of papers.

He was glad "to be here and to see the work going on just as it was   35 in the other schools."

At the first "Amen" from the audience I willed the offender to immediate death by choking on the word. But Amens and Yes, sir's began to fall around the room like rain through a ragged umbrella.

He told us of the wonderful changes we children in Stamps had in store. The Central School (naturally, the white school was Central) had already been granted improvements that would be in use in the fall. A well-known artist was coming from Little Rock to teach art to them. They were going to have the newest microscopes and chemistry equipment for their laboratory. Mr. Donleavy didn't leave us long in the dark over who made these improvements available to Central High. Nor were we to be ignored in the general betterment scheme he had in mind.

He said that he had pointed out to people at a very high level that one of the first-line football tacklers at Arkansas Agricultural and Mechanical College had graduated from good old Lafayette County Training School. Here fewer Amens were heard. Those few that did break through lay dully in the air with the heaviness of habit.

He went on to praise us. He went on to say how he had bragged that "one of the best basketball players at Fisk sank his first ball right here at Lafayette County Training School."

The white kids were going to have a chance to become Galileos and   40 Madame Curies and Edisons and Gauguins, and our boys (the girls weren't even in on it) would try to be Jesse Owenses and Joe Louises.

Owens and the Brown Bomber were great heroes in our world, but what school official in the white-goddom of Little Rock had the right to decide that those two men must be our only heroes? Who decided that for Henry Reed to become a scientist he had to work like George Washington Carver, as a bootblack, to buy a lousy microscope? Bailey was obviously always going to be too small to be an athlete, so which concrete angel glued to what county seat had decided that if my brother wanted to become a lawyer he had to first pay penance for his skin by picking cotton and hoeing corn and studying correspondence books at night for twenty years?

The man's dead words fell like bricks around the auditorium and too many settled in my belly. Constrained by hard-learned manners I couldn't look behind me, but to my left and right the proud graduating class of 1940 had dropped their heads. Every girl in my row had found something new to do with her handkerchief. Some folded the tiny squares into love knots, some into triangles, but most were wadding them, then pressing them flat on their yellow laps.

On the dais, the ancient tragedy was being replayed. Professor Parsons sat, a sculptor's reject, rigid. His large, heavy body seemed devoid of will or willingness, and his eyes said he was no longer with us. The other teachers examined the flag (which was draped stage right) or their notes, or the windows which opened on our now-famous playing diamond.

Graduation, the hush-hush magic time of frills and gifts and congratulations and diplomas, was finished for me before my name was called. The accomplishment was nothing. The meticulous maps, drawn in three colors of ink, learning and spelling decasyllabic words, memorizing the whole of *The Rape of Lucrece* — it was nothing. Donleavy had exposed us.

We were maids and farmers, handymen and washerwomen, and   45
anything higher that we aspired to was farcical and presumptuous. Then I wished that Gabriel Prosser and Nat Turner had killed all whitefolks in their beds and that Abraham Lincoln had been assassinated before the signing of the Emancipation Proclamation, and that Harriet Tubman had been killed by that blow on her head and Christopher Columbus had drowned in the *Santa Maria*.

It was awful to be Negro and have no control over my life. It was brutal to be young and already trained to sit quietly and listen to charges brought against my color with no chance of defense. We should all be dead. I thought I should like to see us all dead, one on top of the other. A pyramid of flesh with the whitefolks on the bottom, as the broad base, then the Indians with their silly tomahawks and teepees and wigwams and treaties, the Negroes with their mops and recipes and cotton sacks and spirituals sticking out of their mouths. The Dutch children should all stumble in their wooden shoes and break their necks. The French should choke to death on the Louisiana Purchase (1803) while silkworms ate all the Chinese with their stupid pigtails. As a species, we were an abomination. All of us.

Donleavy was running for election, and assured our parents that if he won we could count on having the only colored paved playing field in that part of Arkansas. Also — he never looked up to acknowledge the grunts of acceptance — also, we were bound to get some new equipment for the home economics building and the workshop.

He finished, and since there was no need to give any more than the most perfunctory thank-you's, he nodded to the men on the stage, and the tall white man who was never introduced joined him at the door. They left with the attitude that now they were off to something really important. (The graduation ceremonies at Lafayette County Training School had been a mere preliminary.)

The ugliness they left was palpable. An uninvited guest who wouldn't leave. The choir was summoned and sang a modern arrangement of "Onward, Christian Soldiers," with new words pertaining to graduates seeking their place in the world. But it didn't work. Elouise, the daughter of the Baptist minister, recited "Invictus," and I could have cried at the impertinence of "I am the master of my fate, I am the captain of my soul."

My name had lost its ring of familiarity and I had to be nudged to go   50
and receive my diploma. All my preparations had fled. I neither marched
up to the stage like a conquering Amazon, nor did I look in the audience
for Bailey's nod of approval. Marguerite Johnson, I heard the name again,
my honors were read, there were noises in the audience of appreciation,
and I took my place on the stage as rehearsed.

I thought about colors I hated: ecru, puce, lavender, beige, and
black.

There was shuffling and rustling around me, then Henry Reed was
giving his valedictory address, "To Be or Not to Be." Hadn't he heard the
whitefolks? We couldn't *be*, so the question was a waste of time. Henry's
voice came out clear and strong. I feared to look at him. Hadn't he got the
message? There was no "nobler in the mind" for Negroes because the
world didn't think we had minds, and they let us know it. "Outrageous
fortune"? Now, that was a joke. When the ceremony was over I had to tell
Henry Reed some things. That is, if I still cared. Not "rub," Henry,
"erase." "Ah, there's the erase." Us.

Henry had been a good student in elocution. His voice rose on tides
of promise and fell on waves of warnings. The English teacher had helped
him to create a sermon winging through Hamlet's soliloquy. To be a
man, a doer, a builder, a leader, or to be a tool, an unfunny joke, a crusher
of funky toadstools. I marveled that Henry could go through the speech as
if we had a choice.

I had been listening and silently rebutting each sentence with my
eyes closed; then there was a hush, which in an audience warns that something unplanned is happening. I looked up and saw Henry Reed, the conservative, the proper, the A student, turn his back to the audience and
turn to us (the proud graduating class of 1940) and sing, nearly speaking,

> Lift ev'ry voice and sing
> Till earth and heaven ring
> Ring with the harmonies of Liberty . . .

It was the poem written by James Weldon Johnson. It was the music com-
posed by J. Rosamond Johnson. It was the Negro National Anthem. Out
of habit we were singing it.

Our mothers and fathers stood in the dark hall and joined the hymn   55
of encouragement. A kindergarten teacher led the small children onto the
stage and the buttercups and daisies and bunny rabbits marked time and
tried to follow:

> Stony the road we trod
> Bitter the chastening rod
> Felt in the days when hope, unborn, had died.
> Yet with a steady beat
> Have not our weary feet
> Come to the place for which our fathers sighed?

Every child I knew had learned that song with his ABCs and along with "Jesus Loves Me This I Know." But I personally had never heard it before. Never heard the words, despite the thousands of times I had sung them. Never thought they had anything to do with me.

On the other hand, the words of Patrick Henry had made such an impression on me that I had been able to stretch myself tall and trembling and say, "I know not what course others may take, but as for me, give me liberty or give me death."

And now I heard, really for the first time:

> We have come over a way that with tears has been watered,
> We have come, treading our path through the blood
>   of the slaughtered.

While echoes of the song shivered in the air, Henry Reed bowed his head, said "Thank you," and returned to his place in the line. The tears that slipped down many faces were not wiped away in shame.

We were on top again. As always, again. We survived. The depths   60
had been icy and dark, but now a bright sun spoke to our souls. I was no longer simply a member of the proud graduating class of 1940; I was a proud member of the wonderful, beautiful Negro race.

Oh, Black known and unknown poets, how often have your auctioned pains sustained us? Who will compute the lonely nights made less lonely by your songs, or by the empty pots made less tragic by your tales?

If we were a people much given to revealing secrets, we might raise monuments and sacrifice to the memories of our poets, but slavery cured us of that weakness. It may be enough, however, to have it said that we survive in exact relationship to the dedication of our poets (include preachers, musicians, and blues singers).

CONSIDERATIONS

1. What changes come over the student body as the time for graduation approaches? What phrases convey a special atmosphere? What changes come over Angelou in particular?

2. How do you explain Angelou's immediate response to Donleavy's speech? Does it seem excessive?

3. In what sense is this graduation truly a "commencement" for Angelou? Make your answer detailed and explicit.

WRITING SUGGESTIONS

4. Traditional ceremonies are formal initiations to a new status, as in a graduation, confirmation, bar or bat mitzvah, or wedding. Analyze the customs associated with one such passage you experienced or witnessed. What meanings and ideals are suggested by details of the ritual? If you could,

what parts of the ceremony would you change? Which parts do you think are most important?

5. Angelou and Nora Ephron (see "Shaping Up Absurd," p. 5) recapture the style of adolescent exaggeration. Compare their use of humor to deal with serious subjects.

AMY TAN

Mother Tongue

AMY TAN (b. 1952), the daughter of Chinese immigrants, grew up in California and graduated from San Jose State University. She began a business career writing speeches and reports for corporate executives. She turned to fiction writing as part of her remedy for workaholism. Tan's first novel, *The Joy Luck Club* (1989), recounts interconnected stories of conflict and loyalty between Chinese mothers and their American-born daughters. The novel was made into a popular movie. The Chinese heroine in her second novel, *The Kitchen God's Wife* (1991), resembles Tan's mother as she is represented in "Mother Tongue," which first appeared in *Threepenny Review* (1990). Tan recently published a third novel, *The Hundred Secret Senses* (1995).

I am not a scholar of English or literature. I cannot give you much more than personal opinions on the English language and its variations in this country or others.

I am a writer. And by that definition, I am someone who has always loved language. I am fascinated by language in daily life. I spend a great deal of my time thinking about the power of language — the way it can evoke an emotion, a visual image, a complex idea, or a simple truth. Language is the tool of my trade. And I use them all — all the Englishes I grew up with.

Recently, I was made keenly aware of the different Englishes I do use. I was giving a talk to a large group of people, the same talk I had already given to half a dozen other groups. The nature of the talk was about my writing, my life, and my book, *The Joy Luck Club*. The talk was going along well enough, until I remembered one major difference that made the whole talk sound wrong. My mother was in the room. And it was perhaps the first time she had heard me give a lengthy speech, using the kind of English I have never used with her. I was saying things like "The intersection of memory upon imagination" and "There is an aspect of my fiction that relates to thus-and-thus" — a speech filled with carefully wrought grammatical phrases, burdened, it suddenly seemed to me, with nominalized forms, past perfect tenses, conditional phrases, all the forms of standard English that I had learned in school and through books, the forms of English I did not use at home with my mother.

Just last week, I was walking down the street with my mother, and I again found myself conscious of the English I was using, the English I do use with her. We were talking about the price of new and used furniture and I heard myself saying this: "Not waste money that way." My husband was with us as well, and he didn't notice any switch in my English. And then I realized why. It's because over the twenty years we've been together I've often used that same kind of English with him, and sometimes he even uses it with me. It has become our language of intimacy, a different sort of English that relates to family talk, the language I grew up with.

So you'll have some idea of what this family talk I heard sounds like,   5
I'll quote what my mother said during a recent conversation which I videotaped and then transcribed. During this conversation, my mother was talking about a political gangster in Shanghai who had the same last name as her family's, Du, and how the gangster in his early years wanted to be adopted by her family, which was rich by comparison. Later, the gangster became more powerful, far richer than my mother's family, and one day showed up at my mother's wedding to pay his respects. Here's what she said in part:

"Du Yusong having business like fruit stand. Like off the street kind. He is Du like Du Zong — but not Tsung-ming Island people. The local people call putong, the river east side, he belong to that side local people. That man want to ask Du Zong father take him in like become own family. Du Zong father wasn't look down on him, but didn't take seriously, until that man big like become a mafia. Now important person, very hard to inviting him. Chinese way, came only to show respect, don't stay for dinner. Respect for making big celebration, he shows up. Mean gives lots of respect. Chinese custom. Chinese social life that way. If too important won't have to stay too long. He come to my wedding. I didn't see, I heard it. I gone to boy's side, they have YMCA dinner. Chinese age I was nineteen."

You should know that my mother's expressive command of English belies how much she actually understands. She reads the *Forbes* report, listens to *Wall Street Week*, converses daily with her stockbroker, reads all of Shirley MacLaine's books with ease — all kinds of things I can't begin to understand. Yet some of my friends tell me they understand 50 percent of what my mother says. Some say they understand 80 to 90 percent. Some say they understand none of it, as if she were speaking pure Chinese. But to me, my mother's English is perfectly clear, perfectly natural. It's my mother tongue. Her language, as I hear it, is vivid, direct, full of observation and imagery. That was the language that helped shape the way I saw things, expressed things, made sense of the world.

Lately, I've been giving more thought to the kind of English my mother speaks. Like others, I have described it to people as "broken" or "fractured" English. But I wince when I say that. It has always bothered me that I can think of no other way to describe it other than "broken," as if it were damaged and needed to be fixed, as if it lacked a certain wholeness and soundness. I've heard other terms used, "limited English," for example. But they seem just as bad, as if everything is limited, including people's perceptions of the limited English speaker.

I know this for a fact, because when I was growing up, my mother's "limited" English limited *my* perception of her. I was ashamed of her English. I believed that her English reflected the quality of what she had to say. That is, because she expressed them imperfectly her thoughts were imperfect. And I had plenty of empirical evidence to support me: the fact that people in department stores, at banks, and at restaurants did not take her seriously, did not give her good service, pretended not to understand her, or even acted as if they did not hear her.

My mother has long realized the limitations of her English as well.   10
When I was fifteen, she used to have me call people on the phone to pretend I was she. In this guise, I was forced to ask for information or even to complain and yell at people who had been rude to her. One time it was a call to her stockbroker in New York. She had cashed out her small portfolio and it just so happened we were going to go to New York the next week, our very first trip outside California. I had to get on the phone and say in an adolescent voice that was not very convincing, "This is Mrs. Tan."

And my mother was standing in the back whispering loudly, "Why he don't send me check, already two weeks late. So mad he lie to me, losing me money."

And then I said in perfect English, "Yes, I'm getting rather concerned. You had agreed to send the check two weeks ago, but it hasn't arrived."

Then she began to talk more loudly. "What he want, I come to New York tell him front of his boss, you cheating me?" And I was trying to calm her down, make her be quiet, while telling the stockbroker, "I can't tolerate any more excuses. If I don't receive the check immediately, I am going to have to speak to your manager when I'm in New York next week." And sure enough, the following week there we were in front of this astonished stockbroker, and I was sitting there red-faced and quiet, and my mother, the real Mrs. Tan, was shouting at his boss in her impeccable broken English.

We used a similar routine just five days ago, for a situation that was far less humorous. My mother had gone to the hospital for an appointment, to find out about a benign brain tumor a CAT scan had revealed a month ago. She said she had spoken very good English, her best English, no mistakes. Still, she said, the hospital did not apologize when they said they had lost the CAT scan and she had come for nothing. She said they did not seem to have any sympathy when she told them she was anxious to know the exact diagnosis, since her husband and son had both died of brain tumors. She said they would not give her any more information until the next time and she would have to make another appointment for that. So she said she would not leave until the doctor called her daughter. She wouldn't budge. And when the doctor finally called her daughter, me, who spoke in perfect English — lo and behold — we had assurances the CAT scan would be found, promises that a conference call on Monday would be held, and apologies for any suffering my mother had gone through for a most regrettable mistake.

I think my mother's English almost had an effect on limiting my 15 possibilities in life as well. Sociologists and linguists probably will tell you that a person's developing language skills are more influenced by peers. But I do think that the language spoken in the family, especially in immigrant families which are more insular, plays a large role in shaping the language of the child. And I believe that it affected my results on achievement tests, IQ tests, and the SAT. While my English skills were never judged as poor, compared to math, English could not be considered my strong suit. In grade school I did moderately well, getting perhaps B's, sometimes B-pluses, in English and scoring perhaps in the sixtieth or seventieth percentile on achievement tests. But those scores were not good enough to override the opinion that my true abilities lay in math and science, because in those areas I achieved A's and scored in the ninetieth percentile or higher.

This was understandable. Math is precise; there is only one correct answer. Whereas, for me at least, the answers on English tests were always a judgment call, a matter of opinion and personal experience. Those tests were constructed around items like fill-in-the-blank sentence completion, such as "Even though Tom was _____, Mary thought he was _____." And the correct answer always seemed to be the most bland combinations of thoughts, for example, "Even though Tom was shy, Mary thought he was charming," with the grammatical structure "even though" limiting the correct answer to some sort of semantic opposites, so you wouldn't get answers like, "Even though Tom was foolish, Mary thought he was ridiculous." Well, according to my mother, there were very few limitations as to what Tom could have been and what Mary might have thought of him. So I never did well on tests like that.

The same was true with word analogies, pairs of words in which you were supposed to find some sort of logical, semantic relationship — for example, "*Sunset* is to *nightfall* as _____ is to _____." And here you would be presented with a list of four possible pairs, one of which showed the same kind of relationship: *red* is to *stoplight*, *bus* is to *arrival*, *chills* is to *fever*, *yawn* is to *boring*. Well, I could never think that way. I knew what the tests were asking, but I could not block out of my mind the images already created by the first pair, "*sunset* is to *nightfall*" — and I would see a burst of colors against a darkening sky, the moon rising, the lowering of a curtain of stars. And all the other pairs of words — red, bus, stoplight, boring — just threw up a mass of confusing images, making it impossible for me to sort out something as logical as saying: "A sunset precedes nightfall" is the same as "a chill precedes a fever." The only way I would have gotten that answer right would have been to imagine an associative situation, for example, my being disobedient and staying out past sunset, catching a chill at night, which turns into feverish pneumonia as punishment, which indeed did happen to me.

I have been thinking about all this lately, about my mother's English, about achievement tests. Because lately I've been asked, as a writer, why there are not more Asian Americans represented in American literature. Why are there few Asian Americans enrolled in creative writing programs? Why do so many Chinese students go into engineering? Well, these are broad sociological questions I can't begin to answer. But I have noticed in surveys — in fact, just last week — that Asian students, as a whole, always do significantly better on math achievement tests than in English. And this makes me think that there are other Asian-American students whose English spoken in the home might also be described as "broken" or "limited." And perhaps they also have teachers who are steering them away from writing and into math and science, which is what happened to me.

Fortunately, I happen to be rebellious in nature and enjoy the challenge of disproving assumptions made about me. I became an English major my first year in college, after being enrolled as pre-med. I started writing nonfiction as a freelancer the week after I was told by my former boss that writing was my worst skill and I should hone my talents toward account management.

But it wasn't until 1985 that I finally began to write fiction. And at first I wrote using what I thought to be wittily crafted sentences, sentences that would finally prove I had mastery over the English language. Here's an example from the first draft of a story that later made its way into *The Joy Luck Club*, but without this line: "That was my mental quandary in its nascent state." A terrible line, which I can barely pronounce.

Fortunately, for reasons I won't get into today, I later decided I should envision a reader for the stories I would write. And the reader I decided upon was my mother, because these were stories about mothers. So with this reader in mind — and in fact she did read my early drafts — I began to write stories using all the Englishes I grew up with: the English I spoke to my mother, which for lack of a better term might be described as "simple"; the English she used with me, which for lack of a better term might be described as "broken"; my translation of her Chinese, which could certainly be described as "watered down"; and what I imagined to be her translation of her Chinese if she could speak in perfect English, her internal language, and for that I sought to preserve the essence, but

20

neither an English nor a Chinese structure. I wanted to capture what language ability tests can never reveal: her intent, her passion, her imagery, the rhythms of her speech, and the nature of her thoughts.

Apart from what any critic had to say about my writing, I knew I had succeeded where it counted when my mother finished reading my book and gave me her verdict: "So easy to read."

CONSIDERATIONS

1. The author starts by emphasizing her professional viewpoint. What focus and freedoms does she claim by virtue of her profession?

2. What is Tan's tone toward her mother? Find details that indicate her feelings and attitudes in their relationship. How have they changed through the years?

3. Explain why the author had so much trouble with SAT tests. What is her criticism of them and of other language ability tests?

4. According to Tan, what is the public attitude toward people with limited English? As a child, how did she respond to this attitude?

WRITING SUGGESTION

5. Tan and Richard Rodriguez (see "Public and Private Language," p. 104) write about the difficulties of assimilating American culture. But they succeeded at it. What is gained and what is lost in the process of assimilating? How does it affect family relationships and personal goals? Use evidence from both selections to make your points. If you have personal knowledge of assimilation, add your perspective.

VIRGINIA WOOLF

Professions for Women

VIRGINIA WOOLF (1882–1941) was an important British novelist
noted for her emphasis on the subjective meaning of events rather
than the outward circumstances of plot and appearance. Her novels include *Mrs. Dalloway* (1925) and *To the Lighthouse* (1927). Born
into a distinguished literary family, she was educated at home and
began her writing career as a book reviewer for the London *Times
Literary Supplement.* She spoke out consistently for freedom and
equality for women in works such as *A Room of One's Own* (1929)
and the following address to the Women's Service League. Her
essays appear in the four-volume *Collected Essays* (1967).

When your secretary invited me to come here, she told me that your
Society is concerned with the employment of women and she suggested
that I might tell you something about my own professional experiences. It
is true that I am a woman; it is true I am employed; but what professional
experiences have I had? It is difficult to say. My profession is literature;
and in that profession there are fewer experiences for women than in any
other, with the exception of the stage — fewer, I mean, that are peculiar
to women. For the road was cut many years ago — by Fanny Burney, by
Aphra Behn, by Harriet Martineau, by Jane Austen, by George Eliot[1] —
many famous women, and many more unknown and forgotten, have been
before me, making the path smooth, and regulating my steps. Thus, when
I came to write, there were very few material obstacles in my way. Writing was a reputable and harmless occupation. The family peace was not
broken by the scratching of a pen. No demand was made upon the family
purse. For ten and sixpence one can buy paper enough to write all the
plays of Shakespeare — if one has a mind that way. Pianos and models,
Paris, Vienna and Berlin, masters and mistresses, are not needed by a
writer. The cheapness of writing paper is, of course, the reason why
women have succeeded as writers before they succeeded in the other professions.

But to tell you my story — it is a simple one. You have only got to
figure to yourselves a girl in a bedroom with a pen in her hand. She had
only to move that pen from left to right — from ten o'clock to one. Then
it occurred to her to do what is simple and cheap enough after all — to
slip a few of those pages into an envelope, fix a penny stamp in the corner,

[1]British women novelists of the eighteenth and nineteenth centuries.

and drop the envelope into the red box at the corner. It was thus that I became a journalist; and my effort was rewarded on the first day of the following month — a very glorious day it was for me — by a letter from an editor containing a check for one pound ten shillings and sixpence. But to show you how little I deserve to be called a professional woman, how little I know of the struggles and difficulties of such lives, I have to admit that instead of spending that sum upon bread and butter, rent, shoes and stockings, or butcher's bills, I went out and bought a cat — a beautiful cat, a Persian cat, which very soon involved me in bitter disputes with my neighbors.

What could be easier than to write articles and to buy Persian cats with the profits? But wait a moment. Articles have to be about something. Mine, I seem to remember, was about a novel by a famous man. And while I was writing this review I discovered that if I were going to review books I should need to do battle with a certain phantom. And the phantom was a woman, and when I came to know her better I called her after the heroine of a famous poem, The Angel in the House. It was she who used to come between me and my paper when I was writing reviews. It was she who bothered me and wasted my time and so tormented me that at last I killed her. You who come of a younger and happier generation may not have heard of her — you may not know what I mean by the Angel in the House. I will describe her as shortly as I can. She was intensely sympathetic. She was immensely charming. She was utterly unselfish. She excelled in the difficult arts of family life. She sacrificed herself daily. If there was chicken, she took the leg; if there was a draught, she sat in it — in short she was so constituted that she never had a mind or a wish of her own, but preferred to sympathize always with the minds and wishes of others. Above all — I need not say it — she was pure. Her purity was supposed to be her chief beauty — her blushes, her great grace. In those days — the last of Queen Victoria — every house had its Angel. And when I came to write I encountered her with the very first words. The shadow of her wings fell on my page; I heard the rustling of her skirts in the room. Directly, that is to say, I took my pen in hand to review that novel by a famous man, she slipped behind me and whispered: "My dear, you are a young woman. You are writing about a book that has been written by a man. Be sympathetic; be tender; flatter; deceive; use all the arts and wiles of our sex. Never let anybody guess that you have a mind of your own. Above all, be pure." And she made as if to guide my pen. I now record the one act for which I take some credit to myself, though the credit rightly belongs to some excellent ancestors of mine who left me a certain sum of money — shall we say five hundred pounds a year? — so that it was not necessary for me to depend solely on charm for my living. I turned upon her and caught her by the throat. I did my best to kill her. My excuse, if I were to be had up in a court of law, would be that I acted in self-defense. Had I not killed her she would have killed me. She would have plucked the heart out of my writing. For, as I found, directly I put pen to paper, you cannot review even a novel without having a mind of your own, without expressing what you think to be the truth about human relations, morality, sex. And all these questions, according to the Angel in the House, cannot be dealt with freely and openly by women; they must charm, they must conciliate, they must — to put it bluntly — tell lies if they are to succeed. Thus, whenever I felt the shadow of her wing or the radiance of her halo upon my page, I took up the inkpot and flung it at her. She died hard. Her fictitious nature was of great assistance to her. It is far harder to kill a phantom than a reality. She was always creeping back when I thought I had despatched her. Though I flatter myself that I killed her in the end, the struggle was severe; it took much time that had better have been spent upon learning Greek grammar; or in roaming the world in search of adventures. But it was a real experience; it was an experience that was bound to befall all women writers at that time. Killing the Angel in the House was part of the occupation of a woman writer.

But to continue my story. The Angel was dead; what then remained? You may say that what remained was a simple and common object — a young woman in a bedroom with an inkpot. In other words, now that she had rid herself of falsehood, that young woman had only to be herself. Ah, but what is "herself"? I mean, what is a woman? I assure you, I do not know. I do not believe that you know. I do not believe that anybody can know until she has expressed herself in all the arts and professions open to human skill. That indeed is one of the reasons why I have come here — out of respect for you, who are in process of showing us by your experiment what a woman is, who are in process of providing us, by your failures and successes, with that extremely important piece of information.

But to continue the story of my professional experiences. I made one pound ten and six by my first review; and I bought a Persian cat with the proceeds. Then I grew ambitious. A Persian cat is all very well, I said; but a Persian cat is not enough. I must have a motor car. And it was thus that I became a novelist — for it is a very strange thing that people will give you a motor car if you will tell them a story. It is a still stranger thing that there is nothing so delightful in the world as telling stories. It is far pleasanter than writing reviews of famous novels. And yet, if I am to obey your secretary and tell you my professional experiences as a novelist, I must tell you about a very strange experience that befell me as a novelist. And to understand it you must try first to imagine a novelist's state of mind. I hope I am not giving away professional secrets if I say that a novelist's chief desire is to be as unconscious as possible. He has to induce in himself a state of perpetual lethargy. He wants life to proceed with the utmost quiet and regularity. He wants to see the same faces, to read the same books, to do the same things day after day, month after month, while he is writing, so that nothing may break the illusion in which he is living — so that nothing may disturb or disquiet the mysterious nosings about, feelings round, darts, dashes, and sudden discoveries of that very shy and illusive spirit, the imagination. I suspect that this state is the same both for men and women. Be that as it may, I want you to imagine me writing a novel in a state of trance. I want you to figure to yourselves a girl sitting with a pen in her hand, which for minutes, and indeed for hours, she never dips into the inkpot. The image that comes to my mind when I think of this girl is the image of a fisherman lying sunk in dreams on the verge of a deep lake with a rod held out over the water. She was letting her imagination sweep unchecked round every rock and cranny of the world that lies submerged in the depths of our unconscious being. Now came the experience, the experience that I believe to be far commoner with women writers than with men. The line raced through the girl's fingers. Her imagination had rushed away. It had sought the pools, the depths, and the dark places where the largest fish slumber. And then there was a smash. There was an explosion. There was foam and confusion. The imagination had dashed itself against something hard. The girl was roused from her dream. She was indeed in a state of the most acute and difficult distress. To speak without figure she had thought of something, something about the body, about the passions which it was unfitting for her as a woman to say. Men, her reason told her, would be shocked. The consciousness of what men will say of a woman who speaks the truth about her passions had roused her from her artist's state of unconsciousness. She could write no more. The trance was over. Her imagination could work no longer. This I believe to be a very common experience with women writers — they are impeded by the extreme conventionality of the other sex. For though men sensibly allow themselves great freedom in these respects, I doubt that they realize or can control the extreme severity with which they condemn such freedom in women.

These then were two very genuine experiences of my own. These were two of the adventures of my professional life. The first — killing the Angel in the House — I think I solved. She died. But the second, telling the truth about my own experiences as a body, I do not think I solved. I doubt that any woman has solved it yet. The obstacles against her are still immensely powerful — and yet they are very difficult to define. Outwardly, what is simpler than to write books? Outwardly, what obstacles are there for a woman rather than for a man? Inwardly, I think, the case is very different; she has still many ghosts to fight, many prejudices to overcome. Indeed it will be a long time still, I think, before a woman can sit down to write a book without finding a phantom to be slain, a rock to be dashed against. And if this is so in literature, the freest of all professions for women, how is it in the new professions which you are now for the first time entering?

Those are the questions I should like, had I time, to ask you. And indeed, if I have laid stress upon these professional experiences of mine, it is because I believe that they are, though in different forms, yours also. Even when the path is nominally open — when there is nothing to prevent a woman from being a doctor, a lawyer, a civil servant — there are many phantoms and obstacles, as I believe, looming in her way. To discuss and define them is I think of great value and importance; for thus only can the labor be shared, the difficulties be solved. But besides this, it is necessary also to discuss the ends and the aims for which we are fighting, for which we are doing battle with these formidable obstacles. Those aims cannot be taken for granted; they must be perpetually questioned and examined. The whole position, as I see it — here in this hall surrounded by women practicing for the first time in history I know not how many different professions — is one of extraordinary interest and importance. You have won rooms of your own in the house hitherto exclusively owned by men. You are able, though not without great labor and effort, to pay the rent. You are earning your five hundred pounds a year. But this freedom is only a beginning; the room is your own, but it's still bare. It has to be furnished; it has to be decorated; it has to be shared. How are you going to furnish it, how are you going to decorate it? With whom are you going to share it, and upon what terms? These, I think, are questions of the utmost importance and interest. For the first time in history you are able to ask them; for the first time you are able to decide for yourselves what the answers should be. Willingly would I stay and discuss those questions and answers — but not tonight. My time is up; and I must cease.

CONSIDERATIONS

1. In the first two paragraphs, what relation does Woolf establish with her audience? What details make her appear ingratiating? condescending? earnest?

2. Does the Angel in the House still exist? What has changed, and what remains the same, in present-day expectations of women?

3. Does Woolf assume that male writers encounter no difficulties or conflicts in thinking independently and expressing themselves? Is Woolf a female sexist in some of her observations?

4. What relationships between men and women are implied in Woolf's many references to women in a house and a room? What changes in the future are suggested by the metaphorical use of "house" in the final paragraph?

WRITING SUGGESTION

5. Should young men and women ever be educated separately for part of their lives? At what age can it do the most good or the most harm to change or reinforce gender roles through separate schools or separate classes? Draw on any of your relevant experiences in single-sex associations such as scouting, sports, clubs, and being with just "the boys" or "the girls." Consider what it has meant to you to have these associations, and how they might have been more beneficial, or less limiting, than they were.

TONI CADE BAMBARA

The Lesson

TONI CADE BAMBARA (1939–1995) grew up in the black districts of New York City, where she experienced racism and poverty set in sharp contrast to the opulence of white Manhattan, as the following story reflects. After graduating from Queens College, she studied dance and acting in Italy and France before returning to New York, where she took an M.A. degree at City College. Bambara worked as a welfare investigator and youth counselor, as well as a college teacher of English, while writing short stories. Her selected short fiction, essays, and interviews are collected in *Deep Sightings and Rescue Missions* (1996).

Back in the days when everyone was old and stupid or young and foolish and me and Sugar were the only ones just right, this lady moved on our block with nappy hair and proper speech and no makeup. And quite naturally we laughed at her, laughed the way we did at the junk man who went about his business like he was some big-time president and his sorry-ass horse his secretary. And we kinda hated her too, hated the way we did the winos who cluttered up our parks and pissed on our handball walls and stank up our hallways and stairs so you couldn't halfway play hide-and-seek without a goddamn gas mask. Miss Moore was her name. The only woman on the block with no first name. And she was black as hell, cept for her feet, which were fish-white and spooky. And she was always planning these boring-ass things for us to do, us being my cousin, mostly, who lived on the block cause we all moved North the same time and to the same apartment then spread out gradual to breathe. And our parents would yank our heads into some kinda shape and crisp up our clothes so we'd be presentable for travel with Miss Moore, who always looked like she was going to church, though she never did. Which is just one of the things the grownups talked about when they talked behind her back like a dog. But when she came calling with some sachet she'd sewed up or some gingerbread she'd made or some book, why then they'd all be too embarrassed to turn her down and we'd get handed over all spruced up. She'd been to college and said it was only right that she should take responsibility for the young ones' education, and she not even related by marriage or blood. So they'd go for it. Specially Aunt Gretchen. She was the main gofer in the family. You got some ole dumb shit foolishness you want somebody to go for, you send for Aunt Gretchen. She been screwed into the go-along for so long, it's a blood-deep natural thing with her.

130

Which is how she got saddled with me and Sugar and Junior in the first place while our mothers were in the la-de-da apartment up the block having a good ole time.

So this one day Miss Moore rounds us all up at the mailbox and it's puredee hot and she's knockin herself out about arithmetic. And school suppose to let up in the summer I heard, but she don't never let up. And the starch in my pinafore scratching the shit outta me and I'm really hating this nappy-head bitch and her goddamn college degree. I'd much rather go to the pool or to the show where it's cool. So me and Sugar leaning on the mailbox being surly, which is a Miss Moore word. And Flyboy checking out what everybody brought for lunch. And Fat Butt already wasting his peanut-butter-and-jelly sandwich like the pig he is. And Junebug punchin on Q.T.'s arm for potato chips. And Rosie Giraffe shifting from one hip to the other waiting for somebody to step on her foot or ask if she from Georgia so she can kick ass, preferably Mercedes'. And Miss Moore asking us do we know what money is, like we a bunch of re-tards. I mean real money, she say, like it's only poker chips or monopoly papers we lay on the grocer. So right away I'm tired of this and say so. And would much rather snatch Sugar and go to the Sunset and terrorize the West Indian kids and take their hair ribbons and their money too. And Miss Moore files that remark away for next week's lesson on brotherhood, I can tell. And finally I say we oughta get to the subway cause it's cooler and besides we might meet some cute boys. Sugar done swiped her mama's lipstick, so we ready.

So we heading down the street and she's boring us silly about what things cost and what our parents make and how much goes for rent and how money ain't divided up right in this country. And then she gets to the part about we all poor and live in the slums, which I don't feature. And I'm ready to speak on that, but she steps out in the street and hails two cabs just like that. Then she hustles half the crew in with her and hands me a five-dollar bill and tells me to calculate 10 percent tip for the driver. And we're off. Me and Sugar and Junebug and Flyboy hanging out the window and hollering to everybody, putting lipstick on each other cause Flyboy a faggot anyway, and making farts with our sweaty armpits. But I'm mostly trying to figure how to spend this money. But they all fascinated with the meter ticking and Junebug starts laying bets as to how much it'll read when Flyboy can't hold his breath no more. Then Sugar lay bets as to how much it'll be when we get there. So I'm stuck. Don't nobody want to go for my plan, which is to jump out at the next light and run off to the first bar-b-que we can find. Then the driver tells us to get the hell out cause we there already. And the meter reads eighty-five cents. And I'm stalling to figure out the tip and Sugar say give him a dime. And I decide he don't need it bad as I do, so later for him. But then he tries to take off with Junebug foot still in the door so we talk about his mama something ferocious. Then we check out that we on Fifth Avenue and everybody dressed up in stockings. One lady in a fur coat, hot as it is. White folks crazy.

"This is the place," Miss Moore say, presenting it to us in the voice she uses at the museum. "Let's look in the windows before we go in."

"Can we steal?" Sugar asks very serious like she's getting the ground   5
rules squared away before she plays. "I beg your pardon," say Miss Moore, and we fall out. So she leads us around the windows of the toy store and me and Sugar screamin, "This is mine, that's mine, I gotta have that, that was made for me, I was born for that," till Big Butt drowns us out.

"Hey, I'm goin to buy that there."

"That there? You don't even know what it is, stupid."

"I do so," he say punchin on Rosie Giraffe. "It's a microscope."

"Whatcha gonna do with a microscope, fool?"

"Look at things."   10

"Like what, Ronald?" ask Miss Moore. And Big Butt ain't got the first notion. So here go Miss Moore gabbing about the thousands of bacteria in a drop of water and the somethinorother in a speck of blood and the million and one living things in the air around us is invisible to the naked eye. And what she say that for? Junebug go to town on that "naked" and we rolling. Then Miss Moore ask what it cost. So we all jam into the window smudgin it up and the price tag say $300. So then she ask how long'd take for Big Butt and Junebug to save up their allowances. "Too long," I say. "Yeh," adds Sugar, "outgrown it by that time." And Miss Moore say no, you never outgrow learning instruments. "Why, even medical students and interns and," blah, blah, blah. And we ready to choke Big Butt for bringing it up in the first damn place.

"This here costs four hundred eighty dollars," say Rosie Giraffe. So we pile up all over her to see what she pointin out. My eyes tell me it's a chunk of glass cracked with something heavy, and different-color inks dripped into the splits, then the whole thing put into a oven or something. But for $480 it don't make sense.

"That's a paperweight made of semi-precious stones fused together under tremendous pressure," she explains slowly, with her hands doing the mining and all the factory work.

"So what's a paperweight?" asks Rosie Giraffe.

"To weigh paper with, dumbbell," say Flyboy, the wise man from   15
the East.

"Not exactly," say Miss Moore, which is what she say when you warm or way off too. "It's to weigh paper down so it won't scatter and make your desk untidy." So right away me and Sugar curtsy to each other and then to Mercedes who is more the tidy type.

"We don't keep paper on top of the desk in my class," say Junebug, figuring Miss Moore crazy or lyin one.

"At home, then," she say. "Don't you have a calendar and a pencil case and a blotter and a letter-opener on your desk at home where you do your homework?" and she know damn well what our homes look like cause she nosys around in them every chance she gets.

"I don't even have a desk," say Junebug. "Do we?"

"No, and I don't get no homework neither," says Big Butt.   20

"And I don't even have a home," say Flyboy like he do at school to keep the white folks off his back and sorry for him. Send this poor kid to camp posters, is his specialty.

"I do," says Mercedes. "I have a box of stationery on my desk and a picture of my cat. My godmother bought the stationery and the desk. There's a big rose on each sheet and the envelopes smell like roses."

"Who wants to know about your smelly-ass stationery," say Rosie Giraffe fore I can get my two cents in.

"It's important to have a work area all your own so that . . ."

"Will you look at this sailboat, please," say Flyboy, cuttin her off   25
and pointin to the thing like it was his. So once again we tumble all over each other to gaze at this magnificent thing in the toy store which is just big enough to maybe sail two kittens across the pond if you strap them to the posts tight. We all start reciting the price tag like we in assembly. "Handcrafted sailboat of fiberglass at one thousand one hundred ninety-five dollars."

"Unbelievable," I hear myself say and am really stunned. I read it again for myself just in case the group recitation put me in a trance. Same thing. For some reason this pisses me off. We look at Miss Moore and she lookin at us, waiting for I dunno what.

"Who'd pay all that when you can buy a sailboat set for a quarter at Pop's, a tube of glue for a dime, and a ball of string for eight cents? It must have a motor and a whole lot besides," I say. "My sailboat cost me about fifty cents."

"But will it take water?" says Mercedes with her smart ass.

"Took mine to Alley Pond Park once," say Flyboy. "String broke. Lost it. Pity."

"Sailed mine in Central Park and it keeled over and sank. Had to ask   30
my father for another dollar."

"And you got the strap," laughed Big Butt. "The jerk didn't even have a string on it. My old man wailed his behind."

Little Q.T. was staring hard at the sailboat and you could see he wanted it bad. But he too little and somebody'd just take it from him. So what the hell. "This boat for kids, Miss Moore?"

"Parents silly to buy something like that just to get all broke up," say Rosie Giraffe.

"That much money it should last forever," I figure.

"My father'd buy it for me if I wanted it."   35

"Your father, my ass," say Rosie Giraffe getting a chance to finally push Mercedes.

"Must be rich people shop here," say Q.T.

"You are a very bright boy," say Flyboy. "What was your first clue?" And he rap him on the head with the back of his knuckles, since Q.T. the only one he could get away with. Though Q.T. liable to come up behind you years later and get his licks in when you half expect it.

"What I want to know is," I says to Miss Moore though I never talk to her, I wouldn't give the bitch that satisfaction, "is how much a real boat costs? I figure a thousand'd get you a yacht any day?"

"Why don't you check that out," she says, "and report back to the group?" Which really pains my ass. If you gonna mess up a perfectly good swim day least you could do is have some answers. "Let's go in," she say like she got something up her sleeve. Only she don't lead the way. So me and Sugar turn the corner to where the entrance is, but when we get there I kinda hang back. Not that I'm scared, what's there to be afraid of, just a toy store. But I feel funny, shame. But what I got to be shamed about? Got as much right to go in as anybody. But somehow I can't seem to get hold of the door, so I step away for Sugar to lead. But she hangs back too. And I look at her and she looks at me and this is ridiculous. I mean, damn, I have never ever been shy about doing nothing or going nowhere. But then Mercedes steps up and then Rosie Giraffe and Big Butt crowd in behind and shove, and next thing we all stuffed into the doorway with only Mercedes squeezing past us, smoothing out her jumper and walking right down the aisle. Then the rest of us tumble in like a glued-together jigsaw done all wrong. And people lookin at us. And it's like the time me and Sugar crashed into the Catholic church on a dare. But once we got in there and everything so hushed and holy and the candles and the bowin and the handkerchiefs on all the drooping heads, I just couldn't go through with the plan. Which was for me to run up to the altar and do a tap dance while Sugar played the nose flute and messed around in the holy waters. And Sugar kept giving me the elbow. Then later teased me so bad I tied her up in the shower and turned it on and locked her in. And she'd be there till this day if Aunt Gretchen hadn't finally figured I was lyin about the boarder takin a shower.

Same thing in the store. We all walkin on tiptoe and hardly touchin the games and puzzles and things. And I watched Miss Moore who is steady watchin us like she waiting for a sign. Like Mama Drewery watches the sky and sniffs the air and takes note of just how much slant is in the bird formation. Then me and Sugar bump smack into each other, so busy gazing at the toys, 'specially the sailboat. But we don't laugh and go into our fat-lady bump-stomach routine. We just stare at that price tag. Then Sugar run a finger over the whole boat. And I'm jealous and want to hit her. Maybe not her, but I sure want to punch somebody in the mouth.

"Watcha bring us here for, Miss Moore?"

"You sound angry, Sylvia. Are you mad about something?" Givin me one of them grins like she tellin a grown-up joke that never turns out to be funny. And she's lookin very closely at me like maybe she plannin to do my portrait from memory. I'm mad, but I won't give her that satisfaction. So I slouch around the store bein very bored and say, "Let's go."

Me and Sugar at the back of the train watchin the tracks whizzin by large then small then gettin gobbled up in the dark. I'm thinkin about this

40

tricky toy I saw in the store. A clown that somersaults on a bar then does chin-ups just cause you yank lightly at his leg. Cost $35. I could see me askin my mother for a $35 birthday clown. "You wanna who that costs what?" she'd say, cocking her head to the side to get a better view of the hole in my head. Thirty-five dollars and the whole household could go visit Grandaddy Nelson in the country. Thirty-five dollars would pay for the rent and the piano bill too. Who are these people that spend that much for performing clowns and $1000 for toy sailboats? What kinda work they do and how they live and how come we ain't in on it? Where we are is who we are, Miss Moore always pointin out. But it don't necessarily have to be that way, she always adds then waits for somebody to say that poor people have to wake up and demand their share of the pie and don't none of us know what kind of pie she talkin about in the first damn place. But she ain't so smart cause I still got her four dollars from the taxi and she sure ain't gettin it. Messin up my day with this shit. Sugar nudges me in my pocket and winks.

Miss Moore lines us up in front of the mailbox where we started   45
from, seem like years ago, and I got a headache for thinkin so hard. And we lean all over each other so we can hold up under the draggy-ass lecture she always finishes us off with at the end before we thank her for borin us to tears. But she just looks at us like she readin tea leaves. Finally she say, "Well, what did you think of F.A.O. Schwartz?"

Rosie Giraffe mumbles, "White folks crazy."

"I'd like to go there again when I get my birthday money," says Mercedes, and we shove her out the pack so she has to lean on the mail-box by herself.

"I'd like a shower. Tiring day," say Flyboy.

Then Sugar surprises me by saying, "You know, Miss Moore, I don't think all of us here put together eat in a year what that sailboat costs." And Miss Moore lights up like something goosed her. "And?" she say, urging Sugar on. Only I'm standin on her foot so she don't continue.

"Imagine for a minute what kind of society it is in which some people   50
can spend on a toy what it would cost to feed a family of six or seven. What do you think?"

"I think," says Sugar pushing me off her feet like she never done before, cause I whip her ass in a minute, "that this is not much of a democracy if you ask me. Equal chance to pursue happiness means an equal crack at the dough, don't it?" Miss Moore is besides herself and I am disgusted with Sugar's treachery. So I stand on her foot one more time to see if she'll shove me. She shuts up, and Miss Moore looks at me, sorrowfully I'm thinkin. And somethin weird is goin on. I can feel it in my chest.

"Anybody else learn anything today?" lookin dead at me. I walk away and Sugar has to run to catch up and don't even seem to notice when I shrug her arm off my shoulder.

"Well, we got four dollars anyway," she says.

"Uh hunh."

"We could go to Hascombs and get half a chocolate layer and then   55
to the Sunset and still have plenty of money for potato chips and ice
cream sodas."

"Uh hunh."

"Race you to Hascombs," she say.

We start down the block and she gets ahead which is O.K. by me
cause I'm goin to the West End and then over to the Drive to think this
day through. She can run if she want to and even run faster. But ain't nobody gonna beat me at nuthin.

CONSIDERATIONS

1. Based on details in the first paragraph, about how old is the narrator?
   What particular characteristics lead you to this informed guess?

2. Why does Sylvia continue to resist Miss Moore's efforts to teach the children?

3. What tone do the slang and obscenities add to the story? What attitudes
   do you think the author has toward the kids?

WRITING SUGGESTIONS

4. Consider a movie or novel that changed the way you see the world. Explain how it encouraged new attitudes, challenged old assumptions, or supplied fresh insight.

5. Going to look at the trappings of great wealth — for instance, the elegant
   houses of the very rich, royalty's crown jewels, or a magnificent yacht —
   can be sometimes enjoyable and sometimes disturbing. Think of an example of evidence of wealth that you admired or criticized. What lesson, if
   any, did you take from your exposure? Do you feel differently about it
   today?

DILEMMAS

Problems, Theories, and Opinions

SALLIE TISDALE

We Do Abortions Here

SALLIE TISDALE (b. 1957) received her degree in nursing at the University of Portland in Oregon. She has written two books about health care and the nursing profession: *The Sorcerer's Apprentice* (1986) and *Harvest Moon* (1987). Her writings about the impact of nature on history, and the impact of humanity on nature, include *Lot's Wife: Salt and the Human Condition* (1988) and *Stepping Westward: The Long Search for Home in the Pacific Northwest* (1991). Her most recent book is *Talk Dirty to Me: An Intimate Philosophy of Sex* (1994). Tisdale was a registered nurse in an abortion clinic when she wrote the following reflections about the tasks, the suffering, and the moral issues involved in that work.

We do abortions here; that is all we do. There are weary, grim moments when I think I cannot bear another basin of bloody remains, utter another kind phrase of reassurance. So I leave the procedure room in the back and reach for a new chart. Soon I am talking to an eighteen-year-old woman pregnant for the fourth time. I push up her sleeve to check her blood pressure and find row upon row of needle marks, neat and parallel and discolored. She has been so hungry for her drug for so long that she has taken to using the loose skin of her upper arms; her elbows are already a permanent ruin of bruises. She is surprised to find herself nearly four months pregnant. I suspect she is often surprised, in a mild way, by the

137

blows she is dealt. I prepare myself for another basin, another brief and chafing loss.

"How can you stand it?" Even the clients ask. They see the machine, the strange instruments, the blood, the final stroke that wipes away the promise of pregnancy. Sometimes I see that too: I watch a woman's swollen abdomen sink to softness in a few stuttering moments and my own belly flip-flops with sorrow. But all it takes for me to catch my breath is another interview, one more story that sounds so much like the last one. There is a numbing sameness lurking in this job: the same questions, the same answers, even the same trembling tone in the voices. The worst is the sameness of human failure, of inadequacy in the face of each day's dull demands.

In describing this work, I find it difficult to explain how much I enjoy it most of the time. We laugh a lot here, as friends and as professional peers. It's nice to be with women all day. I like the sudden, transient bonds I forge with some clients: moments when I am in my strength, remembering weakness, and a woman in weakness reaches out for my strength. What I offer is not power, but solidness, offered almost eagerly. Certain clients waken in me every tender urge I have — others make me wince and bite my tongue. Both challenge me to find a balance. It is a sweet brutality we practice here, a stark and loving dispassion.

I look at abortion as if I am standing on a cliff with a telescope, gazing at some great vista. I can sweep the horizon with both eyes, survey the scene in all its distance and size. Or I can put my eye to the lens and focus on the small details, suddenly so close. In abortion the absolute must always be tempered by the contextual, because both are real, both valid, both hard. How can we do this? How can we refuse? Each abortion is a measure of our failure to protect, to nourish our own. Each basin I empty is a promise — but a promise broken a long time ago.

I grew up on the great promise of birth control. Like many women   5 my age, I took the pill as soon as I was sexually active. To risk pregnancy when it was so easy to avoid seemed stupid, and my contraceptive success, as it were, was part of the promise of social enlightenment. But birth control fails, far more frequently than laboratory trials predict. Many of our clients take the pill; its failure to protect them is a shocking realization. We have clients who have been sterilized, whose husbands have had vasectomies; each one is a statistical misfit, fine print come to life. The anger and shame of these women I hold in one hand, and the basin in the other. The distance between the two, the length I pace and try to measure, is the size of an abortion.

The procedure is disarmingly simple. Women are surprised, as though the mystery of conception, a dark and hidden genesis, requires an elaborate finale. In the first trimester of pregnancy, it's a mere few minutes of vacuuming, a neat tidying up. I give a woman a small yellow Valium, and when it has begun to relax her, I lead her into the back, into bareness, the stirrups. The doctor reaches in her, opening the narrow tunnel to the uterus with a succession of slim, smooth bars of steel. He inserts a plastic tube and hooks it to a hose on the machine. The woman is framed against white paper that crackles as she moves, the light bright in her eyes. Then the machine rumbles low and loud in the small windowless room; the doctor moves the tube back and forth with an efficient rhythm, and the long tail of it fills with blood that spurts and stumbles along into a jar. He is usually finished in a few minutes. They are long minutes for the woman; her uterus frequently reacts to its abrupt emptying with a powerful, unceasing cramp, which cuts off the blood vessels and enfolds the irritated, bleeding tissue.

I am learning to recognize the shadows that cross the faces of the women I hold. While the doctor works between her spread legs, the paper drape hiding his intent expression, I stand beside the table. I hold the woman's hands in mine, resting them just below her ribs. I watch her eyes, finger her necklace, stroke her hair. I ask about her job, her family; in a haze she answers me; we chatter, faces close, eyes meeting and sliding apart.

I watch the shadows that creep up unnoticed and suddenly darken her face as she screws up her features and pushes a tear out each side to slide down her cheeks. I have learned to anticipate the quiver of chin, the rapid intake of breath, and the surprising sobs that rise soon after the machine starts to drum. I know this is when the cramp deepens, and the tears are partly the tears that follow pain — the sharp, childish crying when one bumps one's head on a cabinet door. But a well of woe seems to open beneath many women when they hear that thumping sound. The anticipation of the moment has finally come to fruit; the moment has arrived when the loss is no longer an imagined one. It has come true.

I am struck by the sameness and I am struck every day by the variety here — how this commonplace dilemma can so display the differences of women. A twenty-one-year-old woman, unemployed, uneducated, without family, in the fifth month of her pregnancy. A forty-two-year-old mother of teenagers, shocked by her condition, refusing to tell her husband. A twenty-three-year-old mother of two having her seventh abortion, and many women in their thirties having their first. Some are stoic, some hysterical, a few giggle uncontrollably, many cry.

I talk to a sixteen-year-old uneducated girl who was raped. She has 10 gonorrhea. She describes blinding headaches, attacks of breathlessness, nausea. "Sometimes I feel like two different people," she tells me with a calm smile, "and I talk to myself."

I pull out my plastic models. She listens patiently for a time, and then holds out her hands wide in front of her stomach.

"When's the baby going to go up into my stomach?" she asks.

I blink. "What do you mean?"

"Well," she says, still smiling, "when women get so big, isn't the baby in your stomach? Doesn't it hatch out of an egg there?"

My first question in an interview is always the same. As I walk down   15
the hall with the woman, as we get settled in chairs and I glance through
her files, I am trying to gauge her, to get a sense of the words, and the
tone, I should use. With some I joke, and others I chat, sometimes I fall
into a brisk, business-like patter. But I ask every woman, "Are you sure
you want to have an abortion?" Most nod with grim and knowing smiles.
"Oh, yes," they sigh. Some seek forgiveness, offer excuses. Occasionally a
woman will flinch and say, "Please don't use that word."

Later I describe the procedure to come, using care with my language. I don't say "pain" any more than I would say "baby." So many are
afraid to ask how much it will hurt. "My sister told me — " I hear. "A
friend of mine said — " and the dire expectations unravel. I prick the
index finger of a woman for a drop of blood to test, and as the tiny lancet
approaches the skin she averts her eyes, holding her trembling hand out
to me and jumping at my touch.

It is when I am holding a plastic uterus in one hand, a suction tube
in the other, moving them together in an imitation of the scrubbing to
come, that women ask the most secret question. I am speaking in a
matter-of-fact voice about "the tissue" and "the contents" when the
woman suddenly catches my eye and asks, "How big is the baby now?"
These words suggest a quiet need for a definition of the boundaries being
drawn. It isn't so odd, after all, that she feels relief when I describe the
growing bud's bulbous shape, its miniature nature. Again I gauge, and
sometimes lie a little, weaseling around its infantile features until its clinging power slackens.

But when I look in the basin, among the curdlike blood clots, I see an
elfin thorax, attenuated, its pencilline ribs all in parallel rows with tiny
knobs of spine rounding upwards. A translucent arm and hand swim beside.

A sleepy-eyed girl, just fourteen, watched me with a slight and goofy
smile all through her abortion. "Does it have little feet and little fingers
and all?" she'd asked earlier. When the suction was over she sat up
woozily at the end of the table and murmured, "Can I see it?" I shook my
head firmly.

"It's not allowed," I told her sternly, because I knew she didn't really   20
want to see what was left. She accepted this statement of authority, and a
shadow of confused relief crossed her plain, pale face.

Privately, even grudgingly, my colleagues might admit the power of
abortion to provoke emotion. But they seem to prefer the broad view and
disdain the telescope. Abortion is a matter of choice, privacy, control. Its
uncertainty lies in specific cases: retarded women and girls too young to
give consent for surgery, women who are ill or hostile or psychotic. Such
common dilemmas are met with both compassion and impatience; they
slow things down. We are too busy to chew over ethics. One person
might discuss certain concerns, behind closed doors, or describe a particularly disturbing dream. But generally there is to be no ambivalence.

Every day I take calls from women who are annoyed that we cannot see them, cannot do their abortion today, this morning, now. They argue the price, demand that we stay after hours to accommodate their job or class schedule. Abortion is so routine that one expects it to be like a manicure; quick, cheap, and painless.

Still, I've cultivated a certain disregard. It isn't negligence, but I don't always pay attention. I couldn't be here if I tried to judge each case on its merits; after all, we do over a hundred abortions a week. At some point each individual in this line of work draws a boundary and adheres to it. For one physician the boundary is a particular week of gestation; for another, it is a certain number of repeated abortions. But these boundaries can be fluid too: One physician overruled his own limit to abort a mature but severely malformed fetus. For me, the limit is allowing my clients to carry their own burden, shoulder the responsibility themselves. I shoulder the burden of trying not to judge them.

This city has several "crisis pregnancy centers" advertised in the Yellow Pages. They are small offices staffed by volunteers, and they offer free pregnancy testing, glossy photos of dead fetuses, and movies. I had a client recently whose mother is active in the antiabortion movement. The young woman went to the local crisis center and was told that the doctor would make her touch her dismembered baby, that the pain would be the most horrible she could imagine, and that she might, after an abortion, never be able to have children. All lies. They called her at home and at work, over and over and over, but she had been wise enough to give a false name. She came to us a fugitive. We who do abortions are marked, by some, as impure. It's dirty work.

When a deliveryman comes to the sliding glass window by the reception desk and tilts a box toward me, I hesitate. I read the packing slips, assess the shape and weight of the box in the light of its supposed contents. We request familiar faces. The doors are carefully locked; I have learned to half glance around at bags and boxes, looking for a telltale sign. I register with security when I arrive, and I am careful not to bang a door. We are a little on edge here. 25

Concern about size and shape seem to be natural, and so is the relief that follows. We make the powerful assumption that the fetus is different from us, and even when we admit the similarities, it is too simplistic to be seduced by form alone. But the form is enormously potent — humanoid, powerless, palm-sized, and pure, it evokes an almost fierce tenderness when viewed simply as what it appears to be. But appearance, and even potential, aren't enough. The fetus, in becoming itself, can ruin others; its utter dependence has a sinister side. When I am struck in the moment by the contents in the basin, I am careful to remember the context, to note the tearful teenager and the woman sighing with something more than relief. One kind of question, though, I find considerably trickier.

"Can you tell what it is?" I am asked, and this means gender. This question is asked by couples, not women alone. Always couples would abort a girl and keep a boy. I have been asked about twins, and even if I could tell what race the father was.

An eighteen-year-old woman with three daughters brought her husband to the interview. He glared first at me, then at his wife, as he sank lower and lower in the chair, picking his teeth with a toothpick. He interrupted a conversation with his wife to ask if I could tell whether the baby would be a boy or a girl. I told him I could not.

"Good," he replied in a slow and strangely malevolent voice, "'cause if it was a boy I'd wring her neck."

In a literal sense, abortion exists because we are able to ask such questions, able to assign a value to the fetus which can shift with changing circumstances. If the human bond to a child were as primitive and unflinchingly narrow as that of other animals, there would be no abortion. There would be no abortion because there would be nothing more important than caring for the young and perpetuating the species, no reason for sex but to make babies. I sense this sometimes, this wordless organic duty, when I do ultrasounds.

We do ultrasound, a sound-wave test that paints a faint, gray picture of the fetus, whenever we're uncertain of gestation. Age is measured by the width of the skull and confirmed by the length of the femur or thighbone; we speak of pregnancy as being a certain "femur length" in weeks. The usual concern is whether a pregnancy is within the legal limit for an abortion. Women this far along have bellies which swell out round and tight like trim muscles. When they lie flat, the mound rises softly above the hips, pressing the umbilicus upward.

It takes practice to read an ultrasound picture, which is grainy and etched as though in strokes of charcoal. But suddenly a rapid rhythmic motion appears — the beating heart. Nearby is a soft oval, scratched with lines — the skull. The leg is harder to find, and then suddenly the fetus moves, bobbing in the surf. The skull turns away, an arm slides across the screen, the torso rolls. I know the weight of a baby's head on my shoulder, the whisper of lips on ears, the delicate curve of a fragile spine in my hand. I know how heavy and correct a newborn cradled feels. The creature I watch in secret requires nothing from me but to be left alone, and that is precisely what won't be done.

These inadvertently made beings are caught in a twisting web of motive and desire. They are at least inconvenient, sometimes quite literally dangerous in the womb, but most often they fall somewhere in between — consequences never quite believed in come to roost. Their virtue rises and falls outside their own nature: They become only what we make them. A fetus created by accident is the most absolute kind of surprise. Whether the blame lies in a failed IUD, a slipped condom, or a false impression of safety, that fetus is a thing whose creation has been actively worked against. Its existence is an error. I think this is why so few women,

30

even late in a pregnancy, will consider giving a baby up for adoption. To do so means making the fetus real — imagining it as something whole and outside oneself. The decision to terminate a pregnancy is sometimes so difficult and confounding that it creates an enormous demand for immediate action. The decision is a rejection; the pregnancy has become something to be rid of, a condition to be ended. It is a burden, a weight, a thing separate.

Women have abortions because they are too old, and too young, too poor, and too rich, too stupid, and too smart. I see women who berate themselves with violent emotions for their first and only abortion, and others who return three times, five times, hauling two or three children, who cannot remember to take a pill or where they put the diaphragm. We talk glibly about choice. But the choice for what? I see all the broken promises in lives lived like a series of impromptu obstacles. There are the sweet, light promises of love and intimacy, the glittering promise of education and progress, the warm promise of safe families, long years of innocence and community. And there is the promise of freedom: freedom from failure, from faithlessness. Freedom from biology. The early feminist defense of abortion asked many questions, but the one I remember is this: Is biology destiny? And the answer is yes, sometimes it is. Women who have the fewest choices of all exercise their right to abortion the most.

Oh, the ignorance. I take a woman to the back room and ask her to undress; a few minutes later I return and find her positioned discreetly behind a drape, still wearing underpants. "Do I have to take these off too?" she asks, a little shocked. Some swear they have not had sex, many do not know what a uterus is, how sperm and egg meet, how sex makes babies. Some late seekers do not believe themselves pregnant; they believe themselves *impregnable*. I was chastised when I began this job for referring to some clients as girls: It is a feminist heresy. They come so young, snapping gum, sockless and sneakered, and their shakily applied eyeliner smears when they cry. I call them girls with maternal benignity. I cannot imagine them as mothers.

35

The doctor seats himself between the woman's thighs and reaches into the dilated opening of a five-month pregnant uterus. Quickly he grabs and crushes the fetus in several places, and the room is filled with a low clatter and snap of forceps, the click of the tanaculum, and a pulling, sucking sound. The paper crinkles as the drugged and sleepy woman shifts, the nurse's low, honey-brown voice explains each step in delicate words.

I have fetus dreams, we all do here: dreams of abortions one after the other; of buckets of blood splashed on the walls; trees full of crawling fetuses. I dreamed that two men grabbed me and began to drag me away: "Let's do an abortion," they said with a sickening leer, and I began to scream, plunged into a vision of sucking, scraping pain, of being spread and torn by impartial instruments that do only what they are bidden. I woke from this dream barely able to breathe and thought of kitchen tables and coat hangers, knitting needles striped with blood, and women all alone clutching a pillow in their teeth to keep the screams from piercing the apartment-house walls. Abortion is the narrowest edge between kindness and cruelty. Done as well as it can be, it is still violence — merciful violence, like putting a suffering animal to death.

Maggie, one of the nurses, received a call at midnight not long ago. It was a woman in her twentieth week of pregnancy; the necessarily gradual process of cervical dilation begun the day before had stimulated labor, as it sometimes does. Maggie and one of the doctors met the woman at the office in the night. Maggie helped her onto the table, and as she lay down the fetus was delivered into Maggie's hands. When Maggie told me about it the next day, she cupped her hands into a small bowl — "It was just like a small kitten," she said softly, wonderingly. "Everything was still attached."

At the end of the day I clean out the suction jars, pouring blood into the sink, splashing the sides with flecks of tissue. From the sink rises a rich and humid smell, hot, earthy, and moldering; it is the smell of something recently alive beginning to decay. I take care of the plastic tub on the floor, filled with pieces too big to be trusted to the trash. The law defines the contents of the bucket I hold protectively against my chest as "tissue." Some would say my complicity in filling that bucket gives me no right to call it anything else. I slip the tissue gently into a bag and place it in the freezer, to be burned at another time. Abortion requires of me an entirely new set of assumptions. It requires a willingness to live with conflict, fearlessness, and grief. As I close the freezer door, I imagine a world where this won't be necessary, and then return to the world where it is.

CONSIDERATIONS

1. In the detailed description of an abortion, what does the author want the reader to recognize? How does her description affect you?

2. What attitude toward her clients does Tisdale reject? What attitude does she uphold? What problems does she have in controlling her attitudes? Are your responses to her clients different from hers?

3. Explain Tisdale's stance on the public controversy over abortion. What is her attitude toward antiabortionists?

4. What is the author's outlook on humanity? What generalizations does Tisdale assert or imply about the human race?

WRITING SUGGESTION

5. Examine a controversy over abortion within a community, group, or family you know. What issues became important? How were disagreements handled? Present views on both sides fairly. If possible, include details from Tisdale's essay to illustrate how she regards these issues. Explain your own perspective.

HENDRIK HERTZBERG AND HENRY LOUIS GATES JR.

The African-American Century

HENDRIK HERTZBERG (b. 1943) is the editorial director of *The New Yorker* and has served as editor of *The New Republic* and as a speechwriter during the Carter administration. HENRY LOUIS GATES JR. (b. 1950) is a professor of Afro-American studies at Harvard University. In addition to his publications on racial issues, Gates has written a memoir about his early life in West Virginia, *Colored People* (1994). The following selection appeared in *The New Yorker* in 1996, introducing a special issue on black experiences in America.

The story of America, according to the narrative enshrined in our civic religion, goes something like this. A great wilderness was gradually populated by waves of hardy immigrants fleeing the oppressions of the Old World to build a better life in the New. Throwing off subordination to a distant throne, they made a commonwealth, the first in history to be founded explicitly on principles of self-government and political equality. Over the next two hundred years and more, they worked and sometimes fought to ensure that their "new nation, conceived in Liberty, and dedicated to the proposition that all men are created equal," would increasingly live up to its moral and material promise. And they succeeded, creating a nation not only of unparalleled personal and political freedom but also (a recent flourish) of wonderful, enriching diversity — a powerful nation, universally looked to as an example and a protector.

A pretty story; and, like all folk tales, this one tells a kind of truth. But the reality is more complicated, darker (in more ways than one), more painful, and, ultimately, more heroic. The myth ignores the tragic dimension of the American condition, the dimension that challenges the moral seriousness of American thinkers and makes American art and culture, high and low, the most dynamic and pervasive on the planet — makes American culture American, in fact. Not all Americans' ancestors came here to escape tyranny; many were brought here in furtherance of tyranny. Not all crossed the ocean to better themselves and their families; many were forcibly carried here — their families torn apart, their social structures smashed, their languages suppressed — to labor without recompense for the benefit of their oppressors. Yet those of us whose forebears came here in chains have much deeper roots in American soil, on the average, than do those of us whose forebears came here in and for freedom; the vast majority of African Americans are descended from men and women who arrived before 1776. Except for American Indians, only a shrinking minority of other Americans can say the same. (And, of course, scores of millions of us — no one knows how many — of every hue are termed "black" or "white" in our country's arbitrary racial shorthand but are in reality a mixture of, at a minimum, both.)

The history of settlement in what is now the United States dates back nearly four hundred years, but the twentieth will be the first century unpolluted by chattel slavery. When the century began, most adult African Americans were former slaves, and had known not only the degradation of bondage but also the exultation of Emancipation, the giddy hopefulness of Reconstruction, and the calamity of a reactionary and increasingly violent regime of legalized white supremacy. The grandchildren of the grandchildren of those African Americans are the African Americans of today. The line is short, the connection between past and present inescapable.

Even so, there have been titanic changes, and they have been accompanied by unexpected ironies. The most striking change has been the growing centrality of the black experience to the maturing national culture of the United States; the most striking irony has been the degree to which blacks, despite that centrality, have remained economically marginal.

An observer from 1900 transported forward in time to this century's end would be astonished at the ubiquity of the black presence in artistic, cultural, and quasi-cultural endeavors of every kind, from the frontiers of modern art (born when Picasso laid eyes on African masks), through the written word (more books by and about African Americans will be published this year than appeared during the whole of the Harlem Renaissance), to the iconography of mass marketing (with Michael Jordan looking down from giant billboards like some beneficent Big Brother). The prime example, of course, is music, the most accessible of the arts. In 1900, ragtime was only just coming into its own, beginning the long and steady fusion of African-American themes and forms with those of European origin. In the early decades of the century, Negro music came to dominate the new technologies of sound recording and radio so thoroughly that, in 1924, an alarmed music establishment sought out a syncopationally challenged bandleader by the comically apt name of Paul Whiteman and designated him "the King of Jazz." But jazz and its offshoots could not be so easily tamed. The wildly creative creolization of African-American and European-American strains produced a profusion of mulatto musics — one thinks of Ellington and Gershwin, Joplin and Stravinsky, Miles Davis and Gil Evans, Chuck Berry and Jerry Lee Lewis, Jimi Hendrix and Bruce Springsteen — that spread their dominion across the whole world.

Economically, however, African Americans remain left out. The successes of integration and affirmative action created a substantial black middle class: There are now four times as many black families with incomes above fifty thousand dollars a year as there were in 1964. But those same successes have contributed to a distillation of ever more concentrated pools of poverty and despair in the inner cities — a process greatly worsened by the catastrophic decline of decent manufacturing jobs and the growing hardheartedness and insolvency of social policy at every level of government. The sufferings and pathologies associated with this process are well known. Half of all African-American children live in poverty. A third of all black men between the ages of twenty and twenty-nine are entangled in the criminal-justice system. The leading cause of death among young black men is gunshot wounds.

Our market economy has shown no ability to solve these problems, and our gridlocked, fragmented political system has shown very little. After a century of struggle, African Americans have at last achieved more or less equal political rights. But our majoritarian electoral system generally prevents them from attaining real power except in geographic areas where they are a majority or a near-majority. Although African Americans constitute some thirteen per cent of the population, their representation in state governorships is zero. In the United States Senate it is one per cent. In the House of Representatives, which now has forty African-American members, black progress has come at the price of racial gerrymandering. It's a high price: It drains (liberal) black voting strength from neighboring districts, often tipping them over into the control of politicians indifferent to black interests; it discourages grass-roots interracial coalition-building; and it creates a black political class with a vested interest in patterns of residential segregation. And even this progress, such as it is, is under mortal threat from a Supreme Court piously bent on making the Constitution "color-blind," especially in cases where a bit of color consciousness might do black folks some good.

For African Americans, the country of oppression and the country of liberation are the same country. Fleeing to some faraway land of liberty is not a possibility, though something like that impulse is implicit in black nationalism, in ironic tribute to the power of the immigrant myth. (Marcus Garvey wanted to call his promised land the United States of Africa.) It is bootless to compare African Americans to "other" immigrant groups and to speak of "assimilating" them: African Americans are not an immigrant group, and, as the success of the cultural synthesis shows, the responsibility for doing the assimilating is not theirs alone. The history that is at the root of the "differentness" of blacks — what might be called African-American exceptionalism — cannot be changed. There is only one option, and it is to make our country live up to its nominal creed.

CONSIDERATIONS

1. Explain the term "civic religion" (paragraph 1). Come up with words that either increase or decrease the implications of the term.

2. According to Gates and Hertzberg, why is gerrymandering a flawed method to increase black political power? What alternatives do the authors favor?

3. In what ways do the authors argue that African Americans are distinct from immigrant groups?

WRITING SUGGESTION

4. Examine one practical way — such as affirmative action — in which our society can or does respond to the "exceptionalism" of African Americans. Explain the benefits and flaws of the measure. How might you recommend changing the policy?

GEORGE ORWELL

Shooting an Elephant

GEORGE ORWELL (1903–1950) was the pen name of Eric Blair, who was born in India and sent by his English parents to England for his education at Eton. He returned to India as an officer in the Imperial Police, but he became bitterly disenchanted with service to the empire and he soon abandoned his career in the government. His first book, *Down and Out in Paris and London* (1933), recounts his struggles to support himself while he learned to write. His lifelong subject, however, is not bohemian life as a writer but his personal encounters with totalitarianism, which he addressed in his novel *Burmese Days* (1935) and his book *Homage to Catalonia* (1938), a chronicle of his developing despair over all political parties after he participated in the Spanish Civil War. His feelings toward politics and government are also expressed in his fiction, *Animal Farm* (1945) and *1984* (1949). The following essay is a memoir of his early period of conflicting loyalties as a British magistrate in Burma.

In Moulmein, in lower Burma, I was hated by large numbers of people — the only time in my life that I have been important enough for this to happen to me. I was subdivisional police officer of the town, and in an aimless, petty kind of way anti-European feeling was very bitter. No one had the guts to raise a riot, but if a European woman went through the bazaars alone somebody would probably spit betel juice over her dress. As a police officer I was an obvious target and was baited whenever it seemed safe to do so. When a nimble Burman tripped me up on the football field and the referee (another Burman) looked the other way, the crowd yelled with hideous laughter. This happened more than once. In the end the sneering yellow faces of young men that met me everywhere, the insults hooted after me when I was at a safe distance, got badly on my nerves. The young Buddhist priests were the worst of all. There were several thousands of them in the town and none of them seemed to have anything to do except stand on street corners and jeer at Europeans.

All this was perplexing and upsetting. For at that time I had already made up my mind that imperialism was an evil thing and the sooner I chucked up my job and got out of it the better. Theoretically — and secretly, of course — I was all for the Burmese and all against the oppressors, the British. As for the job I was doing, I hated it more bitterly than I can perhaps make clear. In a job like that you see the dirty work of Empire at close quarters. The wretched prisoners huddling in the stinking cages of the lockups, the grey, cowed faces of the long-term convicts, the scarred buttocks of the men who had been flogged with bamboos — all these oppressed me with an intolerable sense of guilt. But I could get nothing into perspective. I was young and ill-educated and I had had to think out my problems in the utter silence that is imposed on every Englishman in the East. I did not even know that the British Empire is dying, still less did I know that it is a great deal better than the younger empires that are going to supplant it. All I knew was that I was stuck between my hatred of the empire I served and my rage against the evil-spirited little beasts who tried to make my job impossible. With one part of my mind I thought of the British Raj as an unbreakable tyranny, as something clamped down, in *saecula saeculorum*, upon the will of prostrate peoples; with another part I thought that the greatest joy in the world would be to drive a bayonet into a Buddhist priest's guts. Feelings like these are the normal by-products of imperialism; ask any Anglo-Indian official, if you can catch him off duty.

One day something happened which in a roundabout way was enlightening. It was a tiny incident in itself, but it gave me a better glimpse than I had had before of the real nature of imperialism — the real motives for which despotic governments act. Early one morning the subinspector at a police station the other end of the town rang me up on the phone and said that an elephant was ravaging the bazaar. Would I please come and do something about it? I did not know what I could do, but I wanted to see what was happening and I got on to a pony and started out. I took my rifle, an old .44 Winchester and much too small to kill an elephant, but I thought the noise might be useful *in terrorem*. Various Burmans stopped me on the way and told me about the elephant's doings. It was not, of course, a wild elephant, but a tame one which had gone "must." It had been chained up, as tame elephants always are when their attack of "must" is due, but on the previous night it had broken its chain and escaped. Its mahout, the only person who could manage it when it was in that state, had set out in pursuit, but had taken the wrong direction and was now twelve hours' journey away, and in the morning the elephant had suddenly reappeared in the town. The Burmese population had no weapons and were quite helpless against it. It had already destroyed somebody's bamboo hut, killed a cow, and raided some fruit-stalls and devoured the stock; also it had met the municipal rubbish van and, when the driver jumped out and took to his heels, had turned the van over and inflicted violences upon it.

The Burmese subinspector and some Indian constables were waiting for me in the quarter where the elephant had been seen. It was a very poor quarter, a labyrinth of squalid bamboo huts, thatched with palm-leaf, winding all over a steep hillside. I remember that it was a cloudy, stuffy morning at the beginning of the rains. We began questioning the people as to where the elephant had gone and, as usual, failed to get any definite information. That is invariably the case in the East; a story always sounds clear enough at a distance, but the nearer you get to the scene of events the vaguer it becomes. Some of the people said that the elephant had gone in one direction, some said that he had gone in another, some professed not even to have heard of any elephant. I had almost made up my mind that the whole story was a pack of lies, when we heard yells a little distance away. There was a loud, scandalized cry of "Go away, child! Go away this instant!" and an old woman with a switch in her hand came round the corner of a hut, violently shooing away a crowd of naked children. Some more women followed, clicking their tongues and exclaiming; evidently there was something that the children ought not to have seen. I rounded the hut and saw a man's dead body sprawling in the mud. He was an Indian, a black Dravidian coolie, almost naked, and he could not have been dead many minutes. The people said that the elephant had come suddenly upon him round the corner of the hut, caught him with its trunk, put its foot on his back, and ground him into the earth. This was the rainy season and the ground was soft, and his face had scored a trench a foot deep and a couple of yards long. He was lying on his belly with arms crucified and head sharply twisted to one side. His face was coated with mud, the eyes wide open, the teeth bared and grinning with an expression of unendurable agony. (Never tell me, by the way, that the dead look peaceful. Most of the corpses I have seen looked devilish.) The friction of the great beast's foot had stripped the skin from his back as neatly as one skins a rabbit. As soon as I saw the dead man I sent an orderly to a friend's house nearby to borrow an elephant rifle. I had already sent back the pony, not wanting it to go mad with fright and throw me if it smelt the elephant.

The orderly came back in a few minutes with a rifle and five cartridges, and meanwhile some Burmans had arrived and told us that the elephant was in the paddy fields below, only a few hundred yards away. As I started forward practically the whole population of the quarter flocked

5

out of the houses and followed me. They had seen the rifle and were all shouting excitedly that I was going to shoot the elephant. They had not shown much interest in the elephant when he was merely ravaging their homes, but it was different now that he was going to be shot. It was a bit of fun to them, as it would be to an English crowd; besides they wanted the meat. It made me vaguely uneasy. I had no intention of shooting the elephant — I had merely sent for the rifle to defend myself if necessary — and it is always unnerving to have a crowd following you. I marched down the hill, looking and feeling a fool, with the rifle over my shoulder and an ever-growing army of people jostling at my heels. At the bottom, when you got away from the huts, there was a metalled road and beyond that a miry waste of paddy fields a thousand yards across, not yet ploughed but soggy from the first rains and dotted with coarse grass. The elephant was standing eight yards from the road, his left side towards us. He took not the slightest notice of the crowd's approach. He was tearing up bunches of grass, beating them against his knees to clean them and stuffing them into his mouth.

I had halted on the road. As soon as I saw the elephant I knew with perfect certainty that I ought not to shoot him. It is a serious matter to shoot a working elephant — it is comparable to destroying a huge and costly piece of machinery — and obviously one ought not to do it if it can possibly be avoided. And at that distance, peacefully eating, the elephant looked no more dangerous than a cow. I thought then and I think now that his attack of "must" was already passing off; in which case he would merely wander harmlessly about until the mahout came back and caught him. Moreover, I did not in the least want to shoot him. I decided that I would watch him for a little while to make sure that he did not turn savage again, and then go home.

But at that moment, I glanced round at the crowd that had followed me. It was an immense crowd, two thousand at the least and growing every minute. It blocked the road for a long distance on either side. I looked at the sea of yellow faces above the garish clothes — faces all happy and excited over this bit of fun, all certain that the elephant was going to be shot. They were watching me as they would watch a conjuror about to perform a trick. They did not like me, but with the magical rifle in my hands I was momentarily worth watching. And suddenly I realized that I should have to shoot the elephant after all. The people expected it of me and I had got to do it; I could feel their two thousand wills pressing me forward, irresistibly. And it was at this moment, as I stood there with the rifle in my hands, that I first grasped the hollowness, the futility of the white man's dominion in the East. Here was I, the white man with his gun, standing in front of the unarmed native crowd — seemingly the leading actor of the piece; but in reality I was only an absurd puppet pushed to and fro by the will of those yellow faces behind. I perceived in this moment that when the white man turns tyrant it is his own freedom that he destroys. He becomes a sort of hollow, posing dummy, the conventionalized figure of a

sahib. For it is the condition of his rule that he shall spend his life in trying to impress the "natives," and so in every crisis he has got to do what
the "natives" expect of him. He wears a mask, and his face grows to fit it. I
had got to shoot the elephant. I had committed myself to doing it when I
sent for the rifle. A sahib has got to act like a sahib; he has got to appear
resolute, to know his own mind and do definite things. To come all that
way, rifle in hand, with two thousand people marching at my heels, and
then to trail feebly away, having done nothing — no, that was impossible.
The crowd would laugh at me. And my whole life, every white man's life
in the East, was one long struggle not to be laughed at.

But I did not want to shoot the elephant. I watched him beating his
bunch of grass against his knees, with that preoccupied grandmotherly air
that elephants have. It seemed to me that it would be murder to shoot
him. At that age I was not squeamish about killing animals, but I had
never shot an elephant and never wanted to. (Somehow it always seems
worse to kill a *large* animal.) Besides, there was the beast's owner to be
considered. Alive, the elephant was worth at least a hundred pounds;
dead, he would only be worth the value of his tusks, five pounds, possibly.
But I had got to act quickly. I turned to some experienced-looking Burmans who had been there when we arrived, and asked them how the elephant had been behaving. They all said the same thing: He took no notice
of you if you left him alone, but he might charge if you went too close to
him.

It was perfectly clear to me what I ought to do. I ought to walk up to
within, say, twenty-five yards of the elephant and test his behavior. If he
charged, I could shoot; if he took no notice of me, it would be safe to
leave him until the mahout came back. But also I knew that I was going to
do no such thing. I was a poor shot with a rifle and the ground was soft
mud into which one would sink at every step. If the elephant charged and
I missed him, I should have about as much chance as a toad under a
steamroller. But even then I was not thinking particularly of my own skin,
only of the watchful yellow faces behind. For at that moment, with the
crowd watching me, I was not afraid in the ordinary sense, as I would have
been if I had been alone. A white man mustn't be frightened in front of
"natives"; and so, in general, he isn't frightened. The sole thought in my
mind was that if anything went wrong those two thousand Burmans
would see me pursued, caught, trampled on, and reduced to a grinning
corpse like that Indian up the hill. And if that happened it was quite probable that some of them would laugh. That would never do. There was
only one alternative. I shoved the cartridges into the magazine and lay
down on the road to get a better aim.

The crowd grew very still, and a deep, low, happy sigh, as of people   10
who see the theater curtain go up at last, breathed from innumerable
throats. They were going to have their bit of fun after all. The rifle was a
beautiful German thing with cross-hair sights. I did not then know that in
shooting an elephant one would shoot to cut an imaginary bar running

from ear-hole to ear-hole. I ought, therefore, as the elephant was sideways on, to have aimed straight at his ear-hole; actually I aimed several inches in front of this, thinking the brain would be further forward.

When I pulled the trigger I did not hear the bang or feel the kick — one never does when a shot goes home — but I heard the devilish roar of glee that went up from the crowd. In that instant, in too short a time, one would have thought, even for the bullet to get there, a mysterious, terrible change had come over the elephant. He neither stirred nor fell, but every line of his body had altered. He looked suddenly stricken, shrunken, immensely old, as though the frightful impact of the bullet had paralyzed him without knocking him down. At last, after what seemed a long time — it might have been five seconds, I dare say — he sagged flabbily to his knees. His mouth slobbered. An enormous senility seemed to have settled upon him. One could have imagined him thousands of years old. I fired again into the same spot. At the second shot he did not collapse but climbed with desperate slowness to his feet and stood weakly upright, with legs sagging and head drooping. I fired a third time. That was the shot that did for him. You could see the agony of it jolt his whole body and knock the last remnant of strength from his legs. But in falling he seemed for a moment to rise, for as his hind legs collapsed beneath him he seemed to tower upward like a huge rock toppling, his trunk reaching skywards like a tree. He trumpeted, for the first and only time. And then down he came, his belly towards me, with a crash that seemed to shake the ground even where I lay.

I got up. The Burmans were already racing past me across the mud. It was obvious that the elephant would never rise again, but he was not dead. He was breathing very rhythmically with long rattling gasps, his great mound of a side painfully rising and falling. His mouth was wide open — I could see far down into caverns of pale pink throat. I waited a long time for him to die, but his breathing did not weaken. Finally, I fired my two remaining shots into the spot where I thought his heart must be. The thick blood welled out of him like red velvet, but still he did not die. His body did not even jerk when the shots hit him, the tortured breathing continued without a pause. He was dying, very slowly and in great agony, but in some world remote from me where not even a bullet could damage him further. I felt I had got to put an end to that dreadful noise. It seemed dreadful to see the great beast lying there, powerless to move and yet powerless to die, and not even to be able to finish him. I sent back for my small rifle and poured shot after shot into his heart, and down his throat. They seemed to make no impression. The tortured gasps continued as steadily as the ticking of a clock.

In the end I could not stand it any longer and went away. I heard later that it took him half an hour to die. Burmans were bringing dahs[1]

---

[1]*dahs:* Large knives.

and baskets even before I left, and I was told they had stripped his body almost to the bones by the afternoon.

Afterwards, of course, there were endless discussions about the shooting of the elephant. The owner was furious, but he was only an Indian and could do nothing. Besides, legally I had done the right thing, for a mad elephant has to be killed, like a mad dog, if its owner fails to control it. Among the Europeans opinion was divided. The older men said I was right, the younger men said it was a damn shame to shoot an elephant for killing a coolie, because an elephant was worth more than any damn Coringhee coolie. And afterwards I was very glad that the coolie had been killed; it put me legally in the right and it gave me sufficient pretext for shooting the elephant. I often wondered whether any of the others grasped that I had done it solely to avoid looking a fool.

CONSIDERATIONS

1. Why did Orwell hate his job even before this incident occurred? What effect was the job having on his feelings and attitudes? How would you describe his state of mind at the time?

2. What details about the elephant suggest a connection with human life? What details in the descriptions of the Burmans connect them with animals? What evokes Orwell's humane, sympathetic responses?

3. Orwell says that he acted "solely to avoid looking a fool." If he had believed in the goals and values of British imperialism, would his actions have had more integrity?

WRITING SUGGESTION

4. You have probably openly or privately opposed something on the grounds of justice, power, equality, or rights. Perhaps it involved your parents or your school. Examine your role as a participant in or observer of a politicized confrontation. Be specific about the stages of your engagement with the issues, and be clear about your response to the outcome. How have your views changed or developed since that confrontation?

MICHAEL DORRIS

For the Indians
No Thanksgiving

MICHAEL DORRIS (b. 1945), a professor of Native American
studies at Dartmouth College, writes about Indian culture and social issues. In *The Broken Cord* (1990), Dorris recounts the circumstances surrounding his adopted son's struggle with fetal alcohol
syndrome. Dorris also writes fiction and essays. His essays have
been collected in *Paper Trail: Collected Essays* (1994).

Maybe those Pilgrims and Wampanoags actually got together for a
November picnic, maybe not. It matters only as a facile, ironical footnote.

For the former group, it would have been a celebration of a precarious hurdle successfully crossed on the path to the political domination
first of a continent and eventually of a planet. For the latter, it would have
been, at best, a naive extravaganza — the last meeting as equals with in-
vaders who, within a few years, would win King Philip's War and decorate the city limits of their towns with rows of stakes, each topped with an
Indian head.

The few aboriginal survivors of the ensuing violence were either
sold into Caribbean slavery by their better armed, erstwhile hosts, or were
ruthlessly driven from their Cape Cod homes. Despite the symbolic ideal-
ism of the first potluck, New England — from the emerging European
point of view — simply wasn't big enough for two sets of societies.

An enduring benefit of success, when one culture clashes with another, is that the victorious group controls the record. It owns not only
the immediate spoils but also the power to edit, embellish, and concoct
the facts of the original encounter for the generations to come. Events,
once past, reside at the small end of the telescope, the vague and hazy an-
tecedents to accepted reality.

Our collective modern fantasy of Thanksgiving is a case in point. It 5
has evolved into a ritual pageant in which almost every one of us, as children, either acted or were forced to watch a seventeenth-century vision
that we can conjure whole in the blink of an eye.

The cast of stock characters is as recognizable as those in any
Macy's parade: long-faced Pilgrim men, pre-N.R.A. muskets at their
sides, sitting around a rude outdoor table while their wives, dressed in
long dresses, aprons, and linen caps, bustle about lifting the lids off steaming kettles — pater and materfamilias of New World hospitality.

They dish out the turkey to a scattering of shirtless Indian invitees. But there is no ambiguity as to who is in charge of the occasion, who could be asked to leave, whose protocol prevails.

Only good Indians are admitted into this tableau, of course: those who accept the manifest destiny of a European presence and are prepared to adopt English dining customs and, by inference, English everything else.

These compliant Hollywood extras are, naturally enough, among the blessings the Pilgrims are thankful for — and why not? They're colorful, bring the food, and vanish after dessert. They are something exotic to write home about, like a visit to Frontierland. In the sound bite of national folklore, they have metamorphosed into icons, totems of America as evocative, and ultimately as vapid, as a flag factory.

And these particular Indians did not all repair to the happy hunting   10
grounds during the first Christmas rush. They lived on, smoking peace pipes and popping up at appropriate crowd-pleasing moments.

They lost mock battles from coast to coast in Wild West shows. In nineteenth-century art, they sat bareback on their horses and watched a lot of sunsets. Whole professional teams of them take the home field every Sunday afternoon in Cleveland or Washington.

They are the sources of merit badges for Boy Scouts and the emblem of purity for imitation butter. They are, and have been from the beginning, predictable, manageable, domesticated cartoons, inventions without depth or reality apart from that bestowed by their creators.

These appreciative Indians, as opposed to the pesky flesh and blood native peoples on whom they are loosely modeled, did not question the enforced exchange of their territories for a piece of pie. They did not protest when they died by the millions of European diseases.

They did not resist — except for the "bad" ones, the renegades — when solemn pacts made with them were broken or when their religions and customs were declared illegal. They did not make a fuss in courts in defense of their sovereignty. They never expected all the fixings anyway.

As for Thanksgiving 1988, the descendants of those first partygoers   15
sit at increasingly distant tables, the pretense of equity all but abandoned. Against great odds, Native Americans have maintained political identity — hundreds of tribes have Federal recognition as "domestic, dependent nations."

But, in a country so insecure about heterogeneity that it votes its dominant language as "official," this refusal to melt into the pot has been an expensive choice.

A majority of reservation Indians reside in [some of] the most impoverished counties in the nation. They constitute the ethnic group at the wrong peak of every scale: most undernourished, most short-lived, least educated, least healthy.

For them, that long ago Thanksgiving was not a milestone, not a promise. It was the last full meal.

CONSIDERATIONS

1. According to Dorris, American history distorts the reality of Indian experience. How does he explain this distortion?

2. What is the essay's tone? Find phrases that best express the author's attitude.

3. Dorris, as well as Hertzberg and Gates in "The African-American Century" (p. 145), criticizes myths of American experience. Are they talking about the same myths? Compare the way they treat these false stories.

WRITING SUGGESTION

4. Have you ever attended a celebration where the victors sympathize with the vanquished? Design such a celebration for Thanksgiving. Invent customs, images, or other embellishments that acknowledge the Indians' experience from their viewpoint. Consider how your additions will affect family enjoyment of the national holiday.

STEPHEN L. CARTER

Schools of Disbelief

STEPHEN L. CARTER (b. 1954) was educated in the public schools of Washington, D.C., New York City, and Ithaca, New York. He graduated from Stanford University and received his law degree from Yale University. After serving as law clerk to the Supreme Court Justice Thurgood Marshall, Carter joined the Yale faculty, where he teaches constitutional law. His articles and legal research have been published widely. His first book was *Reflections of an Affirmative Action Baby* (1991), and his new book, *The Dissent of the Governed*, will be published in 1997. "Schools of Disbelief"[1] is excerpted from *The Culture of Disbelief: How American Law and Politics Trivialize Religious Devotion* (1993).

Contemporary American politics faces few greater dilemmas than deciding how to deal with the resurgence of religious belief. On the one hand, American ideology cherishes religion, as it does all matters of private conscience, which is why we justly celebrate a strong tradition against state

[1]Editor's title.

interference with private religious choice. At the same time, many political leaders, commentators, scholars, and voters are coming to view any religious element in public moral discourse as a tool of the radical right for reshaping American society. But the effort to banish religion for politics' sake has led us astray: In our sensible zeal to keep religion from dominating our politics, we have created a political and legal culture that presses the religiously faithful to be other than themselves, to act publicly, and sometimes privately as well, as though their faith does not matter to them. . . .

Religion is the first subject of the First Amendment. The amendment begins with the Establishment Clause ("Congress shall make no law respecting an establishment of religion . . ."), which is immediately followed by the Free Exercise Clause ("or prohibiting the free exercise thereof"). Although one might scarcely know it from the zeal with which the primacy of the other First Amendment freedoms (free press, free speech) is often asserted, those projections come *after* the clauses that were designed to secure religious liberty, which Thomas Jefferson called "the most inalienable and sacred of all human rights." What this means in practice, however, is often quite complicated.

Consider an example: At a dinner party in New York City a few years ago, I met a Christian minister who told me about a drug-rehabilitation program that he runs in the inner city. His claim — I cannot document it — was that his program had a success rate much higher than other programs'. The secret, he insisted, was prayer. It was not just that he and his staff prayed for the drug abusers they were trying to help, he told me, although they naturally did that. But the reason for the program's success, he proclaimed, was that he and his staff taught those who came to them for assistance to pray as well; in other words, they converted their charges, if not to Christianity, then at least to religiosity. But this program, he went on with something close to bitterness, could receive no state funding, because of its religious nature.

Well, all right. To decide that the program should not receive any funds, despite the success of its approach, might seem to be a straightforward application of the doctrine holding that the Constitution sets up a wall of separation between church and state. After all, the program is frankly religious: It uses prayer, and even teaches prayer to its clients. What could be more threatening to the separation of church and state than to provide a government subsidy for it? The Supreme Court has said many times that the government may neither "advance" religion nor engage in an "excessive entanglement" with it. On its face, a program of drug-rehabilitation therapy that relies on teaching people to pray would seem to do both.

It is doubtless frustrating to believe deeply that one has a call from 5
God to do what one does, and then to discover that the secular society often will not support that work, no matter how important it is to the individual. Yet that frustration is itself a sign of the robustness of religious

pluralism in America. For the most significant aspect of the separation of church and state is not, as some seem to think, the shielding of the secular world from too strong a religious influence; the principal task of the separation of church and state is to secure religious liberty.

The separation of church and state is one of the great gifts that American political philosophy has presented to the world, and if it has few emulators, that is the world's loss. Culled from the writings of Roger Williams and Thomas Jefferson, the concept of a "wall of separation" finds its constitutional moorings in the First Amendment's firm statement that the "Congress shall make no law respecting an establishment of religion." Although it begins with the word "Congress," the Establishment Clause for decades has been quite sensibly interpreted by the Supreme Court as applying to states as well as to the federal government.

For most of American history, the principal purpose of the Establishment Clause has been understood as the protection of the religious world against the secular government. A century ago, Philip Schaff of Union Seminary in New York celebrated the clause as "the Magna Carta of religious freedom," representing as it did "the first example in history of a government deliberately depriving itself of all legislative control over religion." Note the wording: not religious control over government — government control over religion. . . .

Over the years, the Supreme Court has handed down any number of controversial decisions under the Establishment Clause, many of them landmarks of our democratic culture. The best known are the cases in which the Justices struck down the recital of organized prayer in the public school classrooms, decisions that for three decades have ranked (in surveys) as among the most unpopular in our history. But the decisions were plainly right, for if the state is either able to prescribe a prayer to begin the school day or to select a holy book from which a prayer must be taken, it is casting exercising control over the religious aspects of the life of its people — precisely what the Establishment Clause was written to forbid. But although the separation of church and state is essential to the success of a vibrant, pluralistic democracy, the doctrine does not entail all that is done in its name. . . . [A] school district in Colorado . . . thought it the better part of valor to forbid a teacher to add books on Christianity to a classroom library that already included works on other religions. The town of Hamden, Connecticut, where I live, briefly ruled that a church group could not rent an empty schoolhouse for Sunday services. (Cooler heads in the end prevailed.) These rulings were both defended as required by the separation of church and state; so is the intermittent litigation to strike the legend IN GOD WE TRUST from America's coins or the phrase "under God" from the Pledge of Allegiance, an effort, if successful, that would wipe away even the civil religion. In short, it is not hard to understand the frequent complaints that the secular world acts as though the constitutional command is that the nation and its people must keep religion under wraps. . . .

Justice Hugo Black, in *Everson v. Board of Education* (1947), ... wrote these words: "The First Amendment has erected a wall between church and state. That wall must be kept high and impregnable. We could not approve the slightest breach." A year later, Justice Stanley Reed warned that "a rule of law should not be drawn from a figure of speech." One critic wrote years later that Black had simply penned a few "lines of fiction." The critics are not quite right, but they are not quite wrong, either. There is nothing wrong with the metaphor of a wall of separation. The trouble is that in order to make the Founders' vision compatible with the structure and needs of modern society, the wall has to have a few doors in it. ...

What *should* the public schools say about religion generally? One 10
problem with the public school curriculum — a problem, happily, that has lately had much attention — is that the concern to avoid even a hint of forbidden *endorsement* of religion has led to a climate in which teachers are loath to *mention* religion. A number of studies have concluded that the public school curriculum is actually biased against religion. But one need not to go that far in order to appreciate the importance of teaching children about the role of religion at crucial junctures in the nation's history, from the openly religious rhetoric of the Founding Generation, through the religious justifications for the abolition of slavery, the "social gospel" movement to reform American society and industry, or even the civil rights movement of the 1950s and 1960s. (Of course, children should study the negative side as well: from the religion-based prohibition movement that culminated in the Eighteenth Amendment and the Volstead Act to the destruction of many Native American religious traditions to what the historian Jon Butler has called the "African spiritual holocaust" — that is, the willed destruction during the nineteenth century of the African religious traditions that the slaves brought with them and tried to preserve.)

The movement to teach about religions in the public schools is not, as some might imagine, a smokescreen for infiltration of the education system by the religious right. On the contrary, John Buchanan of People for the American Way — a liberal organization that normally exists in a relationship of mutual antipathy with the right — agrees that there is a problem. Says Buchanan: "You can't have an accurate portrayal of history and leave out religion."

Both supporters and opponents of teaching about religion in the classroom have worried about the constitutional status of such instruction. But there is nothing to worry about, and, indeed, it would be bizarre if the command of the Establishment Clause turned out to be that religion may never be mentioned in the classroom, even when it is historically relevant. Nothing in the Supreme Court's decisions on school prayer or school curriculum is inconsistent with the idea that public schools can teach about religion, or even that the schools can use religious materials and texts in doing so....

It ought to be embarrassing, in this age of celebration of America's diversity, that the schools have been so slow to move toward teaching about our nation's diverse religious traditions. But matters are beginning to change. In 1988, a gathering of business, political, and religious leaders produced the Williamsburg Charter, which calls for greater attention to the role of religion in American life, including the establishment of a public school curriculum on the history of religions. That same year, a diverse group of religious and education organizations joined to issue a set of guidelines for teaching "about" religion without indoctrination. And all across the country, public schools are working to incorporate into their curricula a more sensitive understanding of the role of religion in American history and culture. In 1991, schools across the country began using new primary school textbooks developed by Houghton Mifflin Company (in response to pressure from California, the largest market for school texts). The new books emphasize the contributions of Christianity, Judaism, and many of the nation's other religious traditions.

Still, the new goal of teaching about religion is not without its problems — especially if the goal remains, as advocates insist it does, to teach about religion "objectively." Richard Baer of Cornell University has warned that although teaching respect for all religions "has a nice democratic ring to it," it could, if taken literally, lead to "intolerable consequences from those persons who take seriously the truth claims of the Christian gospel." Baer worries that a requirement of "objectivity" would make it illegitimate for teachers to criticize any religions, including Satanism, fanatical apocalypticism, or snake handling.

There is, moreover, the tricky problem of what to do when children begin to ask the hard questions. After all, if the material is well taught, many children will surely be intrigued by what will be for many their first exposure to religious traditions different than their own—or, in some instances, to any religious traditions at all. Sooner or later, teachers using the new books and other programs will be asked questions like, "But is it true?" or "What happens when we die?" or "Who made God?" The only safe answers will be those that so frustrate school children searching for certainty: "Well, many people believe that . . . and on the other hand, many others think . . . ." Few teachers are likely to enjoy picking their way through this particular minefield, but keeping the nation's religious heritage out of the classroom is not the answer. As one observer has put it, "The challenge will be finding consensus on an educational approach that describes religious doctrine without indoctrinating. But the option, denying children a piece of their culture and past, is more dangerous." 15

CONSIDERATIONS

1. Who is the intended audience for this essay? Find details that give you an impression of Carter's targeted audience.

2. Which clause in the First Amendment does Carter think is currently undermined?

3. What is Carter's main argument in favor of presenting religion in schools? What problems does he foresee?

WRITING SUGGESTIONS

4. Explain a few differences between *knowing about* and *believing in* a concept of God or a specific religious text (such as the Book of Exodus, the Gospels, or the Koran). Consider *knowing* and *believing* as comparable but distinct activities of the mind, and try to characterize them.

5. Propose your solution to what Carter regards as a great American dilemma. Where and how, if at all, should religion be taught?

TILLIE OLSEN

I Stand Here Ironing

TILLIE OLSEN (b. 1913) dropped out of high school in Nebraska at fifteen in order to help support her family during the Depression. She held jobs as a factory worker or secretary while she organized labor unions, got married, raised four children, and continued to read prodigiously. "Public libraries were my college," she has said. When she was forty, she resumed her early efforts to write fiction. Her volume of stories, *Tell Me a Riddle* (1961), established her as a champion of the poor and overburdened. In *Silences* (1978), a collection of essays, Olsen examines the injustices of social class, racism, and sexism that hinder creativity, particularly in women. The cruelty of harmful social conditions is a theme in all her work, including the following story.

I stand here ironing, and what you asked me moves tormented back and forth with the iron.

"I wish you would manage the time to come in and talk with me about your daughter. I'm sure you can help me understand her. She's a youngster who needs help and whom I'm deeply interested in helping."

"Who needs help." . . . Even if I came, what good would it do? You think because I am her mother I have a key, or that in some way you could use me as a key? She has lived for nineteen years. There is all that life that has happened outside of me, beyond me.

And when is there time to remember, to sift, to weigh, to estimate, to total? I will start and there will be an interruption and I will have to gather it all together again. Or I will become engulfed with all I did or did not do, with what should have been and what cannot be helped.

She was a beautiful baby. The first and only one of our five that was   5
beautiful at birth. You do not guess how new and uneasy her tenancy in her now-loveliness. You did not know her all those years she was thought homely, or see her poring over her baby pictures, making me tell her over and over how beautiful she had been — and would be, I would tell her — and was now, to the seeing eye. But the seeing eyes were few or nonexistent. Including mine.

I nursed her. They feel that's important nowadays. I nursed all the children, but with her, with all the fierce rigidity of first motherhood, I did like the books then said. Though her cries battered me to trembling and my breasts ached with swollenness, I waited until the clock decreed.

Why do I put that first? I do not even know if it matters, or if it explains anything.

She was a beautiful baby. She blew shining bubbles of sound. She loved motion, loved light, loved color and music and textures. She would lie on the floor in her blue overalls patting the surface so hard in ecstasy her hands and feet would blur. She was a miracle to me, but when she was eight months old I had to leave her daytimes with the woman downstairs to whom she was no miracle at all, for I worked or looked for work and for Emily's father, who "could no longer endure" (he wrote in his good-bye note) "sharing want with us."

I was nineteen, it was the pre-relief, pre-WPA world of the Depression. I would start running as soon as I got off the streetcar, running up the stairs, the place smelling sour, and awake or asleep to startle awake, when she saw me she would break into a clogged weeping that could not be comforted, a weeping I can hear yet.

After a while I found a job hashing at night so I could be with her   10
days, and it was better. But it came to where I had to bring her to his family and leave her.

It took a long time to raise the money for her fare back. Then she got chicken pox and I had to wait longer. When she finally came, I hardly knew her, walking quick and nervous like her father, looking like her father, thin, and dressed in a shoddy red that yellowed her skin and glared at the pockmarks. All the baby loveliness gone.

She was two. Old enough for nursery school they said, and I did not know then what I know now — the fatigue of the long day, and the lacerations of group life in the kinds of nurseries that are only parking places for children.

Except that it would have made no difference if I had known. It was the only place there was. It was the only way we could be together, the only way I could hold a job.

And even without knowing, I knew. I knew the teacher that was evil because all these years it has curdled into my memory, the little boy hunched in the corner, her rasp, "why aren't you outside, because Alvin hits you? that's no reason, go out, scaredy." I knew Emily hated it even if she did not clutch and implore "don't go Mommy" like the other children, mornings.

She always had a reason why we should stay home. Momma, you   15
look sick. Momma, I feel sick. Momma, the teachers aren't there today, they're sick. Momma, we can't go, there was a fire there last night. Momma, it's a holiday today, no school, they told me.

But never a direct protest, never rebellion. I think of our others in their three-, four-year-oldness — the explosions, the tempers, the denunciations, the demands — and I feel suddenly ill. I put the iron down. What in me demanded that goodness in her? And what was the cost, the cost to her of such goodness?

The old man living in the back once said in his gentle way: "You should smile at Emily more when you look at her." What *was* in my face when I looked at her? I loved her. There were all the acts of love.

It was only with the others I remembered what he said, and it was the face of joy, and not of care or tightness or worry I turned to them — too late for Emily. She does not smile easily, let alone almost always as her brothers and sisters do. Her face is closed and somber, but when she wants, how fluid. You must have seen it in her pantomimes, you spoke of her rare gift for comedy on the stage that rouses a laughter out of the audience so dear they applaud and applaud and do not want to let her go.

Where does it come from, that comedy? There was none of it in her when she came back to me that second time, after I had had to send her away again. She had a new daddy now to learn to love, and I think perhaps it was a better time.

Except when we left her alone nights, telling ourselves she was old   20
enough.

"Can't you go some other time, Mommy, like tomorrow?" she would ask. "Will it be just a little while you'll be gone? Do you promise?"

The time we came back, the front door open, the clock on the floor in the hall. She rigid awake. "It wasn't just a little while. I didn't cry. Three times I called you, just three times, and then I ran downstairs to open the door so you could come faster. The clock talked loud. I threw it away, it scared me what it talked."

She said the clock talked loud again that night I went to the hospital to have Susan. She was delirious with the fever that comes before red measles, but she was fully conscious all the week I was gone and the week after we were home when she could not come near the new baby or me.

She did not get well. She stayed skeleton thin, not wanting to eat, and night after night she had nightmares. She would call for me, and I would rouse from exhaustion to sleepily call back: "You're all right, darling, go to sleep, it's just a dream," and if she still called, in a sterner voice, "now go to sleep, Emily, there's nothing to hurt you." Twice, only twice, when I had to get up for Susan anyhow, I went in to sit with her.

Now when it is too late (as if she would let me hold and comfort her   25
like I do the others) I get up and go to her at once at her moan or restless stirring. "Are you awake, Emily? Can I get you something?" And the answer is always the same. "No, I'm all right, go back to sleep, Mother."

They persuaded me at the clinic to send her away to a convalescent home in the country where "she can have the kind of food and care you can't manage for her, and you'll be free to concentrate on the new baby." They still send children to that place. I see pictures on the society page of sleek young women planning affairs to raise money for it, or dancing at the affairs, or decorating Easter eggs or filling Christmas stockings for the children.

They never have a picture of the children so I do not know if the girls still wear those gigantic red bows and the ravaged looks on the every other Sunday when parents can come visit "unless otherwise notified" — as we were notified the first six weeks.

Oh it is a handsome place, green lawns and tall trees and fluted flower beds. High up on the balconies of each cottage the children stand, the girls in their red bows and white dresses, the boys in white suits and gigantic red ties. The parents stand below shrieking up to be heard and the children shriek down to be heard, and between them the invisible wall "Not To Be Contaminated by Parental Germs or Physical Affection."

There was a tiny girl who always stood hand in hand with Emily. Her parents never came. One visit she was gone. "They moved her to Rose Cottage," Emily shouted in explanation. "They don't like you to love anybody here."

She wrote once a week, the labored writings of a seven-year-old. "I   30
am fine. How is the baby. If I write my leter nicly I will have a star. Love." There never was a star. We wrote every other day, letters she could never hold or keep but only hear read — once. "We simply do not have room for children to keep any personal possessions," they patiently explained when we pieced one Sunday's shrieking together to plead how much it would mean to Emily, who loved so to keep things, to be allowed to keep her letters and cards.

Each visit she looked frailer. "She isn't eating," they told us.

(They had runny eggs for breakfast or mush with lumps, Emily said later, I'd hold it in my mouth and not swallow. Nothing ever tasted good, just when they had chicken.)

It took us eight months to get her released home, and only the fact that she gained back so little of her seven lost pounds convinced the social worker.

I used to try to hold and love her after she came back, but her body would stay stiff, and after a while she'd push away. She ate little. Food sickened her, and I think much of life too. Oh she had physical lightness and brightness, twinkling by on skates, bouncing like a ball up and down up and down over the jump rope, skimming over the hill; but these were momentary.

She fretted about her appearance, thin and dark and foreign-looking   35 at a time when every little girl was supposed to look or thought she should look like a chubby blonde replica of Shirley Temple. The doorbell sometimes rang for her, but no one seemed to come and play in the house or be a best friend. Maybe because we moved so much.

There was a boy she loved painfully through two school semesters. Months later she told me how she had taken pennies from my purse to buy him candy. "Licorice was his favorite and I brought him some every day, but he still liked Jennifer better'n me. Why, Mommy?" The kind of question for which there is no answer.

School was a worry to her. She was not glib or quick in a world where glibness and quickness were easily confused with ability to learn. To her overworked and exasperated teachers she was an over-conscientious "slow learner" who kept trying to catch up and was absent entirely too often.

I let her be absent, though sometimes the illness was imaginary. How different from my now-strictness about attendance with the others. I wasn't working. We had a new baby, I was home anyhow. Sometimes, after Susan grew old enough, I would keep her home from school, too, to have them all together.

Mostly Emily had asthma, and her breathing, harsh and labored, would fill the house with a curiously tranquil sound. I would bring the two old dresser mirrors and her boxes of collections to her bed. She would select beads and single earrings, bottle tops and shells, dried flowers and pebbles, old postcards and scraps, all sorts of oddments; then she and Susan would play Kingdom, setting up landscapes and furniture, peopling them with action.

Those were the only times of peaceful companionship between her   40 and Susan. I have edged away from it, that poisonous feeling between them, that terrible balancing of hurts and needs I had to do between the two, and did so badly, those earlier years.

Oh there are conflicts between the others too, each one human, needing, demanding, hurting, taking — but only between Emily and Susan, no, Emily toward Susan that corroding resentment. It seems so obvious on the surface, yet it is not obvious. Susan, the second child, Susan, golden- and curly-haired and chubby, quick and articulate and assured, everything in appearance and manner Emily was not; Susan, not able to resist Emily's precious things, losing or sometimes clumsily breaking them; Susan telling jokes and riddles to company for applause while Emily sat silent (to say to me later: That was *my* riddle, Mother, I told it to Susan); Susan, who for all the five years' difference in age was just a year behind Emily in developing physically.

I am glad for that slow physical development that widened the difference between her and her contemporaries, though she suffered over it. She was too vulnerable for that terrible world of youthful competition, of preening and parading, of constant measuring of yourself against every other, of envy, "If I had that copper hair," "If I had that skin. . . ." She tormented herself enough about not looking like the others, there was enough of the unsureness, the having to be conscious of words before you speak, the constant caring—what are they thinking of me? without having it all magnified by the merciless physical drives.

Ronnie is calling. He is wet and I change him. It is rare there is such a cry now. That time of motherhood is almost behind me when the ear is not one's own but must always be racked and listening for the child cry, the child call. We sit for a while and I hold him, looking out over the city spread in charcoal with its soft aisles of light. "*Shoogily*," he breathes and curls closer. I carry him back to bed, asleep. *Shoogily*. A funny word, a family word, inherited from Emily, invented by her to say: *comfort*.

In this and other ways she leaves her seal, I say aloud. And startle at me saying it. What do I mean? What did I start to gather together, to try and make coherent? I was at the terrible, growing years. War years. I do not remember them well. I was working, there were four smaller ones now, there was not time for her. She had to help be a mother, and housekeeper, and shopper. She had to set her seal. Mornings of crisis and near hysteria trying to get lunches packed, hair combed, coats and shoes found, everyone to school or Child Care on time, the baby ready for transportation. And always the paper scribbled on by a smaller one, the book looked at by Susan then mislaid, the homework not done. Running out to that huge school where she was one, she was lost, she was a drop; suffering over her unpreparedness, stammering and unsure in her classes.

There was so little time left at night after the kids were bedded   45
down. She would struggle over books, always eating (it was in those years she developed her enormous appetite that is legendary in our family) and I would be ironing, or preparing food for the next day, or writing V-mail to Bill, or tending the baby. Sometimes, to make me laugh, or out of her despair, she would imitate happenings or types at school.

I think I said once: "Why don't you do something like this in the school amateur show?" One morning she phoned me at work, hardly understandable through the weeping: "Mother, I did it. I won, I won; they gave me first prize; they clapped and clapped and wouldn't let me go."

Now suddenly she was Somebody, and as imprisoned in her difference as she had been in anonymity.

She began to be asked to perform at other high schools, even in colleges, then at city and statewide affairs. The first one we went to, I only recognized her that first moment when thin, shy, she almost drowned herself into the curtains. Then: Was this Emily? The control, the command, the convulsing and deadly drowning, the spell, then the roaring, stamping audience, unwilling to let this rare and precious laughter out of their lives.

Afterwards: You ought to do something about her with a gift like that—but without money or knowing how, what does one do? We have left it all to her, and the gift has as often eddied inside, clogged and clotted, as been used and growing.

She is coming. She runs up the stairs two at a time with her light   50
graceful step, and I know she is happy tonight. Whatever it was that occasioned your call did not happen today.

"Aren't you ever going to finish the ironing, Mother? Whistler painted his mother in a rocker. I'd have to paint mine standing over an ironing board." This is one of her communicative nights and she tells me everything and nothing as she fixes herself a plate of food out of the icebox.

She is so lovely. Why did you want me to come in at all? Why were you concerned? She will find her way.

She starts up the stairs to bed. "Don't get me up with the rest in the morning." "But I thought you were having midterms." "Oh, those," she comes back in, kisses me, and says quite lightly, "in a couple of years when we'll all be atom-dead they won't matter a bit."

She has said it before. She *believes* it. But because I have been dredging the past, and all that compounds a human being is so heavy and meaningful in me, I cannot endure it tonight.

I will never total it all. I will never come in to say: She was a child   55
seldom smiled at. Her father left me before she was a year old. I had to work her first six years when there was work, or I sent her home and to his relatives. There were years she had care she hated. She was dark and thin and foreign-looking in a world where prestige went to blondeness and curly hair and dimples, she was slow where glibness was prized. She was a child of anxious, not proud, love. We were poor and could not afford for her the soil of easy growth. I was a young mother, I was a distracted mother. There were the other children pushing up, demanding. Her younger sister seemed all that she was not. There were years she did not want me to touch her. She kept too much in herself, her life was such she had to keep too much in herself. My wisdom came too late. She has much to her and probably little will come of it. She is a child of her age, of depression, of war, of fear.

Let her be. So all that is in her will not bloom—but in how many does it? There is still enough left to live by. Only help her to know—help make it so there is cause for her to know—that she is more than this dress on the ironing board, helpless before the iron.

CONSIDERATIONS

1. Who has phoned Emily's mother? How has the caller's request affected the mother?

2. Does the mother blame herself too much or too little for causing Emily's hardships? At which points do you disagree with the mother's judgment of her own actions?

3. How did Emily differ from her brothers and sisters? What explanations does the mother have for Emily's difference? Which of her explanations do you think are most valid and important?

4. In the final two paragraphs, why does the mother refuse to consult about Emily?

WRITING SUGGESTIONS

5. What is your view of the mother by the end of the story? Is she cynical? defeatist? courageous? insightful? Does she change through the course of the story?

6. "I Stand Here Ironing" presents a mother's internal monologue about her daughter. Jamaica Kincaid's "Girl" (p. 26) sets out the thoughts and voices running through the head of a young girl. Compare the treatment of comparable dilemmas as seen by different generations. Consider problems such as economic hardship, blame and guilt, growth and sexuality.

Acknowledgments (continued from p. iv)

Raymond Carver, "What We Talk About When We Talk About Love." From *What We Talk About When We Talk About Love* by Raymond Carver. Copyright © 1981 by Raymond Carver. Reprinted by permission of Random House, Inc.

Joan Didion, "On Keeping A Notebook." From *Slouching Towards Bethlehem* by Joan Didion. Copyright © 1968 by Joan Didion. Reprinted by permission of Farrar, Straus & Giroux, Inc.

Michael Dorris, "For the Indians No Thanksgiving." Copyright © 1988 by Michael Dorris. This article first appeared in the *New York Times* in 1988. Reprinted by permission of the author.

Barbara Ehrenreich, "In Praise of Best Friends." From *Ms.* by Barbara Ehrenreich.

Nora Ephron, "Shaping Up Absurd." Reprinted by permission of International Creative Management, Inc. Copyright © 1975 by Nora Ephron.

Marc Feigen Fasteau, "Friendships Among Men." From *The Male Machine* by Marc Feigen Fasteau. Copyright © 1974 by Marc Feigen Fasteau. Reprinted by permission of The McGraw-Hill Companies.

Nancy Friday, "Competition." From *My Mother/My Self* by Nancy Friday. Copyright © 1977, 1987 by Nancy Friday. Used by permission of Dell Books, a division of Bantam Doubleday Dell Publishing Group, Inc.

Hendrik Hertzberg and Henry Louis Gates, Jr., "The African-American Century." Copyright © 1996 The New Yorker, Inc.

James Weldon Johnson and J. Rosamond Johnson, "Lift Every Voice and Sing." Used by permission of Edward B. Marks Music Company.

Jamaica Kincaid, "Girl." From *At the Bottom of the River* by Jamaica Kincaid. Copyright © 1983 by Jamaica Kincaid. Reprinted by permission of Farrar, Straus & Giroux, Inc.

Tillie Olsen, "I Stand Here Ironing." Copyright © 1956, 1957, 1960, 1961 by Tillie Olsen. From *Tell Me a Riddle* by Tillie Olsen. Introduction by John Leonard. Used by permission of Delacorte Press/Seymour Lawrence, a division of Bantam Doubleday Dell Publishing Group, Inc.

George Orwell, "Shooting an Elephant." From *Shooting an Elephant and Other Essays* by George Orwell, copyright 1950 by Sonia Brownell Orwell and renewed 1978 by Sonia Pitt-Rivers, reprinted by permission of Harcourt Brace & Company. Copyright © the estate of the late Sonia Brownell Orwell and Martin Secker and Warberg Ltd.

Richard Rodriguez, "Public and Private Language." Copyright © 1981 by Richard Rodriguez. Reprinted by permission of George Borchardt, Inc. for the author.

Scott Russell Sanders, "The Men We Carry in Our Minds." Copyright © 1984 by Scott Russell Sanders; first appeared in *Milkweed Chronicle*; reprinted by permission of the author and the Virginia Kidd Agency, Inc.

Thomas Simmons, "Motorcycle Talk." From *The Unseen Shore* by Thomas Simmons. Copyright © 1991 Thomas Simmons. Reprinted by permission of Beacon Press, Boston.

Brent Staples, "Black Men and Public Space." First appeared in *Ms.* Reprinted with permission of the author.

Shelby Steele, "On Being Black and Middle Class." Reprinted from *Commentary*, January 1988, by permission; all rights reserved.

RHETORICAL INDEX

Definition

Description

Division or Analysis

Example

INDEX OF
AUTHORS AND TITLES

THE
SPRINGFIELD
READER

PREPARED BY DAVID CAVITCH and DEBRA SPARK

Resources for Teaching

THE SPRINGFIELD READER

Prepared by

David Cavitch, *Tufts University*

Debra Spark, *Colby College*

Bedford Books   **Boston**

For information, write: Bedford Books, 75 Arlington Street, Boston, MA 02116
(617–426–7440)

ISBN: 0–312–15041–5

PREFACE

The Springfield Reader is organized with the goal of taking students from writing personal pieces — probably unlike anything they were asked to do in high school — to writing critical, argumentative, and research essays. Students will start with the material they have on hand — their own lives — and then branch out to consider material that needs more effort, whether that means simply the close reading of an essay to discover an author's thoughts or library research to explore an issue.

Close examination of the structure of the *Springfield* essays should help students see how what they've learned about writing in the past — that you need a thesis sentence; that paragraphs have topic sentences that support the thesis; that sentences have examples and ideas that support the topic sentence — can be expanded on in the present. In these essays, pay special attention to how ideas are developed (not merely repeated), how transitions are made from subject to subject, and how ideas are supported. Emphasize the importance of the particular: how the "smaller" the subject, the deeper the possible point; how the more specific the example, the tighter and more effective the argument.

It may be helpful to prepare students for class discussion and their assignments by using in-class writing exercises. One option is to use the material that follows each selection to initiate "directed, automatic writing." In "automatic writing," students are, for a brief period of time, required to write as fast as possible, never lifting pen from paper, even if it means scribbling nonsense words. Automatic writing is "directed" when it isn't entirely free form, when, for instance, it is done in response to a question. Automatic writing periods might be followed by short sessions where students may start discussion by reading their work aloud.

CONTENTS

Contents

IDENTITY

Self-Image and Reflections

Starting the Course

The essays in this chapter are first and foremost pieces of personal reflection, though they touch on the issues of sexuality, aging, race, identity, and physical appearance. When students mimic these pieces, they will already have their "material" with them, so they can postpone for a time the learning of some of the skills necessary for writing a college paper (such as textual analysis and research). Students can concentrate instead on self-reflection and the requirements of the personal essay form.

While some students may enjoy the opportunity to write creative nonfiction, others may be quite uneasy — and not only because they are being asked to consider their selves, families, and partners. They may feel locked into the five-paragraph structure for essays that they learned in high school: Introduce your topic and thesis in one paragraph, present three points in three subsequent paragraphs, and repeat your thesis in the final paragraph. In encouraging students to go beyond this structure, you may find the personal essay a useful starting point, since it seems so unnatural to talk about one's life in three clear-cut paragraphs.

This raises the question, of course, of what a personal essay *is*. Students' reading will help them form their own definitions. As a provisional definition, they might consider a personal essay to be an emotionally and intellectually significant piece of prose in which the author discloses aspects of the self to the reader. In the best essays, the disclosure represents a genuine discovery for the reader and the writer, that is, while writing the writer learns something about himself or herself. As Flannery O'Connor said, "I write because I don't know what I think till I read what I say."

Since later you will ask students to produce other kinds of nonfiction, you might emphasize now how the strengths of the personal essay — good, clear writing, honesty, and intelligence — are the strengths of the analytic piece and of the argumentative essay as well. You might note too that, like statistics or experiment results in a scientific piece or evidence in an argumentative work, anecdote and observation in a personal essay often have a cumulative effect, moving the reader to the central insight that, more often than not, was the writer's impetus for producing the piece in the first place.

John Updike

THE DISPOSABLE ROCKET, p. 1

As an initial piece to discuss in class, John Updike's "The Disposable Rocket" is tricky. The author's treatment of his subject is quite intimate — at times, embarrassingly so — and his meaning, on the first reading, at least, isn't completely transparent. Both of these problems can easily be turned into opportunities: first, for a discussion of the value of careful reading; and second, for a discussion of the various levels on which nonfiction can be written.

Students may accuse Updike of saying something here that he is, in fact, not saying, and they should be asked to carefully articulate his points before launching into discussion. Ostensibly, his subject is a man's relationship with his body — and the different relationship a woman has with her body. Quickly, however, he makes it clear that he means to make this comparison "from the standpoint of reproduction." You may need to help students sort out when Updike is talking about reproduction, when he's looking at the larger issue of male-female differences, or, indeed, when he is using biology to make claims about general differences between the sexes.

If looked at without considering the rhetorical strategies, some of Updike's points will probably strike the reader as infuriating or outrageous. What his figurative language, occasional hedging, and hyperbole indicate, however, is that his meaning is somewhat subtler than is initially apparent.

Updike's central metaphor is of the male body as a disposable rocket. "Once the delivery is made," he writes, "men feel a faint but distinct falling-off of interest." The metaphor here is both about the sexual act — desire falls away soon after — and about reproduction in general — after the delivery of sperm, a man is more or less uninvolved in the creation process. Women, then, are the heroes of the story of birth, a fact Updike wants to oppose with his own sense of male bravery. There's purposeful self-deprecation alongside the bravado, exaggeration coupled with crudeness: all meant, one suspects, to be taken at least partially as self-mockery. You might ask your students whether such mockery strikes them as particularly modest and whether the comparison that Updike sets up — for all its elevated language about pregnancy — slights women's active participation in the mating game.

Updike continues to use elevated language as he develops his rocket metaphor, writing about the "release from gravity" that men seek. He uses personal anecdote to equate falling with flying and then makes the claims that males exhibit a "superior recklessness" and that the male sense of space is outer while the female sense of space is inner.

Ask your students to translate Updike's claims into less elegant language; at heart, his views can be seen as mundane and old-fashioned. Have students consider the difference made by language — the great rush of the penultimate sentence in paragraph 3, a line that seems to mimic the very activity it describes or the grand, detailed elaboration of examples of "outer" space in paragraph 4. Students who dislike this essay will concede that Updike's skill enables him to get away with what may be a reductive view of the sexes, just as the relative formality of his language allows him to talk about his penis. (Many of your students, however, may be embarrassed by talking too closely about his claims, no matter how elegant the vehicle.) Metaphors and similes allow him to make possible communication that might otherwise seem inappropriate.

You might move from discussing the central metaphor to a discussion of figurative language in general. Updike twice writes of people being tenants in their bodies. He opens by comparing the healthy body to a bank account and closes by comparing a man and his body to a boy and his buddy out for a car ride. Ask why Updike uses these comparisons — all examples of figurative language. (Metaphors and similes compare in order to explain. Writers use figurative language to illustrate the unseen in terms of the seen. "A parsnip looks like a large white carrot" assumes that the person who has never seen a parsnip will be familiar with a carrot. With more inchoate experiences or perceptions, figurative language works in much the same way, helping the writer communicate an otherwise private moment or vision through shared experiences or perceptions.) In his essay, Updike doesn't shy away from a direct discussion of genitals and sex, but his figurative language may help him convey what is, for reasons other than propriety, hard to communicate more directly.

That said, Updike's verbal skills end up, ironically enough, clothing — perhaps cloaking — the author. Despite the personal subject, "The Disposable Rocket" doesn't reveal that much about the author as it touches on penises, vaginas, erection, ejaculation. The most naked moment of the essay is when Updike discusses his ankles. This detail — so much better than the equivalent abstraction "I'm surprised I'm growing old" — is given with real emotion and without the rhetorical flights one sees earlier in the essay.

In the final two paragraphs, Updike shifts his topic from sex to aging. Ask students to identify the two transitions — one in paragraph 6, about time, and one in paragraph 7, about the different ways the sexes age. You may want to point out that this shift is anticipated in the essay's opening simile, since we associate aging with declining health. But in making the shift, Updike hasn't left his central point behind: the self-possessed, hidden wholeness of woman is what man lacks. Man's anatomy leaves him in a vulnerable position: his desires are exposed, his body is split in two. This split is a result of both the sex act, which splits the sperm from the man, and the placement of the genitals outside the body. Man's experience of his own body is similarly divided; even in relative health, he feels not himself but "like a boy and the buddy who has a driver's license and the use of his father's car for the evening; [he] goes along, gratefully, for the ride." Given the broad reaches of the male's sense of space, according to paragraph 4, and the "superior recklessness" described in paragraph 3, the boy's gratefulness here reminds one that this essay is as much about falling as flying, as much as about failure, exposure, and death as it is about being a man.

Writing Suggestions: Think of a time when your sense of your physical self was sharpened, changed, or enhanced. It might be a memory of a sports success, a physical difficulty, an illness, or a growth spurt. How did (or does) that memory affect your sense of self?

What does it mean when someone claims that biology is destiny? Explain the phrase, relating it, where appropriate to Updike's "A Disposable Rocket." Do you agree or disagree with the statement's implications?

Nora Ephron

SHAPING UP ABSURD, p. 5

Nora Ephron's "Shaping Up Absurd," like Updike's "A Disposable Rocket," focuses on the body as wellspring of identity. But Ephron's essay is both less intimate and more revelatory than Updike's. You may have students who are embarrassed to discuss the body, however, no matter how buried in humor such discussion is.

In "Shaping Up Absurd," the style is informal, the content quite personal. Ephron doesn't shy away from giving private details about herself. Indeed, she almost eagerly confesses her adolescent fears and dissimulations as well as her adult experiences and neuroses. Given her direct disclosures, this essay has the potential to make some students uncomfortable, but everything about Ephron's approach to her subject — her tact, humor, sensitivity, and candor — encourages a similarly open, easy response on the part of her readers.

3

If students write their own personal essays for class, they'll have to decide where to place their narrator — their remembering self — in relation to the remembered self. Beginning writers often choose one of two obvious extremes. They either write as if they are still the person of the memory (using, for instance, a child's voice if they are remembering something from their early years) or write as a reminiscent narrator, looking back on times past. Both points of view have advantages and pitfalls. The child's voice may seem more direct, as if it can access, more honestly, the emotions of the memory, but such a voice can easily seem boring or cloying to the adult reader. The adult voice can be used to summarize and reflect, to arrive at fairly sophisticated conclusions, but it may lose some immediacy or authenticity in the process.

Ephron resolves the point of view problem in an interesting way. At intervals, she uses the language of an early adolescent, re-creating the exaggerations, lingo, and abruptness of response that characterized her young self. She is frightened of "gumming" things up, she has an "utterly-hateful-about-bras mother," and she uses phrases like "That was the killer." But one never forgets that it is the adult Ephron, not the adolescent, who is writing this piece, and it is the adult's humor, shrewdness, and maturity, rather than the adolescent's embarrassment, that determine what to tell and what to omit.

Ephron's opening sentence nicely mimics adolescent self-absorption. It also suggests a degree of self-consciousness regarding the act of writing. This self-consciousness continues throughout the essay with lines such as "That is a true story." Given her subject, this self-referential quality seems appropriate. But point out to students that she avoids potentially wooden constructions ("as you can see" or "for these three reasons") as she supports her general observations with anecdotes and details.

In considering the structure of this essay, you might note how Ephron develops her piece's theme as well as her narrative. She tells a story *and* she develops an argument. In the end, it is the shape of the story and the shape of the argument that determine the shape of the essay. Ephron moves forward in time (telling us about how her concerns with flat-chestedness played out over the years), and she moves from a discussion about fear of androgyny to fear of rejection by men. Given the latter concern, why are men dispensed with so quickly in paragraphs 29 and 30? What does the brevity of those paragraphs reveal about the nature of her concern about breast size? How does the stylistic choice of constructing a paragraph that isn't even a sentence long help make her point?

Since the author presents her views primarily through telling her story, you might ask students why certain details are included. For instance, in paragraph 10, why the lengthy list of food? Also, why the decision to shift to present tense in paragraph 11? Here Ephron breaks a "rule," since verb tenses should be consistent. There's a typographical shift as well in paragraphs 21–27. What accounts for the use of italics for this particular anecdote? Finally, look at the amusing final paragraph, where Ephron purposefully undercuts her claim that she's grown past her adolescent obsession with her chest. Note that she doesn't use her essay's closing to sum up her argument or story. Instead, she keeps things moving and changing until the very last minute. The humor of the final line comes from its brevity and informality after the reasoned, careful lines prior to it. Ephron lets the contradictions in her own thoughts emerge as (admitted) contradictions in her essay.

Ask students if they find the piece dated (and what they know about the fifties). Are the opening lines of paragraph 3 still true? Has the vogue of androgyny changed things?

In considering this question, students might be interested in Tracy Young's "A Few (More) Words About Breasts" (*Esquire*, September 1992). Young starts out by reminding us that Ephron's essay was originally published in 1972 under the title "A Few Words About Breasts." Young goes on to write, "If you read the piece today, what strikes you is how well it works both as a nostalgic artifact and as an uncanny prediction of where we've ended up: In 1992, a smart, successful, flat-chested feminist of sorts feels exactly the way Ephron did twenty years ago — only by now she's had implants."

Another option for considering the contemporary relevance of Ephron's piece would be to read this essay against James Baldwin's complicated thoughts on androgyny in "Here Be Dragons," first published in 1985 in Baldwin's collection *The Price of the Ticket.*

Since Ephron's essay was originally published in *Esquire* ("The Magazine for Men"), one might use "Shaping Up Absurd" to address the question of audience. Is there anything about the piece that suggests it was written for male, rather than female, readers? If so, how might the piece be different if its original home had been *Glamour* or *Elle*?

Finally, assumed connections between physical traits and character traits — such as those Ephron encounters in herself and other people and those Updike reads from the differences between the sexes — may lead to classroom consideration of stereotypes (and provide a segue into Brent Staples's "Black Men and Public Space"). When we stereotype another, we are guilty of prejudice. What, you might ask the class, are we guilty of when we stereotype ourselves?

Writing Suggestion: Ephron says of big breasts, "If I had had them, I would have been a completely different person. I honestly believe that." Write a description of an Ephron who, like her friend Diana Raskob, "shaped up" at age eleven. Focus on the character traits that Ephron claims were most influenced by her body type.

Brent Staples

BLACK MEN AND PUBLIC SPACE, p. 12

In the opening lines of paragraph 1, readers are led to believe that they are witnessing a crime to which the writer is confessing. There is no clue that we should take the words "my first victim" and "I came upon her" as sarcastic or ironic. Instead, Staples lets these words create a kind of suspense; we feel we're going to get insight into the criminal mind at the moment of violence. What we discover, of course, is that the tall, broad black man, not the skittish white woman, is the victim in this brief, tense drama. The author's strategy is to have us make the same fearful assumptions about the black man on the street that the white woman does. He convinces us our assumptions our wrong, at least initially, by letting our preconceptions about young graduate students at the University of Chicago replace our preconceptions about large, bearded black men in military jackets. Or, perhaps, students realize even sooner — with the phrase "discreet, uninflammatory distance" — that the author is not who he first appears to be.

Structuring his piece around a central incident, Staples reckons with his "unwieldy inheritance" — the ability to alter public space in ugly ways — and tries to understand why it took him so long to recognize that he had this problematic power. Racism has given him the power, but it is a complicated form of racism, one that both blacks and whites share in, since blacks as well as whites lock their cars when they see a young black man on the street, since both races find black men "ever the suspect." And Staples concedes that there is some reason for the young woman's fear in the opening scene. After all, "Women are particularly vulnerable to street violence, and young black males are drastically overrepresented among the perpetrators of that violence." This admission, however, does little to comfort Staples. He's still alienated by the terrified woman's reaction. She has still made him "an accomplice in tyranny." What's more, her reaction

— considered in light of the anecdotes in paragraphs 8, 9, and 10 — is on a continuum with the more obviously racist behavior of the jewelry store proprietor and the Waukegan police officers. Nor are these responses "merely" unpleasant for Staples and other black men, for, as Staples notes, "being perceived as dangerous is a hazard in itself." It invites the very sort of violence that Staples, from an early age, has tried to avoid.

Despite his analysis, Staples refrains from explicitly chastising the white woman in the opening scene or from openly characterizing her behavior as racist. You might ask students if Staples's essay nonetheless implies reproach. If so, where? If not, why?

In this essay, instead of offering a solution to a large sociological problem, Staples's goal is to identify the problem and then to describe his response to it. Anger, though he has felt it, doesn't help — not if self-preservation is his goal. It is better to find ways to keep himself safe from others' fear. He closes his essay by returning to his opening anecdote and describing how, during his nighttime strolls, he whistles classical music, thus yoking himself with the "equivalent of the cowbell that hikers wear when they know they are in bear country." With this final metaphor, Staples reminds us again that white fear is dangerous for black men; it is the bear, not the hiker, who attacks when bear and hiker meet.

Staples's "tension-reducing measure[s]" — his willingness to alter his movements or whistle at night — may be a conformist ploy or even an abdication of self. They may also be a reflection of his education, taste, humor, and savvy. Students should note that Staples closes with an image of himself whistling in the dark. Their evaluation of his behavior will, no doubt, rest on whether they view the closing irony as intended or not.

Writing Suggestions: In the opening scene of this essay, Staples describes himself as "surprised, embarrassed, and dismayed all at once." Later, it becomes clear that he also has reason to fear those who fear him. Why? What is the danger of being perceived as hazardous? What is the danger of trying to compensate for the way in which one is perceived?

Tell a story about a time when you were, for some reason, misperceived by others. How did you respond to the misperception, and what do you now think of your behavior?

E. B. White

ONCE MORE TO THE LAKE, p. 16

In this classic essay, E. B. White revisits an old haunt, both literally and metaphorically; a return to a childhood space prompts thoughts about mortality.

Because White's essay centers on time, you may want to point out that his narrative sticks to a clear, chronological ordering of events. White may be confused about time, but his essay never is. He begins at the beginning, "one summer," describing his family's trip to a camp on a Maine lake. Then, jumping forward a few decades, he tells us that "a few weeks ago" he felt an urge to return to the lake. As an adult, White is more fond of salt than fresh water, but the lake's placidity beckons him even as the sea — with its "restlessness," "fearful cold," and "incessant wind" — pushes him away. Without saying so directly, White hopes that the trip to the lake will be a retreat.

Until the essay's final paragraphs, White tells the story of his journey to the lake and his stay there in a logical fashion, describing events as they happen. Memories, when they occur, are instigated by specific details in the "now" of the story. We don't have a sense of the author adding details about the past when he sat down to write. Rather, we feel that the memories have accompanied him on his journey.

White starts by recalling the thoughts that came to him as he traveled to the lake, most notably his suspicion that everything would be different when he got there. "The tarred road would have found it out," he writes, expressing his conviction (and fear) that the conveniences of contemporary life will have altered the "remote and primeval" place of his memory. Time will have worked its changes on the lake as it works its changes on everything.

Instead, he finds the lake much the same. Two things make this clear to him: a physical sensation (the smell of his bedroom) and his son's activity, which neatly mimics White's own youth at the lake. As the essay proceeds, these same two things suggest White's shifting sense of identity. He feels at one point that his son "was I, and therefore, by simple transposition, that I was my father." The lake's power seems to be related to its timelessness — so much hasn't changed — and to its being a place the older man associates with his own childhood. In the end, the lake easily lends itself to the appealing illusion that time hasn't passed.

While the essay continues to move ahead in chronological time, the illusion about time grows so strong that White lets himself drop the language that suggests he is referring to a hallucination. It is no longer "as if" time hasn't passed. Instead, he insists, several times, "There had been no years." The things of memory and of the present are one and the same. "Everywhere we went," he writes of himself and his son, "I had trouble making out which was I, the one walking at my side, the one walking in my pants" (para. 11).

"Once More to the Lake" closes with a thunderstorm, and you may want to spend time with your students closely analyzing this description. Everything about it reminds him of long-ago storms: "It was all the same," repeats the by-now-familiar refrain. His description of the storm is a good example of the virtues of concrete language and of how a single well-placed abstraction is better than a lengthy explanation. The first line of description — "This was the big scene, still the big scene" — suggests that values haven't changed. The penultimate line describing the storm is an abstraction: White tells us that the repeated experience has the effect of "linking the generations in a strong indestructible chain." The final image, "the comedian who waded in carrying an umbrella," moves from abstract to concrete. Ask students what they make of this shift. Does the final image trivialize what comes before?

The powerful final paragraph may demand some in-class discussion as well. As he watches his son pulling on his wet swimming trunks, White feels "the chill of death" in his groin. Your students may be shocked by these final words; if so, point out that we've been prepared for them by the word "deathless" and by White's earlier confession that the week's persistent sense of transposition is "creepy," that it makes him, at moments, "dizzy." The sensual language describing the lake visit — from the tennis courts, to the fishing, to the storm — and the rapture about summertime lead us in the usually happy direction of nostalgia. The genius of "Once More to the Lake" lies in its insistence on the implications of the past.

Writing Suggestions: People often have complicated feelings about their age. Birthdays can be a source of real joy or anguish. Consider your own age. Do you think your personality matches your chronological age? Why or why not? If not, write about your "virtual age," explaining why it's more appropriate for your personality.

Do you remember a birthday that had special significance for you? What was that birthday? Explain why it was important for you. Do you feel the same today about that birthday?

Joseph Steffan

HONOR BOUND, p. 22

Because "Honor Bound" is excerpted from a longer work, it doesn't have the well-crafted wholeness of some of the other essays in this chapter, but it is a good example of a young man's thoughts on an abstract subject. A straightforward narrative combines with a simple but direct argument to explain the author's decision to tell the truth when a lie might have furthered his professional and personal goals.

Steffan's narrative moves through the day he decides to disclose his homosexuality to his superior officer. You may want to call your students' attention to his writing style — Steffan is not as skilled a writer as the other authors in this section, and his weaknesses are most apparent when he's telling his story. Despite his appealing honesty, he uses clichés, particularly when describing intense emotion ("the moment of truth," para. 11, and "a moment I will never forget, one of agony and intense pride," para. 13). Use these and other examples to open discussion about how to represent emotion in personal writing. We all cry alike, after all, and what moves us is not tears but something sad.

Steffan also makes a few grammatical errors and occasionally gives information that seems unnecessary. For instance, the details about Captain Habermeyer's office in paragraph 3 seem appropriate, but why are we told, in paragraph 5, about the captain's interest in Japanese culture? There are other places (paragraph 15, for example) where the essay would be more concrete if it gave more examples.

But Steffan's piece is an argument as well as a narrative, and the selection's strength lies in the clear, logical presentation of that argument. As Steffan sees it, the commandant's question — "Are you willing to state at this time that you are a homosexual?" — is a challenge to Steffan's identity and to his honor as a midshipman. Steffan is at his best in paragraph 16, where he explains exactly how the question challenges his honor. Here he details the "Honor Concept at Annapolis," and later he elaborates, saying that the concept of honor has its foundation in human dignity. In the end, Steffan decides, "the only way to retain my honor and identity, both as a midshipman and a person, was to tell the truth." As the piece makes clear, however, he cannot have an identity as a midshipman if he tells the truth. He's in a catch-22: Lying will invalidate his graduation; telling the truth will mean he can't graduate. His decision to tell the truth is based on his conviction that the intangibles of honor and identity are more important than the tangibles of graduation and a military career.

Interestingly, Steffan doesn't feel that he has been victimized by the academy or that there is "someone to hate, a person to blame for everything that was happening." Instead, "there was only a military policy, a rule like countless others that define life in the military, rules that we learn to instinctively enforce and obey" (para. 20). Of course, rules have their origin in decisions by people, so you might ask students to consider why Steffan doesn't critique military policy or the "instinctive" obedience that military life requires.

In the hours after Steffan's disclosure, he takes actions to make it clear that he is not ashamed of his sexual identity. Given that, you might ask students how they read his prior secrecy about his sexual identity. Are they surprised that his friends and family don't know about it?

Writing Suggestions: Tell the story of a rebellious act that was committed in your hometown or your current place of residence. Do some research to uncover different responses to the act, then discuss where you think responsibility for the act lies.

Describe the circumstances around a difficult decision you had to make. Explain your reasons for making the decision, then try to articulate the values or beliefs that underscored your reasoning.

Jamaica Kincaid

GIRL, p. 26

This unusual short story consists of a single (very long) sentence in which a series of commands and bits of advice stream from a mother to her daughter. Twice in the space of the monologue, the daughter speaks up — once to protest an accusation and once to ask a question. Students will disagree (as instructors may also) about what is going on. Are we listening to the actual voice of a mother badgering the girl as she works and listens, or are we listening to the often-heard phrases that now play in the more grownup girl's head as she recalls her upbringing? As is evident in the textbook questions, we treat the story as the girl's responses to an internalized maternal voice. The monologue — with its obsessiveness, contradictions, and repetition — reactivates the limited but spirited rebelliousness of the developing girl who suffered indignities for many years.

The nature of the mother's instructions varies as the story proceeds. At first, the advice concerns domestic chores such as washing clothes, cooking, sewing, gardening, and housecleaning — but the mother soon incorporates advice about manners, giving the reader a bit of a shock when she says, "On Sundays try to walk like a lady and not like the slut you are so bent on becoming." This moral warning quickly becomes the refrain of the piece.

This refrain is surprising in part because the daughter seems, at first, quite young and rather well-behaved; but clearly the girl is not the same age at the beginning as she is at the end of the story. You may want to have your class find the clues "Girl" provides about the age of the daughter. Your discussion will probably include the mother's fears. Explain possible inconsistencies in her advice, such as when the mother tells the daughter how "to make a good medicine to throw away a child before it even becomes a child" and "how to love a man." Earlier the mother warned the daughter about singing benna in Sunday school, but now she is telling her daughter how to spit in the air when she feels like it. This advice is delivered just as the previous advice is. The construction of the phrases is still the same — using the command form or beginning with the words "this is how." How come? What, for instance, is the effect of using the same construction for talking about how to make pepper pot and how to give yourself an abortion? What is the mother telling the daughter about what life is like for women? What kind of knowledge does the mother have?

Writing Suggestion: The daughter in "Girl" constantly hears her mother's advice about how to act appropriately. How is this advice specific to a girl? What might a father's advice to a boy sound like? Write a monologue entitled "Boy" in the same style as Kincaid's story. How does the impact of your monologue differ from that of "Girl"?

| 2 |

HOME

Family and Groups

Recognizing Knots in the Ties

This chapter's selections deal with the complications of family relationships and group identity. Barbara Dafoe Whitehead and Thomas Simmons ask us to consider the parental role — from the points of view of the social critic and the loving, disappointed son. Nancy Friday uses memories of competing with her sister and mother to try to understand their adult relationships. Shelby Steele reminds us that our families extend beyond our family of origin, even if identification is sometimes complicated. And Alice Walker poses the question of belonging in a well-crafted short story that gives no easy answers.

To help students make the transition from the writing of personal essays to analytic, argumentative, and research papers, you may want to use the selections in this chapter to assign *analytic* personal response essays in which students use their experiences to suggest or illustrate a general point rather than focusing on confessional or anecdotal exchanges.

Students may need reminding that papers which relate reading to experience require different skills than personal essays. Instead of using the reading primarily as a jumping off point for their own memories and ideas, students should analyze the essays for "truth value," and they should compare and contrast the ideas and experiences of the authors with their own. They should find a way of focusing their sense of the similarities and differences between the reading and their experiences, rather than simply responding to the essay, point by point, with observations and personal anecdotes. To do this, they'll have to read the essays carefully, distill the essence of each, identify key ideas, summarize relevant points, and evaluate argumentative strategy. Now is probably the time to talk to students about how to smoothly integrate references to and discussions of other sources into their work. This will require a discussion of how to paraphrase and how to quote. (It might be a good time, too, to talk about plagiarism — unintentional and otherwise — since plagiarism is, essentially, about a failure to appropriately attribute paraphrases and quotations.)

Thomas Simmons

MOTORCYCLE TALK, p. 29

Thomas Simmons opens by telling us that his father was an unhappy and difficult man with one significant virtue: his devotion to machines. While another writer might indulge in parental analysis, asking what he was depressed about or what made him so hard to get along with, Simmons chooses instead to focus on his father's skill with machines. This talent was a medium of affection for father and son, and more — it allowed them to communicate.

10

From what is left unsaid, we can see this essay as Simmons's attempt to look past the problems in his relationship with his father. You might ask students to characterize these difficulties. What has Simmons left out? Do students feel that Simmons's omissions detract from the essay? Why or why not?

Our sense of the father is expanded by scattered details about him and by the story of his childhood go-cart, the story he frequently tells about himself despite its disastrous ending. Why? An important ingredient of the story is Simmons's grandfather's harshness when Simmons's father makes an understandable — if financially devastating — mistake as a result of boyhood exuberance. Might Simmons's father, in repeating the story, be trying to apologize for or explain his own behavior as a father? Is he saying that he still feels "stupid" and "irresponsible"?

We quickly learn that the father is tender with machines. Simmons uses metaphor to describe this tenderness: His father, he sees, is caring for his son the way a flat-truck mechanic cares for his driver. Ask your students what they make of this metaphor. Is it a positive or a negative one, in the context of the essay?

When speaking the language of machines, Simmons connects with his father, but this connection is eventually not enough. First, as Simmons writes, "What we shared through the motorcycle contradicted most of our other encounters in the family." Second, Simmons is "surpassing" his father; he's learning other ways of connecting, and he doesn't want to be limited to his father's often inadequate forms of communication.

In the final paragraph of the essay, however, Simmons seems to accept his father's limited communication by adapting to it. Like an immigrant, or a child who has grown up and out of the ghetto, he has learned the language that will help him get by in the larger world while still appreciating what he left behind.

You may want to raise for the class the significance of Simmons's occupation: He is a writer, a man of words. Indeed, it is wordplay, in paragraph 10 and again in the final metaphor, that allows Simmons to discover the truth of his relationship with his father.

Writing Suggestion: Consider current cultural norms for what a "good" father is. How do they resonate with your own beliefs about what makes a good father? How does the father in Simmons's "Motorcycle Talk" meet or fail your standards?

Barbara Dafoe Whitehead

WOMEN AND THE FUTURE OF FATHERHOOD, p. 33

One way to start class discussion of this essay would be to have the class do some brief research on the "contemporary debate over fatherhood" to which Whitehead refers in her opening sentence. You might split the class into groups and assign different topics — the men's movement, the Million Man March, and so on — and then have students report to class on the *rhetoric* that surrounds current discussion about fatherhood. That way, the class will have a better sense of the debate Whitehead joins with this essay.

Whitehead's criticism of the so-called fatherhood movement isn't thoroughgoing. She admires the "cultural" goal of making responsible, loving parenting a masculine attribute, and she makes no objection to the movement's political goal of acquiring a voice for men. What she objects to is the omission of women as a factor in the fatherhood debate. As Whitehead sees it, "marital disruption" is at the source of "the fatherhood problem." Before you ask students to tackle this premise, ask them exactly what Whitehead means by "the fatherhood problem" and why she chooses not to define this problem. Only after the class has reached a consensus should they try to explain her conclusion about marital disruption. Her argument is that men need marriage for fatherhood in a way that women *don't* need marriage for motherhood. Since marriage is presumably what keeps men in close proximity to their children, the absence of marriage means men don't have a chance to make the contributions (emotional and instrumental) that are necessary for effective parenting. What is more, they don't have "access to the social and emotional intelligence of women in building relationships," and the father who doesn't live at home may be denigrated by the mother who does.

Whitehead feels that her own conclusion about the central role of marriage for fatherhood is troubling, since women aren't particularly willing to solve the fatherhood problem by reinstating marriage to its former glory. Indeed, now that women are no longer economically dependent on marriage, they are no longer willing to stay in unhappy relationships, especially since they can meet many of their emotional and personal goals without marriage. Not, Whitehead says, that women have lost their interest in satisfying marriages; it's just that they have grown cynical and despairing of men — in particular, the demands and the egos of men.

According to Whitehead, the fact that women can have motherhood without marriage — and that men can't have fatherhood without marriage — results in a "virtue gap" between the sexes. Popular culture reflects our sense of the single mother as hard-working and the absent father as selfish, perhaps even a "deadbeat dad." (She cites *Waiting to Exhale* as an example of this. You might ask students for other examples.)

So, what's to be done? Women aren't going to give up the achievements of the last few decades and return to the "old" setup. Nor does Whitehead think they should, for though she thinks the solution to the fatherhood problem will have to include women, she finds men primarily to blame for the problem. *They* have to understand what *they* need to do to make women participate in a solution, a solution that requires some sort of effective arrangement between the sexes. A new kind of marriage? Perhaps. But Whitehead doesn't say what that arrangement will be, only that it will have to consider, notably "some mutual understanding and commitment to an equitable division of tasks" and a discussion of expectations for marriage. In paragraph 15, Whitehead concludes that women want fidelity and emotional intimacy (which presumably men aren't interested in), while men want sexual intimacy (which presumably women don't value as highly). You might ask students about these conclusions. Are these stereotypes or accurate portrayals?

Whitehead also reminds us that to be "fair," the roles of mother and father don't need to be the same, and proposes a new "kind of language" to talk about relationships. Right now, our language focuses on individual needs — which may make some sense for a childless marriage, but less sense when marriage is an arrangement for raising children. When marriage is looked at in this utilitarian way, the language of relationships, Whitehead suggests, needs to recognize "differences, mutuality, complementarity, and, more than anything else, altruism."

While Whitehead's argument may seem reasonably persuasive, students may be irked by her assumptions about the sexes. Ask them to identify and examine them. Also, Whitehead gives ample evidence that divorce is a detriment to fatherhood, since it often leaves the father at a physical distance from the child. Does this mean, necessarily, that marriage improves fatherhood?

Writing Suggestion: Consider Whitehead's claims about the role of women in successful fatherhood. Further or disprove her points using your personal experience or your own observations about families. Alternatively, analyze Whitehead's argument by comparing it with one of the following: Tobias Wolff's memoir *This Boy's Life*, Mary Karr's memoir *The Liar's Club*, or Raymond Carver's essay "My Father's Life."

Nancy Friday

COMPETITION, p. 38

Despite the urgency of her adolescent need for affection and praise, Nancy Friday describes her younger self as more or less unaware of her jealousy toward her sister and her competition with her mother. Apparently, only now, in writing about her adolescence, can Friday look honestly at those years and conclude (with the reader) that she must have been crazy with jealousy, that the competition she so hated in her household — the petty fights between her sister and mother — was not truly one that she managed to avoid. Playing the game on her own terms — looking for affirmation in the social and the academic realms, becoming an overachiever — didn't insulate her from the bad feelings she must have had about losing the game on her sister and mother's terms, about not being "the pretty one." Indeed, Friday's penultimate sentence could be reversed. Never having learned to lose gracefully to the greater beauty of her mother and sister, she did and does not know how to accept her victory over them through other attributes.

But the competition is about more than just beauty — or other attributes. It's about the sisters' competition for the mother's attention and about the competition for the grandfather's attention. It's even, obliquely, about the way competition changes when a power relationship changes, since the mother's relationship with Susie parallels the mother's relationship with her own sister — except with Susie the mother has authority, while she long ago abdicated power to her sister, Susie's aunt.

It's clear this essay has an emotional, confessional purpose as well as an explicitly expository one. Friday demonstrates the pain of competition but also its benefits. Competition in her family meant bad behavior. It also contributed to Friday's intellectual, social and professional successes. The conflict between her mother and her sister allowed the author to become an independent woman. It also resulted in her overeating at the dinner table while her sister and her mother fought. Competition brought the author closer to her grandfather — and left her with terrible guilt about that closeness. Competition keeps the mother and sister fighting with each other through their adult years, but it also draws them closer to one another.

On the whole, Friday seems ambivalent about competition. On one hand, she is ambitious. On the other, she suggests, she doesn't really want to win (which is why she feels so guilty about winning her grandfather's favor and about Susie's removal to boarding school).

The emotional part of Friday's essay closes in paragraph 18 with an awareness of the paradoxes of competition, but the expository part of the essay continues through paragraph 19. Here, Friday seems unambivalent about competition. The problem, she says, is the way in which women are trained to compete. Open competition — instead of the "petty" contests between women — would make competition "safe" for women. The unstated suggestion is that such competition would result in all of the benefits of competition with none of the guilt. Ask students what "safe" competition would be and how parents of girls could promote it.

Writing Suggestions: Consider Friday's sense of the differences between the way males and females compete. Then consider a competitive incident between you and a friend or relation. Describe that incident, then analyze the nature of the competition. Was it "male" or "female"? If neither label fits, explain why, offering, if appropriate, a critique of Friday's views about competition.

Read Toni Cade Bambara's "The Lesson." Identify and describe the kinds of competition portrayed in the story. How does the incident at the toy store affect the narrator's competitive urges, and how do you perceive her competitive nature — as a strength, a weakness or something else?

Shelby Steele

ON BEING BLACK AND MIDDLE CLASS, p. 43

Shelby Steele builds his argument by using his own experience: First, he establishes his authority, his suitability for addressing the matter at hand, by immediately disclosing his skin color. Second, instead of presenting and systematically critiquing the opposing argument, Steele simply lets us know that he once held the view he now opposes — that race completely defined his identity, that "most aspects of [his] life found their explanation, their justification, and their motivation in race."

Steele doesn't feel that his old position was accurate for its time and inappropriate for the present. Rather, he claims, the old position was *always* insufficient to explain the situation of blacks in the United States; race never completely defined identity, for *class* had and has a significant role. In examining why he feels so uncomfortable confessing his beliefs, he concludes that his discomfort is a result of how class and race are defined in this country. (You might ask students who defines such terms. Are their definitions immutable?)

When Steele first sets out to articulate the separate definitions, he gives examples of middle-class values, and he characterizes these values as raceless and assimilationist. When he goes on to define race, Steele first turns his attention to a consideration of racial identity. He notes that the definition of racial identity that emerged in the sixties still holds sway today. It is a definition of the self as victim, as "embattled minority," and as such it encourages an adversarial stance toward the majority and an ethnic consciousness rather than an individual one.

Given these definitions, Steele continues, members of the black middle class are in a position that requires them to feel two opposing things at once: they are to embrace middle-class individualism while giving their ethnic identity primacy.

Steele says that the images required to identify with race are in conflict with those required to identify with class, and vice versa. As a result, members of the black middle class are in a double bind. "There is," Steele writes, "no forward movement on either plane that does not constitute backward movement on the other." Assert your middle-class identity and your ethnic identity suffers. (Blacks who define themselves as middle-class first are bound, as a result, to feel the guilt that Steele experiences in the opening scene, a guilt that suggests betrayal of the group.) Alternatively, the more you assert your ethnic identity, the more your middle-class identity suffers. (This seems to be Steele's point in including the scene with the debate coach, where Steele's need to identify with his people cuts him off from the "resources" of his class and provides him only with the fury of the victim.)

As the essay proceeds to discuss values, Steele enters difficult territory. In paragraph 11, he writes that a sense of identity within a collective (whether of class or race) comes from "embracing a polarity of positive and negative images." He explains, "To identify as middle class, for example, I must have both positive and negative images of what being middle class entails; then I will know what I should and should not be doing in order to be middle class. The same goes for racial identity." Steele lists middle-class values in paragraph 6, but he never gives us the positive and negative images of what being black entails. Or he never gives us anything beyond the "victim" identity of which he disapproves. Instead he writes about "negative images of lower-class blacks" and uses the character of Sam to let us know what those are. As a result, he never presents anything like a positive image associated with racial identity — only the positive values of middle-class life, which leaves him in the very place the guilt he expresses in paragraph 4 would suggest he doesn't want to be.

Steele's closing anecdote reinforces his association of negative values with his race and positive ones with his class, since he identifies his rage at the debate coach as a result of his racial identity, his identity as victim. He concludes that the more dignified approach of the victim to the victimizer belongs to him not as a black man but as a middle-class man. (You may want to ask what the implications of this statement are. Is Steele suggesting that a lower-class black doesn't have the power of the measured, dispassionate response?)

The debate team anecdote seems, in certain ways, like an odd one to use in this essay. The middle-class "propriety" that is referred to in paragraph 20 is indisputably racist, so the anecdote itself seems to claim that class itself is necessarily racist. (Students might be asked if they can think of another example of class and race, according to Steele's paradigm, coming into conflict.)

Since Steele says that race and class are largely a matter of definition, his sense of the "problem" here has, in the end, mostly to do with the way blacks define themselves as victims. If there were another definition, then perhaps Steele would have some positive values to associate with his racial identity. Are there reasons, historical or otherwise, that victim identity might have been necessary? Is still necessary? Can students propose alternate definitions?

In an essay titled "The New Sovereignty," Steele has written about the "narcissism of victims" who hold on to their grievances because grievances are a way to have an identity and — in an age of affirmative action and identity politics — power. Philip Roth, in his essay "Writing About Jews," leveled this same criticism against Jews with persecution complexes. Roth took the insistence on claiming wounds where none necessarily existed to be a way of claiming identity that was an insult to the memory of those who *had* been wounded. Sharing this fact with your class may be a good way to open up discussion from blacks as a social group to other groups that claim victim status in our society.

Another possible way to open discussion of this essay is with the following quotation from the *New York Times* (May 30, 1990): "To many whites and conservative blacks, Mr. Steele has given eloquent voice to painful truths that are almost always left unspoken in the nation's circumscribed public discourse on race. To many black politicians and civil rights figures, he is a turncoat, a privileged black man whose visibility and success stem from his ability to say precisely what white America most wants to hear." A point of interest: The first sentence of this quotation, without the introductory phrase, is used as a blurb on the back of Shelby Steele's book *The Content of Our Character.*

Writing Suggestion: In making his argument about the double bind of the black middle class, Steele offers definitions of race and class in the United States. Explain what his definitions are, and then analyze the definitions for completeness. Do the results of your analysis affect your perception of his argument? Do they lend support to or contradict his conclusions? Explain.

Alice Walker

EVERYDAY USE, p. 50

"Everyday Use" looks at both group identity and family relationships. Your students will most likely focus on racial identity, and you should remind them that there are a variety of ways in which that identity might be defined. In this story, Dee's racial identity (in a historical sense) seems inauthentic within the context of her immediate family. The details that suggest she has embraced the Nation of Islam (changing her name "back" to an African one; dating another adherent, a man who doesn't eat pork or collards) are lightly mocked here. Dee has decided to return to her people, but that return has nothing to do with who her people, in a more intimate sense, are.

Indeed, the details we are given characterize Dee's life by a desire to distance herself from her past. Instead of being literally scarred, as Maggie is, by the loss of her original home, Dee is pleased to see the place burn down. Apparently, Dee moves on from that loss in a way that Maggie and their mother do not. "I have," the mother says of the new place, "deliberately turned my back on the house." When she decides her past is fashionable, Dee doesn't make a distinction between the original house and the house her mother and sister now occupy. When she takes snapshots, she's sure to place this "authentic" detail in every frame.

Given Dee's previous relationship to her past, her current behavior seems false and self-conscious, part of the same slight arrogance and determination that characterized her desire to get away from her family in the first place. The mother's fantasy of herself as the light-skinned, slim woman who Dee would want her to be is meant to show us that Dee is afflicted by racial self-hatred, not racial pride. Dee's new enthusiasm for the very things she once scorned is meant to seem mannered and selfish, particularly when opposed to the appallingly selfless, shuffle-footed generosity of the darker-skinned, burned Maggie. Maggie is somehow the "true" member of her people. She uses the butter churn for butter-making, a quilt for covering. She doesn't abstract her experience. And Dee, now that it has become fashionable to "be" black, is willing to claim her race and its artifacts, but only if both can be used for display.

The mother has limited sympathy for her more glamorous daughter's struggle for identity. When the mother gives the quilts to Maggie, her decision is hardly surprising —her sympathies have been with Maggie all along. Even as she praises Dee's determination, we sense her anger with her.

Ask students to analyze the mother's character. What are her strengths and weaknesses as Maggie's mother? as Dee's mother? In both cases, the answer is more complicated than it might seem. For example, the mother tells us that Dee once hated Maggie, but there's also evidence that Maggie might hate Dee. Maggie sees Dee as friendless at the end of paragraph 14 (though the observation is presented as if it were entirely innocent). And while Dee may be impossibly critical, her mother's pleasure in

Jimmy T's flight from Dee's "faultfinding power" to marry "a cheap city girl from a family of ignorant flashy people" (para. 16) should also be considered.

On first reading, it's clear that Maggie is favored. But ask students what they make of the demeaning language that describes Maggie as a lame dog and, in Maggie's final triumph, as having "a kind of dopey, hangdog look.... with her scarred hands hidden in the folds of her skirt."

Dee is certainly hard on her family. She calls Maggie "backward" and speaks of the family's difficult circumstances as if they were chosen. At the same time, Dee, despite her outbursts of frustration and anger, does seem to struggle with the way the family perceives her. During the discussion of her new name, she finally says, "You don't have to call me by it if you don't want to," and in this moment of abdication, her mother is willing to abdicate, too, saying she'll use the name her daughter wants.

The story doesn't end on this moment of reconciliation, however, but with both sides retreating back to their "positions" on their heritage. The positions are nicely summed when Asalamalakim says, "Well, there you are," and the mother responds, "There I was not." The family conflict in "Everyday Use" is partially explained by how the respective members choose to contextualize their experiences and how that contextual reading influences their perceptions about themselves, their family, and their world.

Writing Suggestion: Evaluate Dee's apparent relationship to class and race. Consider who Dee appears to be before she comes home for her visit (before her mother learns of the changes she's made) and after her visit. How might Shelby Steele's essay help explain her character and the changes she decides to make in herself?

$$\boxed{3}$$

RELATIONSHIPS

Friends and Lovers

Responding to Others

In asking questions about love and friendship, the selections in this chapter touch on race, gender, and class, as well as the more existential "nature" of modern life. The topics here remain personal, and several of the pieces include the kind of reflection that students have encountered in chapters 1 and 2, offering more examples of the personal extended to social and political issues.

You may want to continue to have students compare and contrast their experience with the experiences of the individual authors, or you may want to start to introduce more purely analytic assignments. Either way, students should be encouraged to examine how these writers present their points as well as the role and voice of the speaker in these essays. Even Diane Ackerman — who doesn't talk about her private experience — is "present" in her article.

In making the transition to analytic or argumentative essays, students will be using their course readings less for models to imitate than for material to which they can respond. In this section, Barbara Ehrenreich and Marc Feigen Fasteau come closest to the kind of essays students should start writing. Now the goal will be to analyze the reading with an eye to understanding its content, evaluating its argumentative strategy, and developing an intelligent, well-supported response to its position. Students may want to refrain from first-person narration in order to practice putting opinions on paper without putting themselves on paper.

Barbara Ehrenreich

IN PRAISE OF "BEST FRIENDS," p. 58

A good start to discussion would be to ask for responses to Ehrenreich's remark that "most of us would never survive our families if we didn't have our friends" (para. 1). Students should be able to offer ample evidence that friendships help bring autonomy, by building our personal strength and expanding our ability to resist the considerable power wielded by family and society. But, like other political alliances, friendships require loyalty. (There's the rub.) Ehrenreich knows that in our friendships we may want to get away with disloyalty and neglect. Raising the status of "best friendship" is more than a social problem; it is a psychological and moral difficulty, one that may or may not be affected by changes in the manners and social customs of friendship.

The body of this essay gives an overview of the way in which female friendships have been treated throughout history. According to Ehrenreich, Western tradition and Christianity have always devalued female friendships. The twentieth century, with its ideal of the companionate marriage, did even more damage. You might ask students to what degree the ideal of a companionate marriage still holds. If they think this ideal is still strong, do they share Ehrenreich's conviction that modern marriage is the victim of impossible standards?

Ehrenreich argues that the feminism of the seventies was not a boon to female friendships. Instead, in its zeal to acknowledge and support lesbian relationships, the early feminist movement ignored female friendships or even dismissed them as unexplored sexual relationships. Ehrenreich allows that in recent decades female friendships have been granted a certain value — as a means to a (more important) professional end.

Ehrenreich's quick history is intended to illustrate both the consistent devaluation of female friendship and the consistent value that women nonetheless have placed on friendship. You can't, it seems, keep a good friendship down. That said, Ehrenreich proposes some measures to protect female friendship.

Ehrenreich closes with three practical suggestions for achieving valued and respectful friendships between women. Ask students how reasonable they think Ehrenreich's ideas are. Would they be willing to obey her "rules"?

Writing Suggestion: In Ehrenreich's final paragraph, she claims that friendship "requires no help at all from the powers-that-be." Write an essay, based on your observations and experience, in which you agree or disagree with this contention.

Patricia Williams

MY BEST WHITE FRIEND, p. 62

This is a complicated and, in many ways, confusing essay. On the face of it, it is about two friends getting ready for a party. The title makes it clear that this piece is about the friendship between the author and M.B.W.F., as Patricia Williams calls her. But the subtitle — "Cinderella revisited" — and the placement of the essay in *The New Yorker's* "Annals of Appearances" make it clear that friendship isn't this essay's only subject.

Williams's friendship with M.B.W.F. is in certain ways puzzling. Despite the similarities in their formal education, the two women are quite dissimilar. They want different things out of their lives. They have completely different approaches to their physical selves. They see race in completely different ways. And yet there is a playful tenderness in the way they attend to one another, even though their dialogue is relentlessly flippant. As they address each other, both women seem always to be conscious of their race and class and how those identities define them. To a degree, both women are trying to thwart the expectations of their respective class and race with irony. So, for instance, M.B.W.F. purposefully says rather appalling things. At one point, she characterizes Williams as a would-be "ethnic woman warrior, always on that midnight train to someplace else, intent on becoming the highest-paid Aunt Jemima in history." Williams doesn't seem offended by this. She just chokes on her possible response. Part of Williams's failure to object has to do with M.B.W.F.'s personality, her apparent relish for hyperbolic, outrageous statements. (Of herself, she says that she has always aspired to be "a cunning little meringue of a male prize.")

In turn, Williams says rather unflattering things about her friend, too, using the essay to paint M.B.W.F. as funny, quick, and generous but also narcissistic and somewhat oblivious in her privilege. What, for instance, is the point of disclosing their discussion

19

about aging, particularly the anecdote about M.B.W.F. looking at Princess Diana and exclaiming, "God! Bulimia must work!"?

After an afternoon of making each other up, Williams and M.B.W.F. look at each other with "deep disapproval." They then wonder (as readers must) why they are friends. It seems that it is the commonness of their disapproval that keeps them together. They're joined by the slightly campy shake of the head and the sigh that signals a mutual recognition: they're *soooo* different.

Williams closes her essay by placing herself literally in her white friend's shoes and then rejecting those shoes. Ask your students what they make of the shoe detail given the essay's Cinderella motif. Remind them that Cinderella gets the man when her foot fits the shoe, but Williams doesn't, like an evil stepsister, shove her foot into an overly dainty shoe.

The final paragraph is intriguing and puzzling. "I do not envy her. I do not resent her," Williams writes. Do readers ever suspect her of having either of these emotions about M.B.W.F.? And then: "I do not hold my breath." What does this mean? Is Williams saying she's not going to hold her breath against M.B.W.F.'s husband's cigar, that she's not going to resist *that* world? Is she saying she's not going to hold her breath waiting for the man for whom, supposedly, she has been preparing all evening? What are the other possibilities?

Aside from friendship, the metaphor of the fundraiser as Cinderella's ball guides this essay. Presumably, the white friend's attentions to Williams have a fairy godmother quality, but Williams insists these efforts are wasted on her, because "white knights just don't play the same part in my mythical landscape of desire." What part do white knights play, given what we learn about the author? What does it mean to compare a self-described "over-thirty black professional with an attitude" to Cinderella?

In the context of the party Williams is about to attend, what is the import of the mother's stories? Williams may be saying to her friend, "I don't want what you want for me. I want to be a woman who invents her own ending." But her desires are not all that easily untangled, given the unhappy dreams she relates, dreams in which she's unsuitably placed for love, safety, or power. The dreams, as fears, are acknowledged by M.B.W.F.'s somewhat flippant response — she denies the first dream, and jokingly mentions therapy when she hears the second, but she doesn't engage Williams about the fears. Indeed, when the fears embodied in the dreams are played out — in much milder form — at a cocktail party, M.B.W.F. offers another glib response.

When Williams gives her dramatic "queen" speech, M.B.W.F. does finally address Williams's fear. While it may not be clear how the "queen" analysis accounts for the dreams, the rhetoric does speak directly to Williams's sense of herself as burdened by cultural images and, as a result, "a wee bit tense." The B.W.F. is surprised by the weakness that is implied in Williams's fears, and readers see why the prospect of being "the belle of the ball" seems impossible to Williams — no matter how much primping her "fairy godmother" has helped her do.

Writing Suggestions: Explain Williams's complicated responses to being "made up" by her "Best White Friend." We know Williams both resists the makeover and is looking forward to it. Why?

Do you think the friendship between Williams and M.B.W.F. is a good one? Why? Why not? What qualities does it share, or fail to share, with the "best friendships" that Barbara Ehrenreich describes?

Scott Russell Sanders

THE MEN WE CARRY IN OUR MINDS, p. 68

The ten-paragraph introduction to "The Men We Carry in Our Minds" places Sanders in the present and explains why he's analyzing his perceptions about men. Setting the scene this way offers something of a counterpoint to the rest of the essay and lets readers know that despite what he argues, Sanders does have a sense of "male guilt" about his historical past. Ask students if they think Sanders unnecessarily undercuts his authority with this admission. Does the gain — a sense of Sanders' sensitivity — seem necessary as the essay proceeds?

In the body of his essay, Sanders gives details about his past, details that explain his thesis: Economic hardship makes the plight of men and women equally bad, while improved economic conditions create discrepancies between men and women. Only the privileged can afford to claim a woman's lot is unjust. Sanders doesn't argue that the plights of poor men and women are the same, or even that poor men are innocent of wrongs against women — his point is simply that it makes no sense to talk about the "male privilege" of disenfranchised men. This group includes men "in dirt-poor farm country, in mining country, in black ghettos, in Hispanic barrios, in the shadows of factories, in Third World nations."

In fact, Sanders argues that poor women are *more* privileged than men in some respects. (Under the old division of labor between the sexes, women weren't responsible for earning money, and there was a *relative* freedom to their days. What's more, they didn't have to go to war.) You might ask your students what they think of his argument and his style of presenting it. What, if anything, does Sanders fail to take into account in his analysis of men's and women's relative situations? Do you agree with his analysis of the role of class? One way to consider this issue is to look at how his argument might change if he didn't use the phrase "the joys and privileges" of men to talk about what the women he met at college wanted. Is Sanders the ally to women he claims to be? Why or why not?

Writing Suggestion: Scott Sanders, Shelby Steele, and Patricia Williams all downplay the importance of race and gender in the current cultural climate. What do you think the most important factor is in determining privilege today: race, class, gender, or sexuality, or a combination of these factors? Support your answer with your own experience.

Marc Feigen Fasteau

FRIENDSHIPS AMONG MEN, p. 73

Marc Feigen Fasteau's point that superficial friendships would be taken for great friendships may need some clarification. Taken apart, his point is that mythical male friendships are based on competition developed through adventure or danger, and limited to exchange of loyalty and strength. War buddies who might willingly have died for each other in battle seldom see each other in peacetime. But despite the limited nature of such friendships, legends grow from those situations in which cooperation makes more sense than competition.

Legend aside, Fasteau argues that male friendships are often "shallow and unsatisfying." Avoiding the personal, men keep their talk general and theoretical, even avoiding discussions of workaday problems. (It's no accident that the male archetype has for so long been the mute cowboy.) The reason men avoid self-disclosure is intimately bound up with societal perceptions about masculinity. Men should be strong, well-functioning, independent creatures. Admitting weakness, affection, or vulnerability is seen as threatening the sexual identity of a heterosexual man. All of this stands in the way of friendships between men. Amongst themselves, men can't confide in or get angry with one another, touch, express pleasure, support, or, ultimately, talk to one another. And yet, says Fasteau, men prefer the company of men, since male friendships provide "mutual reassurance of masculinity," even if they don't provide an outlet for personal communication.

Fasteau quotes studies that say men want more out of their male friendships; they'd like to know their male friends better. (Fasteau himself would like to be closer to his male friends.) Since Fasteau treats men's emotional patterns as socially acquired and culturally determined, there is reason for hope. He implies that these conventions can be changed and that men can learn to reinterpret their behavior. Affection, tenderness and vulnerability may eventually be regarded as virile. Students should be asked to examine this premise from all sides, including a sociobiological perspective.

One final thing to note: Fasteau's use of outside sources. Through most of his essay, Fasteau's "evidence" is his own experience, but he uses an occasional quotation to support his argument. How does this lend him authority, even when the quotation is attributed only to "one man" or an anonymous "corporate executive"?

Writing Suggestions: Fasteau's argument hinges on the assumption that nonverbal communication can't lead to true male friendship. Do you agree? Write an essay that focuses on the many different kinds of communication that occur between friends, ranking them from least to most important.

Diane Ackerman

THE CHEMISTRY OF LOVE, p. 82

In "The Chemistry of Love," Diane Ackerman examines the role of three chemicals — oxytocin, PEA, and endorphins — in mother love, romantic love, infatuation and long-term attachment. Though her information is undeniably fascinating, students may resist her seeming reduction of our complex selves — our personalities and desires — to our lowly bodies. Ackerman's purpose is primarily informational, though she does allow herself to speculate about the implications of her information. Students should note how often Ackerman uses qualifying words here. Things "might" or "may" help explain a phenomenon. Chemicals "seem" to have certain effects. Can your students find places where she fails to examine her conclusions or assumptions? Her "facts" are often so pleasingly wild that it's easy to accept her speculations enthusiastically, especially since much of what Ackerman presents *is* factual.

Science writing is often considered dry or dull, and students should look at how Ackerman manages to keep things lively. An analysis of any one paragraph will show her skill at playfully packing a wealth of technical material into readable, entertaining prose. It might be a good idea to do this as a class. In paragraph 4, for example, Ackerman makes interesting information even more so, first by prefacing it with a quotation from Carl

Jung and then by using highly charged language to describe the highly charged effects of PEA. After describing what PEA does, she cites two fascinating studies that elaborate on the chemical's effect. She summarizes what the studies might imply and ends with a funny (but, she encourages us to think, accurate) quip. Love just might be "a sweet fix."

Writing Suggestion: Use Ackerman's essay to explain the various couples' relationships in Raymond Carver's story "What We Talk About When We Talk About Love."

Raymond Carver

WHAT WE TALK ABOUT
WHEN WE TALK ABOUT LOVE, p. 86

This story explicitly borrows from Plato's *Symposium* and James Joyce's "The Dead," but because your students may not have read either, a short summary of the *Symposium*, at least, might make the discussion more interesting. Like Carver's story, Plato's famous dialogue takes place at a drinking party. The gathered Greeks are still hungover from the previous night's debauchery, so they agree to keep their drinking to a minimum and debate a relatively "light" subject: love. Each person present is asked to define it. As with Carver's story, the definitions are as revealing as the manner of delivery.

In "What We Talk About When We Talk About Love," Mel is a cardiologist, an expert, supposedly, on the heart, but we also know that he's interested in absolutes. (Why did he leave the seminary? Why did he join in the first place?) More intensely than any of the other characters, Mel believes in traditional definitions of love, yet he comes to recognize that even his love is not as pure as he wishes. All his life he has been inclined to serve an ideal of pure love — he would like to be a courtly knight — but his experience has shown him so many examples of weird, mixed, irrational love that he is increasingly desperate to redefine "true" love, fearing that no such thing exists. His use of profanity and the details he chooses in describing the elderly couple he treated in the accident show his paradoxical feelings. He is moved by what love has done to the couple, yet repelled by that love's power to persist despite pain and misfortune. Mel's story of the lifelong devotion of the elderly man reawakens Mel's feelings of attachment to his ex-wife, a woman whom he insists he hates and would like to kill. Ironically, he reveals himself as similar to Terri's ex-husband, who was driven by the pain of love to want to kill someone. As the evening goes on, Mel loses his certainty about love and finally ends up feeling the urge to phone his children, as if he does not realize that the call will, for a moment, reconnect him with their mother. The powerful upsurge of buried and illogical ties to former loves frightens all four friends, who find themselves pulling away from or worrying about losing one another. The confident conviviality of the late afternoon vanishes as each character sinks into a somber, anxious recognition of the mixed, intractable nature of love.

The passage of the day — from sunlight to dusk to dark — parallels the stages of love and of life... and of the couples' relative degrees of drunkenness. The one constant in the story is the beating of their hearts. The story's closing words — "when the room went dark" — link the progress of light in this story with the progress of emotions and time. The final words also evoke the ending of a play: The curtain is down, the room has darkened, the drama is over.

In this story, the stages of love are demonstrated by three different couples. Laura and the narrator are like a young couple, still dewy with the fresh bloom of love. Mel and Terri are a middle-stage couple, struggling with their relationship and striving, despite what they say, against each other. The elderly couple seem to be an example of mature affection; their love persists despite pain, despite the impossibility of a physical component to the love. Mel doesn't really differentiate between husband and wife as he tells their story, perhaps indicating to what extent the elderly lovers have become one.

Point out to the students that the narrator does not offer explicit explanations of the story's events but that it touches on many different kinds of love. Even though the story presents a continuous discussion and unbroken flow of time, Carver leaves extra spaces after paragraphs 31, 42, 54, 66, 88, 101, and 121. Ask students what these seven extra spaces emphasize or suggest about each preceding event. What narrative exposition could be inserted at each place? Why does the author omit that exposition?

Writing Suggestions: Like Plato in his *Symposium*, Carver *demonstrates* love while he has his characters discuss *definitions* of love. Sometimes what he shows contradicts what his characters say. Conduct your own "symposium," and gather definitions of love from those you know well. Is there any discrepancy between how these people talk about love and how they conduct themselves in affairs of the heart? What similarities or differences do you find between the people you know and Carver's characters? Given your observations, how do you define love? Try to be as specific as possible.

In "What We Talk About When We Talk About Love," Carver's narrator pays special attention to the quality of light in the room. How come? What do these details have to do with the characters' conversation? How is the subject of love influenced by observations about the passage of time and even death?

LESSONS

Language and Learning

Arguing Audibly

Life's lessons, as the essays in this section make clear, aren't necessarily the lessons of the classroom. Indeed, one of the ways we learn is by articulating our thoughts, and as they read the pieces in this section, students should do the same in argumentative essays of their own. To begin to challenge the *Springfield* authors and themselves, students should question what they read, asking what the author is trying to prove and how the argument is supported. Is the evidence sufficient, relevant, reasonable, and representative? How does the author appeal to the needs and values of the reader? What assumptions underlie the argument?

To argue effectively, students need to state their own opinions clearly, to support their claims fully, and to anticipate and respond to possible objections to their positions. As they prepare to do this, you might want to give them the advice that E. B. White said his teacher Will Strunk gave him. When you write, Strunk said, "Make definite assertions." Avoid, as White himself later wrote, "the vague, the tame, the colorless, the irresolute."

You might also remind your class that Strunk also told White's college composition class, "If you don't know how to pronounce a word, say it loud!" Ask students why a teacher would give such advice. White's own conclusion was that Strunk thought, "Why compound ignorance with inaudibility? Why run and hide?"

Joan Didion

ON KEEPING A NOTEBOOK, p. 97

Joan Didion, though she denies it vehemently, has a practical reason for keeping a notebook. Her notebook recalls her to her earlier self, and in doing so provides her with material for her writing. As Didion explores her subject, she gives a sense both of what it is to be a writer and of the world she inhabits.

Didion's notebook is neither a diary nor a simple recording of daily events and thoughts. Instead, it is a repository for scattered observations that have meaning for her, "bits of the mind's string too short to use, an indiscriminate and erratic assemblage with meaning only for its maker."

These "bits of the mind's string" are hardly meaningless. The vivid moments she shares reveal a good deal in themselves and more when Didion plays them out. They also have a kind of uniformity. The oxymoronic opening image is a "dirty crepe-de-Chine wrapper," an image of dissipation and wealth. Have students think about the world for such an object—by turns glamourous, fashionable, and depressing—and the circumstances surrounding Didion's details. Even the sauerkraut recipe is really a story of existential panic, where the trappings of existence include money (a stay off Fire Island, a resort community for fashionable New York) and alcohol ("we drank a lot of bourbon").

Didion's notebook helps her remember what something *was* to her, how she felt at certain past moments. Though Didion claims there's no point to such remembering for her writing, her very essay — with its wonderful elaboration of the notebook quotes — belies her. As she plays out each detail — things such as "the ground hardening and summer already dead" — she does what every writer most wants to do: she transfers her feelings to her readers. (Indeed, by writing "On Keeping a Notebook," she creates a public audience for the words that she insists have an audience of only one: Didion herself.)

Didion's notebook also serves a personal purpose; she writes, "I think we are well advised to keep on nodding terms with the people we used to be whether we find them attractive company or not." Keeping a notebook, then, is a form of personal education. (That said, as Didion points out, notebook writing is an undeniably narcissistic activity, for we write to put our *own* opinions, perceptions, and thoughts out into the world.)

In another oft-anthologized essay, "Why I Write," Joan Didion explains what she likes about the phrase "Why I Write" (a title she borrows from Orwell's essay by the same name):

> I like the sound of the words [...] three short unambiguous words that share a sound, and the sound they share is this:
>
> I
> I
> I.
>
> In many ways writing is the act of saying *I*, of imposing oneself upon other people, of saying, *listen to me, see it my way, change your mind.*

Writing Suggestion: Keep two records of a week of your life: a conventional diary and a "journal" along the lines of Didion's notebook. Analyze the results, with an eye to uncovering the purposes of these different records.

Richard Rodriguez

PUBLIC AND PRIVATE LANGUAGE, p. 104

Like Shelby Steele in "On Being Black and Middle Class," Richard Rodriguez writes as an insider here, and his qualifications in the subject of bilingual education come from his own experience. He plays his argument out by looking at the question of relative richness. To Rodriguez, supporters of bilingual education, who imply that children "miss a great deal" by not being educated in their family's language, need to look at what these children gain: a public identity. Without denying that his education entailed some personal losses, Rodriguez argues in favor of assimilation (at least on the level of language). He concludes that children should not avoid learning the language of public society, no matter how comforting it may be to stick to the private language of home. He uses his father to exemplify the consequences of not mastering the public language — diminished by his inability to speak English, his father's private identity suffers. Even his family comes to think of him as withdrawn, though his shyness is less a character trait than a result of his uncertainty with English.

Rodriguez feels fortunate that his teachers weren't "sentimental" about educating him. Though such sentimentality would have comforted him in the short run, it would have hurt him in the long run. (The implication here is that resisting the dominant language is somewhat childish, like the wish for continual pampering.)

Rodriguez notes that public language demands words in meaningful order, with communication as important as self-expression. The audience at home — being an intimate one — does not require the precision demanded by a general audience. Before he learns the public language, Rodriguez is relatively silent in public. After, he trades his public silence for a private quiet and some loss of the intimacy in his "pleasing family life." Part of the loss is a result of the way the family defines its identity (at least initially) in opposition to the *gringo* majority. This identity is both comforting and troubling for the family. In the end, the troubles must outweigh the comforts, for the parents have no compunction about giving up Spanish "in an instant." (You might refer students back to Steele's argument to note the similarities and differences between the two writers' takes on how ethnic identity is defined.)

Once the Rodriguez children start to learn English, the literal quiet at home is matched by a new kind of public "silence." Students might find this point a bit confusing, but all Rodriguez means is that when he attended to the content of the English language, he became less conscious of the noise, the sounds, of that language.

Rodriguez closes by repeating his thesis: there are two ways a person is individualized, publicly and privately, and given that, assimilation is both valuable and necessary. Ultimately, he explains his point more than he proves it, for he fails to give us the means to decide which individuality should be sacrificed. In his opening line, Rodriguez oversimplifies his opponents' position and goes on to present his argument without considering the complexities of the bilingualists' argument. Not until his closing paragraph does he expand on the opposing view. What's more, he uses his argument to make some jumps that the reader might not be willing to make with him. In paragraph 18, he speaks of the necessity of assimilation in general, as opposed to the importance of learning the country's dominant language. Does he mean to imply that there are other things a first- or second-generation immigrant needs to "do" in order to have a public identity?

This piece is an excerpt from Rodriguez's book *Hunger of Memory*, which was both vilified and praised when it originally appeared in the early eighties. To his critics, Rodriguez betrayed his blood by buying into white, middle-class myths about what is necessary to participate in public culture. According to Marcelo Rodriguez's article on Rodriguez's subsequent book, *Days of Obligation*, for the *San Francisco Weekly* (Sept. 30, 1992), Richard Rodriguez now says he wrote *Hunger of Memory* in "the heat of youthful anger" and that he would not write the book today. Though he is viewed otherwise by his critics and some of his supporters, Richard Rodriguez does not think of himself as political.

Writing Suggestion: Do some brief research into the arguments of bilingualists to see, first, if Rodriguez has characterized their position fairly, and second, to see if his analysis convincingly refutes their arguments. Then, argue your own position, taking care to address the concerns of the opposing point of view.

Maya Angelou

GRADUATION, p. 109

At the beginning of this essay, Angelou conveys the sense of dignity and even grandeur that she and her classmates felt on the morning of their graduation. You might start by asking students whether they knew disappointment would follow. What do they think explains the children's enthusiasm, given the community's awareness of the limited opportunities for blacks at the time? The answers to these questions will center around the nature of this community: economically depressed but hard-working and self-respecting.

The threat to the community's self-respect comes from the larger white society. The initial contrast between the schools for white and black children (para. 2) introduces the reality of racism, which will undermine the graduates' dreams. The youthful narrator is clearly responding to the atmosphere of both her immediate and her larger worlds when she feels that everything is simultaneously significant and portentous (para. 9).

You might want to ask your students what the young Angelou expects from the world, using the text as evidence. They should note that Angelou lets details do double or triple work. When she describes herself reciting the preamble to the Constitution with Bailey, she's telling the reader that she's a top student and that she has a close, intellectual relationship with her brother. She's also deftly placing information for later. By the end of the essay, the reader will see that Angelou expected the promise of her country to hold true for her, too. (Ask students to find other details that are placed early in the essay so Angelou can use them later. You might steer them to, among other things, early information about Henry Reed's character and the Negro National Anthem.)

The direct threat finally arrives in the person of Edward Donleavy and his colleague. The latter is present, presumably, because Donleavy feels he can not walk among the blacks without another white man for protection. As Donleavy insults the entire graduating class and audience in numerous ways, the pride Angelou had been feeling turns abruptly to self-loathing and sardonic contempt for black delusions. Donleavy's speech is "educational" in that it tells the listeners what their opportunities are in a racist white world. Angelou is crushed. But after Henry Reed speaks, yet another emotional change will open Angelou's heart, perhaps for the first time, to the heroism of her people's struggle for dignity.

It is significant that Henry Reed is able to restore the community's dignity by returning to the moment where the graduation celebrants were "interrupted." The community's earlier failure to sing the Negro National Anthem was, no doubt, a result of Donleavy's backstage presence. Denied the opportunity to express self-respect, the community is disoriented, and the way has been prepared for Angelou's self-loathing. In singing the anthem, Henry Reed turns back the clock on the graduation to the moment when things started to go wrong. In doing this, he recalls the community to the words of the anthem and lets them recapture the enthusiasm that ruled earlier in the day, only now there is no question of this being a naive enthusiasm. The pride is truly about what this community has to celebrate.

On graduation day, the wide swing of Angelou's response — from exultation to degradation to sympathy and solidarity — organizes the memory, which also includes many light touches of humorous characterization and satire. In the end, her graduation *has* been as important as she thought it would be.

Writing Suggestion: If Angelou had ended her essay with paragraph 60, it would have seemed complete. Why does she add paragraphs 61 and 62? How have poets helped the black community survive? Be specific. You might want to address the question of whether contemporary black musicians and poets continue to serve this function for the black community.

Amy Tan

MOTHER TONGUE, p. 119

Like Virginia Woolf in "Professions for Women," Amy Tan starts out with an apparent disclaimer. She emphasizes her professional viewpoint as a writer, almost apologizing, as if the viewpoint is a limitation. By the end of her essay, however, she has suggested the opposite: The scholar's language is insufficiently textured for the richness of the world.

Tan's goal is not so much to critique scholarly language as to express the inestimable value of other underappreciated "Englishes." Her mother tongue — which is her mother's tongue, her native language, and the language of her heart — is "vivid, direct, full of observation and imagery." It has informed Tan's fiction, but has had a limiting effect on Tan and her mother, since limited language is often equated with limited thought. Because her mother's English doesn't resemble standard written English, people incorrectly assume she isn't bright, and, in the case of the rude doctor, that assumption results in substandard treatment. What's more, the language once limited Tan's perception of her mother. "I believed," Tan writes, "that her English reflected the quality of what she had to say. That is, because she expressed them imperfectly her thoughts were imperfect." (You might ask students how this compares to Richard Rodriguez's perceptions about his parents' imperfect English.)

Tan feels that she, too, was once limited by her mother's English, a limitation reflected in her performance on standardized tests. While efforts have been made, in recent years, to create culturally neutral standardized tests, Tan's examples of the kinds of questions that were problematic for her indicate how difficult a task that is. Technically, for instance, her example about analogies does not relate to language; instead it suggests that imaginative people have more trouble on standardized tests than literal-minded people do. (You might ask students if the example seems to undercut her argument.)

Tan, like Scott Russell Sanders in his essay "The Men We Carry in Our Minds," makes the occasion for her thoughts become part of her essay. Paragraphs 3, 4, 8, and 18 all refer to something that happened "recently," "just last week," or "lately." (Ask students why Tan includes these references to time.) The central question, as opposed to the central event, that prompts Tan's considerations is in paragraph 18: Why aren't more Asian Americans represented in American literature? What do students think of Tan's (admittedly incomplete) answer to the question? (Note that this device of getting away with an incomplete answer by simply acknowledging the incompleteness is something students can, when appropriate, use in their own papers.) Why does Tan feel she was able to defeat the odds — and apparent early criticism — to become a writer?

Students should be made aware of the popularity of Tan's fiction. It's significant that the language she pieces together — an English that is a combination of all the Englishes she knows and an English that does try to reflect her experience of her mother, her language, and her world — was well received by many readers. Her mother's final compliment is a compliment given by many non-Chinese-American readers. Ask students why this is important. Alternatively, bring in some sample pages from one of her novels and see whether students agree with Tan's assessment of her own work.

Writing Suggestion: Compare and contrast the language in sections of three novels by contemporary female Asian-American authors. You might consider Tan's *The Joy Luck Club*, Maxine Hong Kingston's *The Woman Warrior*, and Gish Jen's *Typical American*. Does Tan's analysis of her own "Englishes" shed light on these novels? Explain.

Virginia Woolf

PROFESSIONS FOR WOMEN, p. 125

The original circumstances of this talk — it was delivered to the Women's Service League in London in 1931 and only later published in *The Death of the Moth and Other Essays* — influence Woolf's opening. Her rather ordinary title suggests we'll get a dry, straightforward listing of what the opportunities are: something like a 1930s version of what students may have experienced at their school's "career services" office. Instead, we get a powerful image of what keeps the (supposedly) emancipated woman from true freedom — the Angel in the House.

Cleverly, Woolf takes the Society's request and uses it for her own purposes. She "meets the assignment" but talks about what really concerns her. (Something, you might point out, students should also try to do.) Woolf uses the practical concern about the economics of writing to discuss her larger concern about the personal economics of writing. How can one afford to do this? What are the costs to the self, particularly the self that has been told to take care of the needs of others?

Woolf's audience may have known that "The Angel in the House" is the title of a poem by Coventry Patmore (1823–1896). The heroine of that poem was a self-sacrificing individual and, as such, she represented an ideal for nineteenth-century British women. But even for contemporary readers who have not read the poem, Woolf's image should seem apt. Why?

Ask students if the male writer has to deal with the Angel in the House. Why or why not? Then ask if the angel is *still* in the house for women writers. What about the second problem Woolf cites, the problem that is more peculiar to female novelists than to female book reviewers? Can today's women express the truth of their sensual experiences? Can men?

Another way to approach this essay is to discuss the directions and progress of feminism since the days of Woolf. Ask the class what changes in the 1920s were affecting society's attitudes toward professional women. (The most notable was suffrage.) Are Woolf's views consistent with the more contemporary issues of feminism? Or do they seem outdated? How have attitudes toward women who seek careers changed since this address was delivered?

In paragraph 5, Woolf uses the masculine pronoun, even though she is speaking about female writers. Why? (This might be a good time for instructors to broach the topic of nonsexist language.)

In the final paragraph of her essay, Woolf tells the members of her audience that her problems as a writer are their problems. Ask your students if they think these problems exist for working women today. What professions require the same degree of interior and exterior accommodation? What does Woolf seem to be exhorting women to do in the essay's final paragraph?

Writing Suggestion: Update Woolf's essay for your gender. What professional opportunities do you have and what constrictions do you feel as a man or woman? Examine externally and internally imposed restrictions.

Toni Cade Bambara

THE LESSON, p. 130

Sylvia, like many of the young girls in Toni Cade Bambara's short fiction, is appealingly mouthy, self-confident, honest, funny, vulnerable, and streetwise. "The Lesson" opens with Sylvia doing what she does best: dismissing everyone. Except for "me and Sugar," she tells us, her world is cluttered with people who are "old and stupid or young and foolish." Given a different narrator in different circumstances, this pride would be hubris. Here, it seems a wonderful sign of Sylvia's strength, a clue that her circumstances will not defeat her. Even her initial lack of interest in Miss Moore and her lessons has its virtue, for Sylvia's ability to doubt and to resist authority is going to serve her well in a society that is economically and racially unjust. And yet part of her resistance to authority is a resistance to the very idea of education, and that, of course, is something she needs to outgrow.

Ask students exactly what Miss Moore's lesson for the day is and whether she successfully imparts it. At first, it seems Miss Moore simply wants to teach the children about the value of money, but none of the children are unaware of money's importance. (Witness Sylvia's feelings about getting the taxi change and the way in which Mercedes makes it clear that she has more than the others.) Nor are the children completely unaware of their own financial situation. Which is to say, they know they're poor. (Flyboy's specialty, Sylvia tells us, is keeping "the white folks off his back and sorry for him. Send this poor kid to camp posters, is his specialty.") But Miss Moore isn't concerned, of course, about who gets pocket change or how the children might "work" their economic situation. Rather, she wants to make the children aware of the injustice of great luxury in the midst of widespread poverty. Her goal seems to be to make them angry. (Ask students what Miss Moore thinks the children's anger will do for them.)

At first, the children find the sights of Fifth Avenue merely funny. The turning point comes when Flyboy notices the expensive toy sailboat. This stuns Sylvia and attracts the attention of all the children, for a sailboat is something they might want — it is a toy, after all — and it is also something they can weigh the value of; they know what their toy boats cost and how easily they can be destroyed.

The emotions they feel about the toy boat continue in the toy store. A general loss of confidence makes them all uneasy. Sugar and Sylvia hang back, too, and then, in paragraph 41, there is a split in the unity between the two friends. When Sugar touches the boat, Sylvia says, "I'm jealous and want to hit her." This isn't so surprising given that the unity between the friends has always been about a shared self-confidence. Once the self-regard drops away, Sylvia's confused by, and alone with, her emotions.

Though Sylvia articulates Miss Moore's lesson for the reader in paragraph 44, she doesn't do the same for Miss Moore and the other children. (How come?) Instead, it is Sugar who gives Miss Moore what she wants, and Sylvia immediately views her explanation as the betrayal of a goody-goody. ("I am disgusted with Sugar's treachery.") Have students explain why Sylvia views Sugar's behavior this way.

Immediately, the betrayal results in a further split between the friends. Sylvia walks away from Sugar, while Sugar tries to re-cement their bond by suggesting a trip to Hascombs. Sylvia agrees, but the small satisfactions of her life aren't going to mitigate the larger problems anymore. Instead of racing Sugar to the store, Sylvia splits off, but not before she concludes that she isn't going to let anyone beat her at any competition. Here, Sylvia talks about the new rivalry she has with her best friend, but we suspect that unconsciously she refers to a larger socioeconomic competition — the one that, as Miss Moore has already shown Sylvia, she *is* losing.

As readers, we feel that Sylvia's attitude will save her. After the trip, she is roused by anger, shame, and envy to begin to consider the causes and remedies of the inequalities she scarcely recognized earlier. Has Sugar learned the same lesson? Perhaps not — or not in the same way as Sylvia — as Sugar's conciliatory behavior (and attitude toward money) at the end suggests. It may be Sugar's final actions, as much as her betrayal, that create the distance between the girls at the story's close. And though the friends' split might be inevitable, it is a loss that presages future losses, for the wonderful buoyancy and shrewdness of childhood are threatened by the economic and racial injustice of the adult world. If the losses are met with concomitant gains, it will be a result of Sylvia's strength — her ability to resist the messages of adult society.

Writing Suggestion: Evaluate Miss Moore as a teacher. What do you think of the way she goes about imparting her lesson? What is the lesson she means to teach the children? What is the lesson they learn?

5

DILEMMAS

Problems, Theories, and Opinions

Recasting the Problem

The works in this section recast the terms of a much-debated problem in order to shed new light on that problem. Stephen Carter asks us to look at the separation between church and state in light of religious liberty rather than secular freedom. George Orwell's decision to play out the colonizer-colonized debate in terms of personal emotions was, for its time, also new. Sallie Tisdale's essay will probably be most striking for students, since they'll be familiar with the other ways in which the abortion debate has been presented.

For a final assignment, you might ask students to recast a hotly debated dilemma in order to add a new voice to the existing arguments. This will require students to familiarize themselves with the positions in a current debate (they will need to do outside research for class). It will also require students to look intelligently at the *form* of a debate, so they can advance the discussion by helpfully altering it.

To help students reconsider their own thoughts on a matter, you might require them to use several outside sources for their final paper. This will encourage students to examine various sides of an issue while providing them with an occasion to develop research skills and learn how to cite and document sources.

Sallie Tisdale

WE DO ABORTIONS HERE, p. 137

Sallie Tisdale's perspective as an insider governs the content of this essay. "We Do Abortions Here" consists of a description of Tisdale's work, its paradoxical character (monotonous, varied, grim, enjoyable), and the way in which it affects both Tisdale and her clients. But the essay is as striking for its approach as for its content. In paragraph 4, Tisdale introduces the telescope metaphor that guides her views of abortion. She concludes, "In abortion the absolute must always be tempered by the contextual, because both are real, both valid, both hard."

Tisdale lets her essay mimic her approach to abortion and thus the movement of the telescope; she sweeps the horizon and then focuses on small details. The paragraphs that focus on the small details take the reader through the upsetting abortion procedure, start to finish. Here, Tisdale presents the grimness of abortion, the actual basin contents, and the ways in which an abortion is a "failure to protect." The "surveying" paragraphs examine the abortion issue in the context of specific women's lives and particular societal concerns such as the failure of "the great promise of birth control." Taken together, all these paragraphs are Tisdale's "position" on abortion. Most participants in the abortion debate take only one side or another — to admit the validity of the contextual position might damage the absolute position and vica versa. As Tisdale writes, "Privately, even grudgingly, my colleagues might admit the power of abortion to provoke emotion. But they seem to prefer the broad view and disdain the telescope."

At times Tisdale herself has to put the telescope aside, to not even look, to distance herself from the actual abortions and cultivate "a certain disregard." Still Tisdale points out that those involved with abortions need to draw a boundary for themselves, a boundary that is, essentially, about the telescope — a boundary between the "up close" and the "pulled back" views of abortion. This boundary recognizes the other side of the abortion issue, for if no other side existed, no boundary would be needed. Since Tisdale's position already encompasses both the contextual and the absolute, she needs boundaries on both sides. She needs to decide where she is going to place herself given her sympathies with the contextual (she is going to let her clients "carry their own burden") and where she is going to place herself given her sympathies with the absolute (she is not going to "judge" her clients).

Tisdale holds clear beliefs about abortion that she doesn't present as open to debate. She writes, in paragraph 21, "Abortion is a matter of choice, privacy, control." Despite her convictions, her essay isn't about persuasion as much as it is about sympathy, and as such, it doesn't shy away from presenting contradictions. Tisdale describes her own slight dissimulation as a nurse along with the fabrications of the antiabortion/pro-life people who staff "crisis pregnancy centers." In paragraph 17, she admits that in response to the question, "How big is the baby now?" she "sometimes lie[s] a little, weaseling around [the fetus's] infantile features until its clinging power slackens." But she doesn't, then, choose to lie to the reader, for she gives us, in paragraph 18, the very image she withholds from the client. How do we feel about her decision as a nurse here? What about her decision as a writer?

Though Tisdale finds much of her clients' behavior natural — their fear, their relief, their questions about size and shape — she does stumble on the gender question. How come? Is it surprising that the question only comes from couples? Tisdale tells an anecdote in paragraphs 28–29 about a rather unattractive husband who asks the sex of the baby. She then follows it up by using even his ugliness to make her point. What is the effect of this shift from paragraph 29 to paragraph 30? Have students explain what Tisdale means when she writes, "In a literal sense, abortion exists because we are able to ask such questions, able to assign a value to the fetus which can shift with changing circumstances."

Have students look at Tisdale's final paragraph. As she closes the narrative of her day that loosely structures the essay, she also closes her argument. Her final sentence — with its concrete detail ("the freezer door") and its abstract hope (imagining "a world where this won't be necessary") — ends with a phrase that is literal and metaphoric, and on both levels, precise and powerful.

Writing Suggestion: Both a pro-choice and an antiabortion activist might feel disturbed by Tisdale's essay. Why? In what way does Tisdale's article change the traditional form of the abortion debate?

Hendrik Hertzberg and Henry Louis Gates Jr.

THE AFRICAN-AMERICAN CENTURY, p. 145

In the summer of 1996, Hendrik Hertzberg and Henry Louis Gates Jr. guest-edited a special double issue of *The New Yorker* titled "Black in America." This essay is their introduction to that issue, which included portraits of Louis Farrakhan, William Julius Wilson, stock trader Buddy Fletcher, Clarence Thomas, Dennis Rodman, and Angela Bassett, as well as articles about an all-black Oklahoma community and West Indian immigrants, among others. Your students may need extra help contextualizing this essay. As this editors' introduction attempts to define the current state of affairs for African Americans, it might be a good idea to start discussion with where African Americans have been. For Hertzberg and Gates, no definition of the present can ignore the past, especially when that past, though not so distant, is ignored by our present-day "civic religion," which mythologizes America's role as protector of all. (Students should note the difference between a history book, which acknowledges slavery and injustice, and a civic religion, which does not.)

In paragraph 4, Hertzberg and Gates define the current situation as one of "titanic changes" and "unexpected ironies." They write, "The most striking change has been the growing centrality of the black experience to the maturing national culture of the United States; the most striking irony has been the degree to which blacks, despite that centrality, have remained economically marginal." Paragraph 5 details and celebrates the black cultural presence; paragraph 6 looks at economic marginalization. Rather than finding that the growth of a black middle class disputes current claims of economic injustice, Hertzberg and Gates note that middle-class gains have ironically resulted in "a distillation of ever more concentrated pools of poverty and despair in the inner cities."

African Americans' cultural centrality hasn't redeemed this socioeconomic situation, and Hertzberg and Gates don't see where help *is* going to come from, especially when manufacturing jobs are down, when social policy is hard-hearted, and when neither the market economy nor the present political system seems capable of solving the problem. Even political rights are no comfort — in our electoral system, political rights don't translate into political power. The current method of trying to gain political power, "racial gerrymandering," exacts its own price. They conclude that our only option is "to make our country live up to its nominal creed." The practical details are left up to the reader to consider.

Writing Suggestion: What can or should this country do to "live up to its nominal creed"? To answer this question, you might look at the April 29/May 6, 1996, issue of *The New Yorker*. Do you find any solutions there?

George Orwell

SHOOTING AN ELEPHANT, p. 148

Students will easily grasp Orwell's main point: tyranny enslaves the tyrant as well as the oppressed. But they may decide that Orwell himself is a racist rather than a writer using irony to describe the way imperial power influences the mindset as well as the behavior of the imperialist. As a representative of European forces, Orwell is not able to prevent the Burmese from hating him, nor is he able to prevent them from "requiring" a certain sort of behavior from him in the scene with the elephant. Even worse, perhaps, is that he's not ultimately able to keep his own humanistic views operating over the course of his tenure as a subdivisional police officer.

Orwell tells this story from a distance, at a time when his political sympathies and emotions are in accord. While in Burma, Orwell, despite his political sympathies, felt both contempt for and some fear of the Burmese. He begins his essay by writing, "In Moulmein, in lower Burma, I was hated by large numbers of people — the only time in my life that I have been important enough for this to happen to me." Quickly, however, he establishes that he "had already made up [his] mind that imperialism was an evil thing and the sooner [he] chucked up [his] job and got out of it the better." He takes further pains in his second paragraph to identify his own attitudes toward imperialism — he is not, he lets us know, one of the bad guys. And yet he acts like a bad guy. Orwell's use of derogatory language ("sneering yellow faces," "the evil-spirited little beasts") as well as his attitude toward the behavior of the Burmese both show that he is not free of the dehumanizing effects of the imperialism he has to enforce.

In looking back at his younger self, Orwell self-critically reveals his apparent lack of emotional sympathy for the Burmese, despite his political sympathies. He shows, too, that the emotions he withheld from human beings flowed intuitively toward the elephant. One of the piece's great ironies — an intended one — is the lengthy, loving description of the elephant's death. Here, Orwell personifies the elephant — its "preoccupied grandmotherly air," its grave and pitiful death in paragraph 11 — while he adopts the colonizer's dehumanizing language to talk about the Burmese. He sees them, as he has been instructed to, generically. They have "their bit of fun," he writes, over and over again, using an entirely patronizing phrase, and he speaks of their "devilish roar of glee" at the elephant's murder.

Though in the situation with the elephant the real power belongs to the tyrannized Burmese and not the tyrannizer (that is, not to Orwell in his official role). Ultimately the source of tyranny is British imperialism, and the sarcastic close makes the full ugliness and inhumanity of that imperialism apparent.

Ask students to locate the essay's thesis sentence and explain why it is placed where it is. Also, ask them to consider why the essay was written by a reminiscent narrator and not in the "voice" of the young Orwell. Finally, you might have them consider why the piece doesn't begin with paragraph 3.

Writing Suggestion: What is the historical context for this essay? It was written in 1936. What relevance does the essay have for contemporary society?

Michael Dorris

FOR THE INDIANS NO THANKSGIVING, p. 155

Michael Dorris's essay is particularly interesting when read against the opening two paragraphs of "The African-American Century," for both pieces address the hypocrisy of America's "civic religion" and both force us to look at our country's enduring, and at least partially false, mythology. According to Dorris, one reason myth persists is that "when one culture clashes with another... the victorious group controls the record." Are there others? For Dorris, Thanksgiving is "a modern fantasy" and, as Dorris plays it out, a pretty insulting one, depending on death, poverty, and racism. Dorris's tone — sarcastic, angry, funny — may make some students feel he's overstating his case. Is he?

You might ask students why we even celebrate Thanksgiving, especially when we're aware of what the original settlers did to Native Americans. The holiday is so much a part of our culture and our sense of what the country stands for that it is bound to have staunch defenders. It might be interesting to ask students to debate the abolishment of the holiday or to suggest thoroughgoing reforms. What obstacles stand in the way of making even small transformations in the annual holiday?

Writing Suggestion: Do some research on the debate about the use of Native American iconography by sports teams such as the Atlanta Braves and the Cleveland Indians. Then argue your own position about the use of these images, taking care to address the concerns of the opposing point of view.

Stephen L. Carter

SCHOOLS OF DISBELIEF, p. 157

In this excerpt, Stephen L. Carter explains the original intention of the First Amendment, showing himself a clear supporter of the doctrine of separation between church and state. However, Carter argues, in the years since the Constitution was framed, we have become a culture of nonbelievers who think of the amendment — with its Establishment Clause and its Free Exercise Clause — as protecting government and the secular world from religion, rather than protecting religion from government. He concludes that contemporary interpretations of the Constitution, in their zeal to protect the secular world from the religious, may actually violate religious liberty.

The "wall of separation" between church and state needs, Carter writes, "to have a few doors in it," because not all of the decisions made in the name of the Establishment Clause have been just. Carter focuses on the way in which the Establishment Clause could be used to prevent teaching religion in the classroom, and he distinguishes between teaching religion and endorsing a specific religion. Ask students if they think Carter is guilty of presenting a straw argument here. (He gives only one example of a school district that used the First Amendment to supress education about religion.) Students with a public education will be able to discuss whether public schools are loath to teach the history of religion or the place of religion in history. (Try asking if any of them learned about European history without hearing about the Reformation.)

Still, if there really *is* public school resistance to education about religion, Carter's argument in favor of this sort of education seems easy enough to support; certainly he takes great pains — particularly in paragraphs 1 through 7 — to demonstrate the *reasonableness* of his approach to the issue. The one place where he seems to run into a potentially tricky question is when he describes Richard Baer of Cornell University wondering whether the requirement of teacher objectivity in the classroom would make it impossible for teachers "to criticize any religions, including Satanism, fanatical apocalypticism, or snake handling." Ask students what they think of Baer's concern.

It might also be interesting to ask students to give examples beyond public education of ways in which the "political and legal culture... presses the religiously faithful to be other than themselves, to act publicly, and sometimes privately as well, as though their faith does not matter to them." What other social issues involve a clash between a secular right and a religious belief? Whose rights should prevail in such debates?

Writing Suggestion: Find a specific case where religious beliefs and secular rights seem to clash with one another. How, in your view, does the Constitution require you to judge the case? How would you personally judge it?

37

Tillie Olsen

I STAND HERE IRONING, p. 162

This story abruptly plunges us into a mother's internal monologue, stimulated by a phone call from someone who thinks her daughter Emily needs counseling. The mother's first response to the phone call is to do what she says she doesn't have time for, "to remember, to sift, to weigh, to estimate, to total." Twice the mother tells us that Emily was "a beautiful baby." She finally says, as we sense she will, "but." The "but" might be followed by a list of Emily's shortcomings, but it's not. Instead we get a list of the failures of the outside world, the limitations of the "seeing eyes" and the mother's own difficult circumstances.

Ask students whether they have sympathy for the mother. On the surface, the narrator's detailing of her own situation might seem to include a great deal of self-justifying as she recounts the long string of unmanageable circumstances — "of depression, of war, of fear" — that prevented her from being a better mother. The terrible things that happened were simply unavoidable at the time, she says. What emerges from her monologue, however, is not self-pity but understated compassion for Emily, insight into the girl's growing autonomy and trust in her strengths. The mother's love and sympathy for her child increases as a result of the misfortunes they both suffered. The mother was also ridden down by harsh forces — like the dress flattened by the iron — but both women steadily exercised sufficient power to resist the flattening of their spirits. They "bloom" at least partially with pride and wisdom, qualities that arrive late in both their lives — in the mother's second marriage and in the daughter's early adulthood.

Neither of them blooms as a result of the help they received along the way, and this explains, in part, the mother's resistance to the caller. After all, the "help" Emily got at the nursery school and the convalescent home only seemed to hurt her. In the end, the mother says, "I will never total it all." But then she does total it all — for the reader, if not for the phone caller. By the end we know that Emily has been shaped by her unhappy circumstances: her unpopularity, her illness, her fatherlessness, her poverty, her mother's exhaustion, and her rivalry with her siblings. But she also has a gift and is loved and supported by many.

Ask students to discuss the significance of the ironing and its relation to the story's theme. Is the iron a positive or a negative force, smoothing or crushing?

Writing Suggestion: Consider the social background of this piece (as opposed to the "merely" personal background that includes the mother's struggles). What does the specter of nuclear war have to do with Emily's personality? What social circumstances of Emily's life reinforce her personal hardships?